THE UPPER ROOM

Disciplines

1987

Coordinating Editor
Tom Page

Edited by
David Bradley
Janet McNish Bugg
Mary Ruth Coffman
Pamela Crosby
Charla Honea
Tom Page
Shirley Paris
Jill Reddig
Mary Lou Redding
Willie Teague
Doug Tonks

The Upper Room Disciplines 1987

ISBN 0-8358-0531-X

The scripture quotations not otherwise identified are from the Revised Standard Version of the Bible, copyrighted 1946, 1952, and © 1971 by the Division of Christian Education, National Council of the Churches of Christ in the United States of America, and are used by permission.

Quotations from *The New English Bible*, © The Delegates of the Oxford University Press and the Syndics of the Cambridge University Press 1961 and 1970, are reprinted by permission. The initials NEB are used to identify *New English Bible* quotations.

Quotations designated TEV are from the *Good News Bible, The Bible in Today's English Version*, copyright by American Bible Society 1966, 1971, © 1976, and are used by permission.

Quotations from *The New Testament in Modern English*, by J.B. Phillips, are reprinted by permission of the Macmillan Company. Copyright © 1958 by J.B. Phillips.

Scripture quotations marked NIV are from the *Holy Bible: New International Version*. Copyright © 1973, 1978, 1984 International Bible Society. Used by permission of Zondervan Bible Publishers.

The initials KJV are used throughout this book to identify quotations from the King James Version of the Bible.

Any scripture quotation designated AP is the author's paraphrase.

Cover photo by Frances Dorris.

Contents

Foreword 11
Willie S. Teague

January 1-4 13
The Transforming Word
R. Wade Paschal, Jr.

January 5-11 17
God's Promises: Our Responses
James K. Wagner

January 12-18 24
Confirmed in Hope for Beginning Again
Cheryl Hammock

January 19-25 31
The Empty Cross—Emptying the Cross
William Robert Sharman, III

January 26–February 1 38
The Lord Leads
Raymond W. Fenn

February 2-8 45
The Spirit as the Light for Life
Jan Sutermeister Edwards

February 9-15 52
The Indispensable Divine Laws
Jung Young Lee

February 16-22 59
Quality of Life with God
Dorothy J. Mosher

February 23–March 1 66
Some Activities of God
Hugh Irwin

March 2-8 73
Choices for Life
Cathy Burkhardt

March 9-15 80
The Primacy of Faith
Robert M. Holmes

March 16-22 87
Undeserved Gifts
Barbara P. Ferguson

March 23-29 94
Words of Grace and Peace
James W. Holsinger, Jr.

March 30–April 5 101
Prerequisites for Resurrection
Mary Olson

April 6-12 108
Hosanna: Save Now!
Evelyn Laycock

April 13-19 115
Holy Week
Russell T. Montfort

April 20-26 122
Faith, Peace, and Courage
David Maldonado

April 27–May 3 129
On the Road to Emmaus
Marjorie J. Williams

May 4-10 136
Portrait of the First Christians
Dan B. Genung

May 11-17 143
Stones of Remembrance
Thomas P. Harp

May 18-24 150
God Is Not Far from Us
Pamela Hadsall

May 25-31 157
In God's Mighty Presence
Robert D. Ingram

June 1-7 164
Pentecost: The Believer's Birthright
Ruth Heaney

June 8-14 171
Power, Presence, and the Chosen
Leonard Thompson Wolcott

June 15-21 178
New Beginnings!
Ruth Hurtt

June 22-28 185
Strength through Testing
James L. Merrell

June 29–July 5 192
God Delivers
Thomas R. Logsdon

July 6-12 199
Growing in the Spirit
L. June Stevenson

July 13-19 206
The Vision of God
Bruce A. Mitchell

July 20-26 213
Looking for the Kingdom
J. Stephen Lang

July 27–August 2 220
On Being Connected
Norene D. Martin

August 3-9 227
Accepting God's Presence in the Darkness
Lance Webb

August 10-16 234
Our Responsibility in the Covenant
Homer Noley

August 17-23 241
Beyond Doubt and Fear
Donald E. Kohlstaedt

August 24-30 248
Being True to the Christ Within
Sr. Mary Michael, SSM

August 31–September 6 255
A Powerful and Loving God
Harvey and Gayla Estes

September 7-13 262
Paradox of Law, Fear, and Love
Robert L. King

September 14-20 269
Waiting for God
David F. Ensminger

September 21-27 276
A Peculiar People
John M. Gessell

September 28–October 4 283
The Means Justifies the End
Jerry Litherland

October 5-11 290
To Be God's People
David Randell Boone

October 12-18 297
Suffering: Its Place in Life
Douglas Bowling

October 19-25 304
Traits of the Christian Leader
Perry C. Cotham

October 26–November 1 311
Blessed Are
Peter van Eys

November 2-8 318
The Day of the Lord
Donald C. Schark

November 9-15 325
Hush . . . God Is Near!
Roy W. Hall

November 16-22 332
The Good Shepherd
Nancy Carol Miller

November 23-29 339
Thanksgiving
Fred L. Beck

November 30–December 6 346
Shalom through the Word That Endures
Cecilio Arrastía

December 7-13 353
Preparing for New Life in Christ
Marian "Shug" Yagel

December 14-20 360
God's Surprising Choices
Martin Pike

December 21-27 367
A Time for Feeling Good
Robert N. Zearfoss

December 28-31 374
The Light of God
John O. Gooch

FOREWORD

Thy word have I hid in mine heart, that I might not sin against
thee.   —Psalm 119:11 (KJV)

The 1987 *Disciplines* is offered with the prayer that it will
assist you as you seek union with the word of God. The psalmist
suggests that if this union is to happen, we must faithfully
meditate upon the word of God (119:48) and hide it in our hearts
(119:11).

The wisdom of the psalmist is reflected in a saying from the
desert fathers and mothers of fourth- and fifth-century Egypt.
The stories and sayings attributed to them have been a source of
inspiration for western monasticism for centuries. Abba Poemen
is reported to have said:

The nature of water is yielding, and that of a stone is hard. Yet if
you hang a bottle filled with water above the stone so that the
water drips drop by drop, it will wear a hole in the stone. In the
same way the word of God is tender, and our heart is hard. So
when people hear the word of God frequently, their hearts are
opened to the fear of God.*

We do not presume to claim that *Disciplines* is the word. We
hope that you will use it daily as you discipline yourself to read
the scripture, meditate upon the scripture, and pray. The daily
readings and prayers are offered with the hope that the word of
God will quicken your life and give light to your faith journey.

As you frequently meditate upon God's word, may your heart
be "opened to the fear of God."

Willie S. Teague

Editor, *Pockets*

---

*Yushi Nomura, *Desert Wisdom: Sayings from the Desert Fathers* (New York:
Doubleday & Co., Inc., 1982), p. 59.

THE TRANSFORMING WORD

January 1-4, 1987   **R. Wade Paschal, Jr.**†
Thursday, January 1   Read 2 Corinthians 4:1-11.

The "treasure" of Second Corinthians 4 is the presence of the living God. Faith in Jesus Christ allows the same God who created light out of darkness to do a similar creative act in our hearts. Faith unleashes the light of the character of God in the heart of the believer. The Christian experience is nothing less than knowing God in all God's power and glory and light.

Next to the power and glory and light of God we do indeed seem to be "earthen vessels." We are frail and limited. The trials of life perplex and afflict us to the point where we are often tempted to give up. With the pressures of life on the one side, and the glory of God on the other, we can feel weak, insignificant and impotent.

But, God said, "My power is made perfect in weakness" (2 Cor. 12:9). Paul knew from personal experience that when we stand in faith and survive as life is about to crush us, then people can begin to believe us when we give God the credit. When we get by on our own ability, people who are struggling may feel we have nothing in common with them. But, when we allow God to act in our hurts and weaknesses, others who are hurt and weak can find hope in our witness.

The hope Paul has for us is this: the treasure of God's grace operates not in spite of but through "earthen vessels."

Prayer: *Lord God, in this year let our moments of hurt and struggle be times when your grace and glory are most visible in us. Amen.*

---

†Minister of Adult Learning, First United Methodist Church, Tulsa, Oklahoma.

Friday, January 2   Read Ezekiel 36:22-32.

The most difficult problem a pastor faces in counseling is often the person who does wrong and does not care. The father or mother who leaves the family to live with someone else regardless of the effect on spouse or children; the employer who sacrifices people for profit; the friend who recklessly breaks a confidence for the thrill of being "in the know"—all these are examples of people who wreak havoc on others seemingly without thought or care for their feelings.

The "heart of stone" to which Ezekiel 36:26 refers is just this: the willingness to sacrifice others for personal gain. This is the very spirit of sin. Idolatry (the worship of gods in place of the true God) is the prototypical sin because the "heart of stone" picks gods and commandments to suit itself rather than to submit to anything outside of itself no matter how good or how loving. It is important for the "heart of stone" to have "gods" to justify its own intense self-centeredness. Anything which threatens this drive to self-pleasure is rejected, as God was rejected by Israel.

The remarkable point to this passage is the fact that God does not say, "Replace your heart of stone" as if we could simply change ourselves and be better. Rather we read, "A new heart I will give you, and a new spirit I will put within you; and I will take out of your flesh the heart of stone and give you a heart of flesh. And I will put my spirit within you, and cause you to walk in my statutes." This is the message of the incarnation: that God in Christ took our burden upon himself and delivered us from ourselves. Christian faith is not a course in self-help but in God's grace. God exchanges our heart of stone for a heart of flesh.

Prayer: *Almighty God, thank you for your Spirit who dwells within and makes my heart as your heart. Amen.*

Saturday, January 3　　　　　　Read Ephesians 1:3-6.

Paul's words run away with him in Ephesians. From verse three till the end of the chapter, there are only five sentences in the original Greek. Thought is piled upon thought in a breathless manner as if Paul is struggling to find ways to express himself. Language seems incapable of expressing all he thinks and feels about God's act in Christ. He turns to superlatives to capture the overwhelming nature of God's gracious act in Christ. We receive not simply a blessing but "every spiritual blessing in the heavenly places." Grace is not just "grace" but "glorious grace."

The language of Ephesians is excessive because God's act in Christ is excessive: excessively loving, excessively powerful, excessively beyond our deserts, and excessively wonderful in its effects on our lives.

This excessive love of God in Christ has brought us into "sonship." Sonship in both the Jewish and Greco-Roman world meant privilege and responsibility. The son inherited from the father and carried on the father's business. The son worked closely with the father, often acting as the agent or *alter ego* of the father. Ideally, and legally, the father-son relationship was the closest in the ancient world. The excessive love of God in Christ brings all of us into the closest possible relationship of love, privilege, and responsibility. It is a marvelous inheritance, almost beyond words!

Prayer: *Our Lord and Father, help us to live this day as children of yours, excessively loved and excessively blessed. Amen.*

Sunday, January 4   Read 2 Corinthians 5:12-21.

In a typical week there are many claims on our lives: job, family, friends, and church. There are times when one part or another of our lives seems to take over—usually because of some crisis. Many of us find that our lives are controlled by the "urgent," causing us to run from one emergency to another. In the context of such busy lives what can it mean to be controlled by the love of Christ as Paul claims he is?

At the very least we are controlled by the love of Christ when we begin to look at people as individuals for whom Christ died. For Paul this meant that everyone was of value—every single person significant enough to merit the blood of Christ. I am not allowed to devalue people simply because I am too busy or because their needs are inconvenient. Christ died for them— they are important.

The love of Christ also means that we begin to look at people not only for what they are, but also for what they can become in Christ. Paul frankly assumes we all need to become "new crea- tions." But he affirms our potential in Christ. His point is not to pile on guilt but to pile on hope.

Finally, the love of Christ spurs us on to an active appeal to others. People will learn of God's love primarily through other people. And if not through us, then whom will God use? We are God's ambassadors, sharing and showing God's reconciling love to others.

The most urgent emergency in life is the need all people have for the love of God expressed in Jesus Christ. This is the "urgent" that we should allow to control us.

Prayer: *Our God, atune our hearts today to the crisis of love in the lives of those around us, and help us to repond to that crisis with the love of Christ. Amen.*

GOD'S PROMISES: OUR RESPONSES

January 5-11, 1987   **James K. Wagner†**
Monday, January 5   Read Isaiah 42:1-9.

The lectionary readings for the first full week of 1987 are filled with God's promises.

As you study these scripture passages each day, be sensitive to ways that you might respond to these reassuring signs of God's love. Put yourself into the biblical pages. Allow yourself to hear the word addressed to you personally. This will require some unhurried time on your part, but the insights gained will be worth it. The alternative is simply to read the lessons, assuming they were written long ago for someone else: the nation of Israel, or the church, or certain gifted spiritual leaders. Study God's word not primarily for information but more so to be shaped and formed in the mind and spirit of Christ.

On this first Monday of 1987, claim these promises of God:

Isaiah 42:9   "The former things have come to pass, and new things I now declare."

Psalm 29:11   "The Lord will give strength unto his people; the Lord will bless his people with peace" (KJV).

Acts 10:43   "Every one who believes in [Jesus] receives forgiveness of sins."

Consider 1987 as a gift from God, an arena of unlived experiences where you have the potential and the possibility to actualize God's promises in your life.

Devotional exercise: *Make a list of the things you worried about last year. How did each one turn out? Ponder this thought: Today is the tomorrow you worried about yesterday. Read Proverbs 3:5-6.*

---

†Director, Prayer and Healing Ministries, The Upper Room; Executive Director, Disciplined Order of Christ; Nashville, Tennessee.

Tuesday, January 6 (Epiphany)
Read Psalm 29.

The hymn of seven thunders, a song for the new year festival, a majestic psalm of creation. These are some of the titles given to Psalm 29. Probably written for Jerusalem Temple worship and used at the beginning of the new year's rainy season, this sacred poem contains three distinct scenes.

Verses 1-2. The author calls upon "heavenly beings" to glorify the Creator God in the heavenly places.

Verses 3-9. The scene shifts to the world of nature. The reader is transported into the middle of an awesome thunderstorm. Seven times God's voice and power are identified with thunder.

Verses 10-11. The third scene is in the Jerusalem Temple where the congregation can do nothing more nor less than give God glory. The thunderstorm means the end of drought and brings gifts of water, life, and promise of another harvest.

Therefore, concludes the psalmist, God's people can count on the promises of strength and peace. And what is our response? Verse 9 directs us to gather with the people of God and give God glory. We, too, are dependent on God for everything good and helpful. Allowing God to be on the throne of our personal lives and serving God out of love and gratitude are other ways to give God glory.

Could there be a more fitting scripture to help our transition from Christmas into Epiphany? Psalm 29 begins with "glory in the highest" and concludes with "peace on earth."

Suggestion for meditation: *Sit quietly for several unhurried minutes, breathing the phrase "glory and light" over and over. Allow the Christ light to flood your being. Then ask, What are some ways I can glorify God today?*

Wednesday, January 7   Read Isaiah 42:1-9.

This reading from Isaiah, sometimes called "A Servant Song," describes Israel's special mission to the world:

> I [the Lord God] have given you [Israel] as a covenant to the people, a light to the nations.

And what are the designated tasks of servant Israel? To open the eyes of the blind, to bring out the prisoners from the dungeons, to release those who sit in darkness. This divine mandate is a restatement of God's earlier covenant with Abraham:

> I will bless you, ... so that you will be a blessing . . . . by you all the families of the earth shall bless themselves. (Gen. 12:2-3.)

Obviously, most political rulers and many religious leaders of Israel failed to comprehend this ecumenical scope, this worldwide, international inclusiveness of their "chosenness." This is why Jesus felt called to carry out these original covenantal tasks. In his very first recorded public statement, Jesus read from Isaiah (61:1-2), words that echo Isaiah 42:6-7. This set the tone and the direction of his entire ministry.

Those of us who call ourselves Christian have the same challenge before us every day. We are saved not for our salvation alone. We are healed not for our health alone. We are blessed to be a blessing to others. We are made whole to be instruments of health, salvation, and wholeness to others.

This is an awesome task, but we are not alone. The Holy Spirit is with us, empowering and forgiving.

Suggestion for meditation: *One sign of health in my spiritual life is how much love is flowing through me. How have I been spending my love and compassion lately? Am I sharing the blessings of God with others?*

Thursday, January 8   Read Matthew 3:13-17.

Have you ever disagreed with Jesus? Have you ever resisted Jesus' way of doing things? Are you facing a decision today that you have prayed about, even though you know what you want to do (regardless of what God wants you to do)?

Notice in the scripture reading the difference of opinion between John and Jesus. John tried to prevent Jesus from being baptized. Can you feel the tension between John and Jesus? Do you see the possibility here for argument, disagreement, a strained relationship? Then John allowed Jesus to be baptized by him.

This is so characteristic of Jesus that we sometimes overlook it. Jesus could have forced John to baptize him. Jesus could have intimidated John with his special calling and mission. Jesus could have demanded John's services. But he did none of that. Rather, Jesus treated John the same way he treats us—with respect, with dignity, and with sensitivity.

Jesus comes to us today and every day seeking our permission to be our friend, our Savior, our healer, our guiding shepherd, our light and hope. We may want all of that very much, but we may want it on our terms rather than on his. Jesus will not force us to do anything against our will. Neither will he be turned off by our resistance.

Suggestion for meditation: *Take a few minutes to make a mental list of some decisions you are facing today, of some personal problems unresolved, of some personal goals and ambitions unattained. Jesus wants very much to work with you today. Do you want to work and cooperate with Jesus?*

Friday, January 9   Read Matthew 3:1-17.

Today consider the significance and the benefits of baptism
for all Christians. The promise of God declared by John is still
valid today. "The kingdom of heaven is at hand." One way to
respond to this spiritual reality is to repent and be baptized.
Many people did exactly that and "were baptized by [John] in the
Jordan, confessing their sins." John cautioned his converts that
"he who is coming . . . will baptize you with the Holy Spirit and
with fire."

Christian baptism today likewise calls for repentance but also
affirms the action of the Holy Spirit within the life of the
baptized one. On the Day of Pentecost (see Acts 2:1-4) the
symbol of fire changed from one of destruction to one of power.
Baptized Christians are empowered by the Holy Spirit for obedience and service in the kingdom of God on earth.

When was the last time you thought about your baptism and
the benefits you enjoy through your baptism? In the early
church, baptism was called the Great Sacrament because that is
the unique moment when one is:
    —welcomed and received into the Christian family,
    —given a new name, Christian,
    —given citizenship in the kingdom of God,
    —given the gift of the Holy Spirit,
    —made an heir of all the riches of Christ.
Remember your baptism and be thankful!

Suggestion for meditation: *When were you baptized? Where were you
baptized? What do you recall or what have you been told about your
baptism? What difference has being baptized made in your life? Remember your baptism with thanksgiving. Call upon the presence of the
Holy Spirit within you to empower you to be a faithful and obedient
follower of Jesus Christ today.*

Saturday, January 10   Read Acts 10:1-43.

Some of us Christians are slow learners. But so was Peter, one of the original twelve. It took some extra revelation on the part of God to convince him that Jesus is Lord and Christ for all people, including non-Jewish people. After this vision, when Peter begins his sermon in the house of Cornelius, the Roman, his opening sentence represents a radical change in his understanding of the gospel:

> Truly I perceive that God show no partiality. Jesus Christ . . . is Lord of all.

After restating the universal love of God, Peter concludes his sermon, "Every one who believes in [Jesus] receives forgiveness of sins."

The church is a totally inclusive fellowship, announces Peter. But is it really? Is your church free of prejudice? Are you?

Prejudice is a preconceived idea or an opinion that disregards the facts or contradicts the facts. Prejudice comes in many expressions: ethnic, economic, educational, denominational, racial, social, class. By the grace and forgiveness of God, I am able to overcome partiality and favoritism; however, overcoming one kind of prejudice within myself does not mean I am prejudice-free from all forms of preconceptions.

Suggestion for meditation: *Have I experienced favoritism in the church? Am I impartial in my ministry and service? Am I still waiting for some special revelation to convince me of God's universal love and acceptance for all people? Am I doing my part in helping the church become a totally inclusive fellowship? Continue in silent reflection asking the Holy Spirit to bring to your consciousness personal prejudice, favoritism, or partiality.*

Sunday, January 11   Read Acts 10:34-43.

The author of Acts gives us the essentials only of the significant conversation between Peter and Cornelius. It makes you wonder what Peter said that was not recorded. However, we do have in this earliest of sermons about Jesus the very heart of the gospel. Notice the mention of Jesus' healing ministry and of his power over evil.

> [Jesus] went about doing good and healing all that were oppressed by the devil, for God was with him.

This spiritual truth can be powerful therapy when Christians become discouraged for any reason. Reflect a moment on this legend that tells about the time the devil decided to close up shop in one part of the world and open up in another. A "going out of business" sale was announced. One of the first customers, being quite fascinated with the various evil instruments on display, noticed that of all the devil's tools the highest priced one was called "discouragement."

"Why is that one so expensive?" he inquired.

"Quite simple," replied the devil. "With the tool of discouragement I can pry into almost everyone's life and cause all kinds of damage."

The next time you are discouraged for any reason, call on the name of Jesus. Call on his presence and his power to overcome discouragement and to bring encouragement and strength for refreshed and renewed life.

Suggestion for meditation: *Evil discourages; Jesus encourages. Am I discouraged about someone or some situation in my life? Am I allowing discouragement to lead to depression and defeat? Do I call on the presence and the power of Jesus Christ for help?*

CONFIRMED IN HOPE FOR BEGINNING AGAIN

January 12-18, 1987　　　　　　　　**Cheryl Hammock†**
Monday, January 12　　　　　　Read Isaiah 49:1-4.

God, it's Monday, the day of beginning again—beginning work, beginning relationships, beginning the task of beginning one more time. And I am tired.

Out there, I feel as if I am standing on a desolate beach, shouting mutely into the ocean's swirl of sound and movement and resistance to all but itself. I feel as if, by the force of my lungs alone, I must launch tiny paper airplanes across the Sea of Detachment to the distant Continent of Complacency. Scribbled on them all, almost imperceptibly, are your ancient and newborn words: YOU ARE GOD'S, AND YOU MATTER. It's a joyful message, God, but it's a sorrowful task. Isaiah would understand.

I want to retreat from the struggle of calling people to peace with you, with one another, with themselves. It's too hard for human creatures to hear hope. We are afraid to give up the familiar, even when the familiar is failure. We are afraid we will not know what to do *instead*.

Maybe that includes me, too, God. Have disappointment and disillusionment become all too familiar? Have I, too, come to believe that nothing can change or if it does it will be too minute to recognize or too revolutionary to manage? Have I heard only myself and the silencing winds of despair, instead of your words of faithfulness and liberation, of constancy and power, of inclusion and hope?

Prayer: *God of change, God of certainty, help me to trust you even now—in endings and in beginnings again. Amen.*

---

†Ordained minister, Christian Church (Disciples of Christ), currently serving as counselor/consultant, Associates in Ministry, De Land, Florida.

24

Tuesday, January 13   Read Isaiah 49:5-7.

It's Tuesday, God. I must move out of my foggy exhaustion. The week and the work *will* come. Today is not a day of asking why—but how.

By Tuesday, I look beyond my spent strength and vain labors. I affirm again: You made me; you called me out of my mundane world of muddy perceptions and into the brilliant light of seeing life with your eyes.

But there is more to Tuesday than a new look. It is a clear look. On street corners, in headlines, on television I see poverty, hunger, abuse, terror. The boundaries of my self-concerned village vanish into the horizon. And I see your love running, like a fugitive at large, to the ends of the earth.

Can that be where hope has a chance for life and where I have a life of hope? Is it on the frontiers of worlds which name you differently yet seek you desperately? Can that be where beginning again emerges for all who claim a holy inheritance?

Is that where your salvation reclaims, against all odds, what is yours: at the ends of the earth (and the corner of the block); under the harassment of megalomaniacal dictators (and behind our own closed doors); in the company of poverty and pain (the poverty of our neighbors' stomachs as well as the pain of our own anguished spirits); in the bonds of brokenness and disenfranchisement (the cry of tortured bodies as well as the compliance of our own compromised integrity)?

Is that your response to your discounted yet renewed servant—that your work/my task is enlarged, not diminished? What a strange vote of confidence!

Prayer: *God, in the presence of pain, honor in the face of debasement, wealth in the heart of poverty, lead me to your salvation shining even at the doorway of home, even running to the ends of the earth. Amen.*

Wednesday, January 14   Read 1 Corinthians 1:1-9.

God, this day holds potential for so much pain and so much promise. It's Wednesday—the day of The Endless Committee. I feel as if I am standing beside the synagogue at Corinth arguing for truth in the midst of passion and partisanship.

These people want to follow your leadership, God, but they just keep stumbling over their own feet. They are so gifted. You have been so gracious in enriching them. But they have been struggling so long in the marketplace. Now they have a hard time giving up the tactics of commerce when they come to the table of fellowship. And the sacraments of sensuality they have observed are hard to abandon for the sacrifice of Jesus and the slavery to him that is required of them now.

What will subdue their contentiousness and factionalism? What will make them give up their will to control at all costs? What can I say to help them exchange their old conditioned instincts for a new integrity governed by redemption?

Is the key to this struggle for power somewhere beyond the rules of order? Is the answer to confess that we are neighbors and that we must love one another because we are so alike—alike in our frailty, alike in our fear of inadequacy, alike in our pain of rejection? Most of all, can we learn that we are alike in being called out of the bazaar of trading on human need and included in your grace which binds us together in love—even when we disagree? Does the resolution rest where it always does—at the foot of the cross?

Prayer: *God of strength in our weakness, God of peace in our conflict, help us to remember who we are as we confront one another: children who share the same parent in a family with enough love to go around— to each, to all. Amen.*

Thursday, January 15　　　　　　　Read John 1:29-34;
　　　　　　　　　　　　　　　　　　　Ephesians 5:1-2.

It's evening, God. It has been Thursday, the day for visiting hospitals. I doubted I would encounter you in today's mad pace. But I was wrong. Perhaps John at the Jordan had a day like this. Was he surprised, as I was today, to see you face to face?

I saw you first in the eyes of a nurse. Military paramedic back home, he had seen destruction and felt it, too. He went about his duties on one leg and one prosthesis. He gave special tenderness to a teenaged boy, hit by a drunk driver, broken in every way a body can be broken from his teeth to his toes.

The nurse served silently. In the hush of caring, every movement held compassion, every look offered steadfast attention. As the pain became his own, I saw your Spirit touch him. He was a son of yours.

I saw you in the agony of a young obstetrician. Her passion for healing had not yet given way to the business of medicine or cynical distancing from pain. She sat speechless with the new parents, then sent them home without their long-awaited first baby. In the middle of the night, on the graveyard shift, Sudden Infant Death Syndrome had snatched away Joy.

The woman who came to announce life bore the mark of death. In innocent anguish, she turned to the long, empty, early morning corridor and was driven into the wilderness of helplessness. As she walked, carrying a burden for many yet to come her way, I saw your Spirit touch her. She was a daughter of yours.

I saw you today, God, suffering, broken, grief-stricken. I saw your Spirit descend and touch. You were ours in sacrifice. We are yours in hope.

Prayer: *God of mystery, God of vision, preserve in me the eyes to see you present in your children wherever our crosses stand. Amen.*

Friday, January 16

Read Joshua 6:20-25;
Hebrews 11:29–12:3.

The week is coming to a close now, God. I feel as if I am walking through Jericho just after Joshua's big week. Rubble and chaos surround me as I make my way through the city—my desk. Yet a calm rises within me, knowing that walls of defense are absurdities in the path of your certain dominion.

Jericho, reduced to nothing before your ragged warriors. Jericho, the lush city of palms, given to the hands of slaves and wilderness refugees following a liberator God. Surely that same power moves through these streets.

Rahab is here, too. She opens her door with a strange kind of graciousness. She looks with the eyes of wisdom. She knows the limitations of human power. She has survived the pain of living between walls—known but never included, bought but never valued. She has been pushed furthest from the seat of government, closest to the edge of destruction.

She touches us. She gives us friendly welcome in the world between the walls. We skulk around in the night of fear and intrigue, but she offers comfort, safety, and testimony of who you are. Somehow she has always known that liberation could come even to a harlot and her family. Her faith becomes action, even treason. She casts her lot with you and she survives—as treasured as gold and silver, included in your family. Her faith includes her in the company of patriarchs and saints.

And I begin to wonder what would happen if we could all be like Rahab?

Prayer: *God of endurance, help us to move from the life in between into the vast wilderness of your steadfast love, even at the harlot's door, even in the guerilla camp, even at the cross of Jesus. Amen.*

Saturday, January 17 Read Psalm 40:1-11;
Hebrews 10:5-18.

Saturday. Perhaps it is the best of your days, God. It is the day of letting go. Saturday is the day of remembering all the best memories of your investment in who we are and how we are.

Today is a singing day, and the rhythm is new. The pace is quickened, joyful! Saturday's words proclaim delight, not mourning. We move like children unbound by convention, and we gather all your children in the unplanned parade as we laugh along your way. Empty ritual gives way to childlike celebration, dancing unpatterned new steps and giggling unuttered new melodies.

Today we see some results from efforts, not ours but yours. We hear with new ears your assurance of deliverance, and we just cannot keep it to ourselves. Today we know again that worship is not what happens on Sunday but what happens when we breathe in the renewal of your salvation.

In these moments, God, we go running through your world celebrating your unchanging love, flying our hearts like kites high above our earthbound feet. We reach to catch the wind of joy that lifts our spirits toward you.

Prayer: *God of song and dance, God of drumbeats of delight and play of praise, preserve these visions of your mercy within us, your children—in spite of yesterday, in the face of tomorrow. Amen.*

Sunday, January 18   Read Hebrews 10:19-25.

Hear our confession, O God. We have walked the road of despair this week. We have assumed that proclaiming your message of joy would take more energy than you would provide. Confirm us in hope—assured that the task has already been matched by resources in your providence.

Hear our confession, O God. We have loved the escape of failure more than we have embraced the unfinished work of liberation. Forgive our impatient need for completion of your continuing creation. Help us to see with eternal eyes, instead of frustrated finite ones, your eternal purposes. Confirm us in hope—confident because of the completed work of Jesus.

Hear our confession, O God. Even when we have been together as your people, we have squeezed the life out of your church by our death grip on power. Controlling the vote has mattered more than controlling our tempers. Forgive our battle for the priestly office when Jesus already stands beside an empty tomb as final victor in that war. Confirm us in hope—obedient to his rule established by his sacrifice.

Hear our confession, O God. We have not looked for you in places of suffering, in bodies of the broken, in faces of the tormented. We have not seen you at the doorway of the harlot, in the shelter of the refugee camp, in the hearts of all who live between the walls of the almost-living and the almost-dying. Forgive our repeated search for some good feeling, some ritual that bestows acceptability, some configuration that insures security. Confirm us in hope—liberated by Jesus to love one another.

Prayer: *We believe, O God who loves us, who leads us, who delights in us, and we confess our hope—confirmed in you for one more beginning again. Amen.*

THE EMPTY CROSS—EMPTYING THE CROSS

January 19-25, 1987   **William Robert Sharman, III†**
Monday, January 19   Read Isaiah 9:1-4;
Matthew 4:12-23.

As an introduction to this week of meditations which will focus on the idea of the *empty* cross and the problem that Paul states of *emptying* the cross (see 1 Cor. 1:17, RSV), I want to take a look at the Gospel reading from Matthew. Here Matthew records that after Jesus hears about John the Baptist's imprisonment, he leaves his hometown and moves a few miles to the north to Capernaum in Galilee. Matthew then reaches back to the book of the prophet Isaiah to show Jesus' movement as fulfillment of the prophecy that a light will dawn on this "Galilee of the Gentiles."

Matthew then tells us that Jesus begins to preach from that time forward, "Repent, for the kingdom of heaven is at hand." Jesus is making clear that there is one thing to understand even if nothing else is understood. So Jesus begins from that time to preach, telling these people of the prophecy (these Gentiles of Galilee, these people Isaiah spoke of as living in the land along the Jordan on the way to the sea, these people who are in darkness) to repent, to turn, to look the other way because there a light is dawning, slowly, yet surely appealing itself to them.

Jesus is beginning a ministry of diversity and will soon take this diversity with him to the cross. And for everyone who claims it, the resurrection sign of the empty cross will be a sign of hope.

Prayer: *O God, help me to see the hope of the empty cross. Amen.*

---

†Associate Minister, Government Street Presbyterian Church, Mobile, Alabama.

Tuesday, January 20   Read Matthew 4:12-17;
                                           1 Corinthians 1:10-11.

These people of the great prophecy of Isaiah, the Gentiles of Galilee in Jesus' day, became the Gentiles of the Roman world, and they included the Gentiles of the great trade route that passed through Corinth, Greece. Corinth was a city that would have been built for prime-time commercials. It was built to handle all the trade traveling from west to east and vice versa. People were there for two reasons: the money and the immorality. All the whiz kids of business were there, and every size, shape, and style of religion was there, some of these religions so sordid that the Roman Empire would not even grant them a license.

Paul, of course, never bashful, has established a church there and has found that the gospel is not restricted to the small town or the people of a simpler, slower life. The church has made it through the formation stages, and Paul has moved on. However, after a time passes, Paul hears about a few difficulties the church is having, and so he writes to the church.

In the verses that we read for today, Paul begins his plea to the Corinthians with an appeal to a higher authority: "I appeal to you . . . by the name of our Lord Jesus Christ." Paul knows that they can agree on one thing—Jesus Christ—and so this is where he begins: be united in Christ. Jesus' ministry to the Gentiles shows that there is room on the empty cross for diversity among *people*; Paul is telling the Corinthians that there is also room for diversity of *opinion*. Be united in Jesus Christ, and let the empty cross of Christ stand as a witness to that unity!

Prayer: *Thank you, Lord, for our unity in you. May we always take our stand with you as our center, so that our unity may ever be evident to ourselves and to others. Amen.*

Wednesday, January 21   Read 1 Cor. 1:12-16.

After appealing to the Corinthians for unity in Jesus Christ, Paul states his case against them: Some are giving allegiance to Apollos, some to Peter, some to Paul, and others having nothing to do with these three parties declare themselves to be nonpartisan followers of Christ, which actually does as little to keep them out of church politics as self-claimed, nondenominationalists today. But there they are, divided and divisive. The three people they gave allegiance to are interestingly different: Paul is the planner of the group, the vigorous, enthusiastic worker; Apollos, the true Greek arguer, eloquent and sophisticated; and Peter, the earthy apostle of Jesus who had great qualities of leadership. I suppose all three: the man-with-a-plan, the prince-of-the-pulpit, and the good-ole-boy, appeal to all of us at one time or another.

But Paul doesn't speculate as I just have. He cuts through to the dilemma. "Is Christ divided? Was Paul crucified for you? Or were you baptized in the name of Paul?"

This was evidently part of the problem in Corinth. People were forgetting what brought them to the church and were following instead a particular charismatic leader, one who shared with them the intimacy of the sacrament of baptism. People were forgetting the importance of Christ crucified and resurrected. They were forgetting the call of the empty cross: unity in Jesus Christ.

Prayer: *O Lord, who has been crucified for me, and in whose name I have been baptized, guide me in my allegiance to you. Amen.*

Thursday, January 22　　　　　　Read 1 Corinthians 1:17.

As we progress through these verses in First Corinthians, we come now to the most important point that Paul makes. He says that "Christ did not send me to baptize but to preach the gospel, and not with eloquent wisdom." The word *wisdom* here holds the meaning of wise in a human way, as opposed to having a divine wisdom. This is why the phrase is translated "eloquent wisdom" in the RSV; the idea is to distinguish the kind of knowledge that is explainable with charm or eloquence, from the wisdom that cannot be explained with human words, no matter how eloquent. The *New International Version* translates the sense of the phrase clearly: "not with words of human wisdom." This was important for the people of Corinth because of the influence on Christianity of the Greek culture with so many of its silver-tongued teachers and philosophers.

Why does Paul warn of eloquent preaching? Because preaching for the sake of eloquence is not enough. Preaching is often called an art, but when it is beautiful or persuasive for the *sake* of art it ceases to be preaching. There is no artist who has ever properly portrayed the things of God. This is why we preach, teach, and witness to Christ, crucified and resurrected, and this is why the empty cross holds a deeper wisdom than words will ever comprehend.

Prayer: *O Lord, teach me your wisdom so that my knowledge will carry a depth that my soul can comprehend. Then help my mind to rest secure in that challenge, and help my heart to praise you for it. In Jesus' name. Amen.*

Friday, January 23   Read 1 Corinthians 1:17;
                                                          1 John 2:8.

Paul warns us in our preaching and teaching to be shy of human, eloquent wisdom, hinting that there is a wisdom of the gospel that transcends human words. The wisdom of the gospel is a higher wisdom whose knowledge is comprehended by the soul.

The writer of First John shows how the Greek word for *true* can also hold two different senses in the New Testament. In First John 2:8 the new commandment is spoken of as being "true in him and in you"—true as opposed to false. The reason given for this is because the "darkness is passing away and the true light is already shining"—true in the sense of *real*.

It should not surprise us that if Jesus Christ is the true light of the world, the real light, that the gospel of that light should hold a real wisdom, a transcendant wisdom. It should also not surprise us that any attempt to use human wisdom to communicate the gospel of the true light will in some way obscure that light. Thus Paul proclaims that he does not preach with eloquent or human wisdom, "lest the cross of Christ be emptied of its power." Eloquent preaching may bring attention to beauty and creativity and obscure the ugliness of the cross. Eloquent teaching may cause hearers to focus on the teacher; it may hold logical answers and simple solutions, but in the end it will empty power from the cross because the power of the cross cannot be found in logic.

Prayer: *O God, help me to be such a witness of the cross of Christ that it will remain full and powerful. Amen.*

Saturday, January 24   Read 1 Cor. 1:10-17.

What are some ways we as witnesses of the empty cross of Christ empty that cross of its power? One of the ways is by avoiding the true nature of Christianity. We like to think of Christianity as spherical or round—smooth. But Christianity is not smooth and understandable, round and even. It is *jagged* and *angular*. And by smoothing over the rough edges, we empty it of its power. It is so much easier when someone says, for instance, "Christians are such hypocrites," to say, "Yes, we are; we are really no different from non-Christians." But Christianity teaches more than that. We are hypocrites, but there is more to the story. We believe that Jesus Christ cleansed us by his death and that we do not have to feel guilty for our hypocrisy. We believe that the difference between Christians and some other people is that Christians should be sorry for their hypocrisy.

Or what about something that can't be answered such as when someone says, "I know that Christ was a great man, but how did he get to be God also?" It is so easy to say, "It's not important how he is both God and human. I never understood it either, but faith works it all out." No, faith does not smooth the edges of Christ being fully God and yet fully human; faith is what we experience that helps us believe that it is yet true! I believe that is true; I do not understand it, but yet there it stands, jagged and angular, just like the shape and power of the cross.

Prayer: *O God, I thank you that I do not have to be able to fully understand the cross to know that it holds power for me. Help me to be a good witness for that power. Amen.*

36

Sunday, January 25   Read Psalm 27:1-6.

The psalmist has written a song of trust, proclaiming as Isaiah and First John that the Lord is our light. Verse one says that God is the "stronghold" of our lives.

However, the psalmist goes on to describe the difficulties in life that he will be up against: evildoers, adversaries, days of trouble. These verses are descriptive of the tension in which we, too, live. We are thirsty and yet afraid to approach the water; we are invited and yet scared of what will happen; we see the true light yet cower at its brightness. The God who has allowed kings and rulers and domains to rise and fall also beckons us to come between his terrible and yet loving arms for protection. If only we will, we can, as the psalmist says, "dwell in the house of the Lord" forever.

But again, there are no guarantees; there are always risks that we can see and that we cannot see, chances that we must take. Making Christianity too easy or too simple will rob the cross of its power. By eliminating risk and fear, by making our commitment nonsacrificial, we take away from the cross its purpose and we empty it of its power.

Prayer: *Lord, help me to preach, teach, and stand as a witness for you. But don't let me do this in such a way as to cheapen the cross by emptying it of its power. Make me bold in my witness, trusting you to speak through my life as I open myself to you. Amen.*

THE LORD LEADS

January 26–February 1, 1987   **Raymond W. Fenn†**
Monday, January 26   Read Micah 6:1-5.

The Lord leads. This statement is supported throughout the Old Testament. In today's reading the phrase "My people, remember" stands out. The setting is a law court. Micah is the prosecutor acting on God's behalf: "Stand up, plead your case before the mountains." These are a disobedient people, yet the Lord wants them back. God recalls the deliverance from Egypt; the memorable attempt by Balak, the Moabite king, to stop the Israelites' entering the promised land. Balaam, a prophet, is employed by Balak to ritually curse Israel. Instead he blesses them: "I must speak only what God puts in my mouth" (Num. 22:38, NIV)

The mention of Shittim and Gilgal is a reminder of the sequel to the Balaam incident. One is the point of departure, the enemy side of Jordan; the other is the arrival town after the forty-year desert journey.

This week we have the opportunity to recall our commitment to the Lord. For each of us the initial decision is different, but the progress we make is dependent on our obedience. For the act of saying yes to be meaningful it has to be said each day, with the proviso that we obey whatever leading the Lord gives us.

Prayer: *Lord God, teach us to recall what you have done for us and to build on that foundation. Amen.*

---

†Layman, Anglican Church of Canada, Westbank, British Columbia, Canada.

Tuesday, January 27   Read Micah 6:6-8.

When I am reading scripture, I have a habit of selecting what, for me, are the key thoughts. In today's reading two questions stand out. "With what shall I come before the Lord?" (NIV) and "What does the Lord require of you?" (NIV) Both are designed to stimulate thought about what God requires of us. The answers given to the first question are on an ascending value scale. Animals eight days old could be sacrificed, but calves a year old would be of greater value. A royal offering would involve huge numbers of rams and massive quantities of oil. The offering of a first-born child is that of total dedication to God. This offering is in the same tradition as that of the boy Samuel (see 1 Sam. 1:27-28) and the boy Jesus (see Luke 2:22-23).

Following God means accepting God's total claim over our lives. No particular act of self-sacrifice can meet the demands of this obedience. There are three ingredients in Micah's answer: justice, mercy, humility. Justice not only relates with law but with each person's particular challenge. This idea is illustrated in the dialogue between John the Baptist and his listeners (see Luke 3:10-14).

The second, mercy or kindness, is probably best expressed as loyalty in all human relationships. And humility is the willingness to accept whatever God commands us to do. We should ask these two questions often: "With what shall I come before the Lord?" and "What does the Lord require of (me)?"

Prayer: *Lord, grant us strength, courage, and vision to do your will. Amen.*

Wednesday, January 28   Read Psalm 37:1-6.

For Christians the Psalms are an integral part of devotional life. Today's section underlines several directives for the disciple. The first is to trust. If we are not watchful, we find ourselves envying the godless, who seem to be successful materialists with no apparent problems. Accumulating such thoughts wastes time and destroys the spirit. "Trust in the Lord" is the antidote to such poison.

The writer adds, "and do good." Take the faith-step to be practical about changing your attitude. "Delight yourself in the Lord." What an intriguing thought! This is going beyond duty to experience what we each most deeply desire, and discovering that this is a source of deep joy. "Commit your way to the Lord." This involves making a lifelong decision and accepting the urgent task to enter into a full relationship with God. It means bringing our interaction with God into the center of life.

No more will we allow our faith to be on the edge but at the center of everything we do and think. This is the most serious and most rewarding decision we can make.

Prayer: *Enable us, Lord, to live with faithfulness in your love daily. Amen.*

Thursday, January 29   Read Psalm 37:7-11.

Many people seem to fear silent meditation or prayer. They worry about filling in that time space. We know that prayer is conversation with God—that it is speaking and listening, too. But we don't want to be left alone with God in the stillness.

"Be still before the Lord" (NIV). On its own, "being still" is unlikely to benefit our spiritual life. By force a child can be made to sit still, but inside there is likely to be turmoil. Deliberately relaxing in the Lord's presence, putting all distracting thoughts out of mind is the way to inner peace. This is not a defeatist attitude, being resigned to whatever happens; instead it is a positive effort to make the transition from fretting and doubting to fully trusting in God.

When we reach this point we know that without spiritual aid we can do nothing. But our worst obstacle, always, is our impatience; the feverish desire for results. Not only are we to relax before the Lord, but we must wait patiently for God's will to be done in and through us. Many people find this difficult. The value of yearning for stillness depends on waiting for God to be revealed in our situation. Inner strength is needed for this. Only God, loving and caring, can supply it.

Prayer: *Lead us, Lord, through rough or smooth places by your grace. Amen.*

41

Friday, January 30   Read 1 Corinthians 1:18-25.

In reading today's passage the words *wisdom* and *foolishness* stand out. The first verse stirs my heart: "For the message of the cross is foolish to those who are perishing, but to us who are being saved it is the power of God" (NIV). At first it looks as though Paul has made an about-face because the words *cross* and *foolishness* appear to be interrelated. The preaching or proclaiming of this cross, a self-evident fact for Christians, is essential; but for others it is something only an unbalanced person would believe. The unconverted, in their worldly wisdom, see nothing in it but nonsense.

Paul speaks of those who *are perishing* and us who *are being saved* in the present tense. Every person is in one division or the other. This use of the present tense means not everything has been learned of heaven's wisdom, and those who believe it are being brought into a new kind of life. In contrast, the perishing or the lost see only the superficial.

Paul speaks of the gospel as the "wisdom of God" and the "power of God." It is Christ who is both the wisdom and power of God. God leads us by the way of a servant Christ—a way that seems foolish to the world. But we will find God's leading in our lives as we are willing to participate in the way of Christ.

Prayer: *Almighty God, may we lean on your wisdom and accept your power so that we can do your will. Amen.*

Saturday, January 31   Read 1 Corinthians 1:26-31.

A profitable exercise for me is to picture myself sitting in a group of first-century Christians. The word is read from a letter written by Paul. Everyone listens intently: "Think of what you were when you were called" (NIV). In accepting the assurance that the Lord had chosen them in love, they had, perhaps for the first time, experienced self-worth. Many were slaves and knew what it meant to be bought and sold. Now they belonged to the Lord; this was what mattered.

What was I? What were you when God called? Our answer might be descriptive of our work: I was a carpenter or an accountant or a logger. For many of us, it should also be, I was selfish or I was snobbish or I was abusive. How would you describe your pre-Christian life? The answers will be varied, but the central core will be that the gospel light was missing.

Any ill-educated person today would probably be well educated in comparison with most first-century Christians. But the essential thing is that Jesus has chosen each of us. Everything we know is useful only in relation to him. Jesus sees our possibilities, which are beyond both our ignorance and our cleverness. In today's scripture passage the key word is *chose*. In good human relationships there is always equal decision-making. But in our relationship with God, God chooses us. We make the decision to ignore or follow.

Prayer: *Let this be the day, Lord, when we accept your choosing of us. Amen.*

Sunday, February 1   Read Matthew 5:1-12.

The Beatitudes express the way the Christian life is to be lived. They describe attitudes we should have as Jesus' followers. These characteristics are ones we should reveal. They are separate and yet interrelated. Each one refers to a spiritual disposition. That is, the clear distinction is made between the qualities described by Jesus and the natural ones which are superficially like them. This can be difficult to discern because some people have *apparent* Beatitude characteristics while a closer look reveals that this is not so.

All of us can be meek. The meek are those who are aware of their own limitations and trust the Lord completely for strength. We can be peacemakers, doing God's own work in the world. Being poor in spirit means looking to God for strength and courage against all odds. We can be mourners—looking with sorrow on a sorely troubled world *and* looking toward the new age when God will reign supreme. We can be merciful, or thirsting and hungering after right ways which will reach fruition in the future.

If we accept these qualities as the essence of our witness, we shall indeed be happy and blessed.

Prayer: *Give us the will, Lord, to live by the teachings of Jesus. Amen.*

THE SPIRIT AS THE LIGHT FOR LIFE

February 2-8, 1987   **Jan Sutermeister Edwards†**
Monday, February 2   Read Isaiah 58:3-5.

Israel misses the point of the commandment and fasts to get God's and others' attention. God's intention is that the people find the compassion to share and serve during this time of sacrifice. God wants the nation to draw closer to God. They defeat the purpose of fasting; instead of making an effort to show justice, the Jews continue to oppress those who work for them.

God sees what Israel does not recognize: that the nation fulfills the letter of the law but not the spirit of the law. It is not the donning of sackcloth and ashes which pleases God but living a day full of deeds that are acceptable to and advocated by Yahweh.

These words echo down through the ages. We often allocate a place for God in our lives where the Lord won't challenge us. We may fulfill what we see as a duty by offering a portion of our earnings, spending a day in church, sending our children to Sunday school. What does God require of us? The prophet Micah answers in poetic words which capture Isaiah's meaning: "To do what is just, to show constant love, and to live in humble fellowship with our God" (6:8, TEV).

Suggestion for meditation: *How am I an instrument of God's mercy in the world?*

---

†Pastor, Richmond United Methodist Church, Richmond, Pennsylvania.

Tuesday, February 3   Read Isaiah 58:6-9*a*.

The fast or sacrifice that is pleasing to God is the special effort on our part to combat oppression, help a neighbor, serve the poor, shelter the homeless, and nurture our families. This is the beginning of drawing closer to God. This is the beginning of living a life pleasing to God.

Isaiah says that not only will these acts be seen by an approving God, but the one who does them will be like a shining sun at dawn. These acts of justice and mercy will be as balm for our unhealed wounds. They will heal. The rays of sunlight will speak of justice even before we arrive at a place. We will live an integrated life, no longer giving the appearance of righteousness on the one hand while cheating the poor with the other. Our lives will be a beacon of praise to Yahweh, and Yahweh will be with us wherever we go.

Isaiah's image of the shining sun at dawn is an image of hope to a torn world. Isaiah believes that we can change the world by being examples of God's hope and justice. But if we are not the ones to do it, who will do it? Isaiah's own words of response to God echo in our ears, "Here am I, send me" (Isa. 6:9).

Prayer: *O Lord, my God, open my mind and my heart to receive your message, that I may more perfectly be your hands to an oppressed world. Amen.*

Wednesday, February 4   Read Psalm 112:4-9.

This psalm asserts that the one who remains in awe of God and obeys God's commands will be an example for all those who seek to be upright. Here is the basis of fasting or sacrificing to God: honoring God by obedience to the commandments. And it is this obedience which again causes the man or woman of God to shine like a "city set on a hill" (Matt. 5:14).

The characteristics of the obedient culminate in confidence in God. Thus the obedient do not even fear bad news, for God will see them through and be with them.

The psalmist emphasizes that the obedient ones have a character that is unchangeable. The true man or woman of God remains honest and generous forever. This person can never cheat or use others because he or she is truly good and will always be honored for that.

How refreshing a thought to remember that we need never fear bad news. God strengthens and supports us through even the deepest tragedies of our lives: feelings of uselessness, loss of a child, death. Perhaps we are not as steadfast as this righteous one described in the psalm, but certainly we can learn from this relationship with God.

Prayer: *O Lord, help us to be quick in generosity, honest in our dealings, and able to put every situation into your hands. Amen.*

Thursday, February 5 Read 1 Corinthians 2:1-6.

As a Hellenistic Jew, Paul had watched the fall of the pagan gods who could not satisfy the human longing for salvation. He had watched the rise of rationalism and skepticism of religion. He had seen the influence of exotic eastern philosophies, as the Greeks searched in confusion for new direction. The philosophies of the great masters were on the wane; they did not offer vitality. People were searching for something deeper; they had even erected an altar "to an unknown God" (Acts 17:23). They were ripe for a new spirituality, and so was Paul. He recognized the fulfillment of that need in Jesus, and so he brought Christ to the Greek world.

Paul offers the Greeks at Corinth a philosophy and a wisdom they have never heard before. He presents the gospel through his own experience of Jesus, the crucified Christ. He emphasizes that he leaves behind philosophical and rhetorical arguments, which are but human wisdom, and brings the people God's wisdom. "Your faith, then," Paul wrote them, "does not rest on human wisdom but on God's power" (TEV). Our faith, too, depends on the power of God, on grace working in our lives.

Devotional exercise: *Sometimes fasting for a day can help heighten our awareness of the holy in quiet times alone, in circumstances and in people. If the hours we usually eat meals are no longer the dividing points of our day, often we can be more open to the guidance of the Spirit. Try fasting for 24 hours, and use meal times to study the Bible in quiet.*

Friday, February 6   Read 1 Corinthians 2:6-9.

As Paul speaks to the Corinthians, bearing the "hidden wisdom of God," he says an interesting thing: This wisdom is not for everyone, but for those who are mature.

Oftentimes it is the elders in our midst who, knowing and seeing so much over a long period of time, can truly judge the worth of a thing. It is to these that Paul appeals, with the conviction that Christianity is not just a passing trend but that it has eternal wisdom and value. Christianity is not like the esoteric religions sold on the streets; it has something lasting and substantial to offer.

Paul challenges the elders, "those who have reached maturity," to examine Christianity, confident that the elders will attest to its worth and thus give weight to his persuasion. Paul speaks with confidence and yet awe of things beyond the human mind. He does not truly understand the Spirit of God, for it is something wonderful which cannot be grasped with the mind. Paul recognizes that the Spirit's wisdom is beyond his own, and he is compelled to share this discovery.

Paul holds God's wisdom as greater enlightenment than human wisdom. The symbol of the oil lamp has long represented education and knowledge. Now the lamp that Paul holds before his listeners burns brighter than any other.

Suggestion for meditation: *Remember that the Spirit of God moves through your words and actions, bearing witness that you have knowledge of God. Strive to be more aware of God's presence within you at every moment. Respond to that presence.*

Saturday, February 7   Read 1 Corinthians 2:9-11.

God's preparations and plans for those who love are revealed by the Spirit. As Paul relates this to the Corinthians, it is as if the apostle is discovering the mystery for the first time. His fascination is with the Spirit, who knows the depths of everything, even of God. If we cast our lot with this Spirit, we, too, will move to greater knowledge. And it is this for which Paul and many in the Greco-Roman world had been searching—a deeper spirituality.

Paul discontinues his persecution of this new people called Christians. He hears a new, refreshing message, and so he becomes a bearer of that message.

God's wisdom is for the good of the children of God. As God's Spirit speaks within us, we are capable of doing God's work. But not only are we capable of doing God's work, we are also capable of greater self-awareness. Each person's spirit reveals to that person the depths of himself or herself. Listening to our subconscious aids understanding.

God's Spirit reaches and reveals the depths of God. To the extent that our spirits are in tune with God's Spirit, we can also come to know God.

Paul saw ever so clearly that Jesus embodied the characteristics of the Spirit. Jesus shed light on who God was and enabled those around him to gain a glimpse of the holy.

Suggestion for meditation: *Let us borrow from Paul his spirit of discovery and pursue our spirit to the depths of ourselves. God's Spirit bears witness with our spirit that we are children of God (see Rom. 8:16), so let us not fear the unholy as we search within ourselves for the holy.*

Sunday, February 8   Read Matthew 5:13-16.

The Holy Spirit is the light for life. In Isaiah 58 we find that Israel succeeds in obeying the letter of the law, but not the spirit of the law. But God encourages Israel, and encourages us, to walk in justice, promising that we will then be like a shining sun at dawn, radiating mercy and anointing balm to the world. We will be as a beacon of hope, indeed, a light on a stand, a city set on a hilltop.

Matthew reflects the purpose of our being in the world. We can and should be spiritual salt, a necessary seasoning, for the world: And yet if we are saltless, if we ignore God and God's commands, we add to the problems of the world and risk being oppressors instead of healers. God would have us be filled with integrity and honor.

Paul offers for us, in First Corinthians (2:7-16), the hope that we can grow closer to God through the Holy Spirit and that we can even explore our own inner selves through our own spirits. Gaining self-knowledge leads us on the path to integrity, and God stands holding the lamp of knowledge to guide the way. Can we open our lives more to the light of God's lamp each day? Then we can become light in turn. God's wisdom leads us toward good, and God's grace shows itself to others in the way we live out our lives.

Prayer: *Lord, enable us to receive your light and to be your light in the world. Amen.*

THE INDISPENSABLE DIVINE LAWS

February 9-15, 1987   **Jung Young Lee†**
Monday, February 9   Read Deuteronomy 30:15-20.

The core of the covenant relationship between God and human beings is the commandments of God. The people of Israel are told that by obeying the commandments, they will honor the covenant. If they disobey the commandments, they will breach the covenant. Therefore, the covenant relationship presupposes free choice. People are not puppets but responsible human beings.

Many idols in the world constantly tempt us to breach the covenant. They are no longer the Baal gods or the fertility gods but the powers and principalities manifested in today's money, success, and self-glorification. We have the free will to resist their temptations and to keep the divine laws by loving God and God's ordinances.

God's commandments are more than simple moral or ethical precepts. They are directly connected with human existence. Those who obey the commandments will live and receive blessings, but those who do not obey them will be cursed and die. Our disobedience—breaking our promises to God—leads to the breach of the covenant. The Babylonian exile is often attributed to the Israelites' disobedience of God's commandments. The people of Israel chose curse rather than blessing.

Prayer: *God of the covenant, help us to take your laws seriously in our lives. May your grace be our help in our efforts to follow your law of love. Amen.*

---

†Professor of Religious Studies, University of North Dakota; Minister, Korean Fellowship; Grand Forks, North Dakota.

Tuesday, February 10   Read 1 Corinthians 3:1-3.

Spiritual development seems to follow a pattern similar to our bodily development. In childhood we need milk rather than solid food. In our early spiritual development we need certain basic guidelines to follow. In other words, as milk is essential for physical development, discipline is essential for spiritual development.

Discipline is a process of training our inner will to restrain certain external activities. The needs of the flesh, according to Paul, work against the development of the spirit. Therefore, it is essential to restrain the activities of the flesh through various forms of discipline.

Meditation, for example, is a discipline which begins with strict rules of posture and breathing techniques. As beginners we feel the pain of sitting in a certain posture, but we become more and more comfortable as we continue to develop the discipline of meditation. Beyond the preliminary stage of meditation, we no longer feel any constraint of rules and guidelines; we become spontaneous and natural. Laws are burdensome for beginners, but when we reach a deeper spiritual level, the laws no longer impose any burden. We begin our spiritual life with definite rules and regulations, but a mature spiritual life is spontaneous and beyond rules.

Prayer: *Help us, O God, to accept discipline for the training of our spiritual life. Amen.*

Wednesday, February 11   Read 1 Corinthians 3:4-9.

As those who are spiritually immature begin their Christian life, they have a tendency to form their own groups whenever a disagreement develops within the church. One of the most difficult problems that new congregations confront is this tendency toward schism. When a congregation reaches a certain number, two groups often develop—the people who are faithful to the pastor and the people who dislike the pastor. The latter group usually looks for another pastor or yet another new congregation.

In our text we find that the new congregation of Corinth is in the process of schism. The people of one group think that they belong to Paul, and those of another group think that they belong to Apollos. Paul tells them that all of them work together for the same God, who is not divided. There is no division in God's work, for God is the God of all people.

The growth of a plant is compared with the growth of our spiritual life. Just as the plant needs water and soil for growth, our spiritual life also needs external assistance for our spiritual growth. However, what makes the plant grow is none other than God. Our spiritual growth is also the result of God's grace and the presence of the Holy Spirit. We can only provide conditions for our spiritual growth, but the actual growth is the work of God. Therefore, we need to be united together to support God's work.

Prayer: *O God, help us to recognize that you alone make our spiritual growth possible. May we be united in our efforts to proclaim your love. Amen.*

Thursday, February 12   Read Matthew 5:17-19.

Some people think that Jesus came to abolish the old laws of Moses and make it easier for people to follow God's way. This is a mistaken notion of Jesus' teachings. Jesus did not come to abolish the laws that had been in existence. He did not come to add a new law to them either. His teaching reinforces the importance of obeying the laws; every law has to be kept. Here, Jesus asserts the absoluteness of the divine laws given to the chosen people of God.

This passage stresses the perfection of the divine laws. Because they are perfect and indispensable for our salvation, Jesus came to fulfill these laws. By fulfilling the laws on our behalf, Jesus saved us from our sin and opened to us the possibility of our salvation.

This is very closely related to the classical theory of atonement, which attempts to describe the death of Christ as a sufficient sacrifice for the sins of all humankind. In other words, Christ is our substitute, fulfilling all the requirements of the divine laws that we have failed to fulfill by ourselves. The perfect fulfillment of the laws was possible only by Jesus, for he was the Son of God. God does not compromise. Because the laws are indispensable for our salvation, God had to sacrifice Jesus Christ, who alone was capable of fulfilling God's laws.

Prayer: *Thanks be to you, God, for sending Christ to fulfill all of your laws which we have failed to fulfill in our lives. Help us to accept salvation by your grace alone. Amen.*

Friday, February 13   Read Matthew 5:20.

The fulfillment of the divine laws is possible because of a higher righteousness. Jesus not only fulfilled the laws through his higher righteousness but also asks us to do the same.

Jesus noticed that the Pharisees and scribes were unable to fulfill the laws. Their righteousness was based on works. But no matter how hard they worked to fulfill the laws, they failed to do so. Therefore, Jesus introduced a new and higher form of righteousness, which does not depend on our work but depends on God's grace. This higher righteousness is based on love.

How does this higher righteousness make it possible to fulfill the laws? The higher righteousness goes directly to the root of that which violates the laws. It prevents any actions that may go against the laws. In other words, the higher righteousness creates harmony and peace that do not give rise to acts of injustice. As long as people help each other and love each other as the family of God, there is no need for laws. The higher righteousness is *agape* love, the love that reaches out for others. With this kind of self-caring love of others, the laws are not really needed. By our practice of self-giving love, we can fulfill all the laws that the scribes and Pharisees were unable to fulfill. We can even go beyond the laws.

Prayer: *O God, bestow upon us the higher righteousness of your love so that we can truly fulfill your will for us. Amen.*

Saturday, February 14   Read Matthew 5:21-22.

Jesus gives a new guideline for his higher righteousness in this text. The higher righteousness which is based on the *agape* motive is preventive. The new guideline based on love deals with the root of human problems and troubles. Since laws are made to judge the consequence of acts already committed, they do not deal with the condition prior to action. The new law or the new guideline that Jesus suggests here deals with the human condition prior to the actual commitment of crimes. The new law deals with the motivation rather than the consequence of action.

Before committing a crime, a person may feel hate or anger. The best way to prevent the crime is to deal with the root of this act of crime, that is, to deal with the subtle attitude and emotional violence which eventually manifest themselves in action. The old laws deal with the external acts, while the new law deals with the inner motivations. In this respect, Jesus goes beyond the laws practiced in his day. The inner crime, a psychological or emotional violence, is also subject to judgment, according to this new law. Therefore, the law of Jesus is more difficult to observe than the laws of Moses. However, by observing this new law, we can also fulfill the old laws.

Prayer: *Thank you, O God, for your new law of love. Help us to observe it by your grace. Amen.*

Sunday, February 15   Read Matthew 5:23-26.

Since the old laws stand for judgment of actions already committed, reconciliation before judgment is a way to go beyond the old laws. In other words, reconciliation can resolve conflicts before judgment is required. In this respect, reconciliation is a means to fulfill the laws, for it is a way of resolving the issues through the new law of Jesus.

There is no way for us to fulfill the divine laws or please God unless we first are reconciled with our brothers and sisters. The act of reconciliation begins with our intimate group and moves out to our communal and societal life. Unless we practice reconciliation concretely, within our most intimate circle, we deceive ourselves. This idea is closely connected with the Confucian teaching that the most intimate circle, the family, is the core of all other societal and communal life. Confucius stressed the idea of filial piety as the cornerstone for all other virtues in life. Jesus here seems to stress the same idea.

Our reconciliation with our brothers and sisters is the precondition of our reconciliation with God. Some seek instant salvation through faith in God alone. These people stress reconciliation with God before reconciliation with our brothers and sisters. This, it seems to me, is contrary to what Jesus says in this passage.

Prayer: *O God, help us remember that we must first be reconciled with our brothers and sisters before we seek reconciliation with you. Amen.*

QUALITY OF LIFE WITH GOD

February 16-22, 1987   **Dorothy J. Mosher†**
Monday, February 16   Read Psalm 62:5-8, 11-12.

The industrialized West has discovered a new phrase in recent years: "quality of life." As a price is paid for pollution of streams and oceans; as wildlife is threatened by new development, the "quality of life" comes into sharper focus. A national magazine in the field of ecology keeps a scorecard from year to year to determine whether water resources, air, and wildlife habitats are becoming more or less endangered. Ecologists realize that when the chain of life is threatened, all creatures suffer.

What about the quality of life with God? One definition of the word *quality* is "excellence." Through daily prayer and Bible reading, we are able to live a quality of life with God which transcends all barriers. The psalmist affirms that kind of life. God, he says, is able to be protector, comforter, fortress, rock, and salvation for us. God is to be sought in silence and in trust. Life with God is never dull! Each day can be an adventure. God is able to point us in new directions. God wants this quality of life for us. Do we want it enough to discipline ourselves for it?

This week we will explore some of the movements in this quality of life with God. The movement can be toward relationship or away from it. As our lives change, we can determine how the quality of our life expands or contracts.

Prayer: *Teach us, O Generous Provider of all good gifts, to wait for you in silence. Amen.*

---

†Free-lance writer, Englewood, New Jersey.

Tuesday, February 17   Read Isaiah 49:8-9.

From exile to freedom

There was a dog who was never allowed out of his yard. This dog became so well trained that even after the fence was removed he behaved as if the fence were still there. We smile at such a story, until we realize that the fences in people's minds enslave too, like the fence enclosing the dog.

The writer of today's prophecy lived in a time of exile for the people of the promised land. How could they worship a God so distant from them? they asked. The new land was hard, but they had gotten used to it. They felt God was silent and unconcerned about their welfare. The prophet needed to shake them out of their lethargy. Perhaps, he told them, God is silent now, but God would not be silent forever. A new day was coming. They would not be an insignificant people any longer. God would use them as part of the redemption of all other peoples of the world. "Now therefore, if you will obey my voice and keep my covenant, you shall be my own possession among all people; for all the earth is mine, and you shall be to me a kingdom of priests and a holy nation" (Exod. 19:5-6). This prophet's vision put new heart in his people. No longer did they have to hide as prisoners—they were free. No longer did they live in the darkness of exile—they could show themselves. They were people of worth. God would go with them on the trip back to their land. Exile was coming to a close; new freedom and new responsibility called them to prepare.

Prayer: *Creator and preserver of all humankind, we ask you to throw open the doors of our prisons and allow us to come out. Shake us out of our self-imposed exile, so we can live as people of freedom and love. Amen.*

Wednesday, February 18   Read Isaiah 49:10-13.

From despair to direction

The writer of this section of Isaiah knew his people lived without hope as exiles in Babylon. Despair over their circumstances forced them not to face the future. The quality of their life had shrunk into a dull routine of slavery. They needed a new direction, new energy to hope and dream of a life beyond their servitude. To these people the prophet spoke words of hope. "I will make a highway across the mountains and prepare a road for my people to travel" (TEV).

God loved them so much that God wanted them to return to their own land. When the Israelites said, "The Lord has abandoned us!" the prophet painted a beautiful picture of God's providence. God cared so much for them that God had written their names on the palms of his hand. God could never forget them. God loved them even more than a mother loves her baby. "Can a woman forget her suckling child, that she should have no compassion on the son of her womb? Even these may forget, yet I will not forget you. Behold, I have graven you on the palms of my hands."

When people despair, they cannot envision a future. Someone else must give them a direction to follow. Only God, who understands all they have experienced in exile, can give them a new perspective. Suffering and despair are gone, the prophet told them; hope and direction would change their lives.

Prayer: *Help us to see signs of hope, O God, in the confusion of our world. Amen.*

Thursday, February 19   Read 1 Corinthians 3:10-11.

From one hand to another

The quality of life Paul lived with God shines with startling clarity. Once Paul had met Jesus face to face, his life literally turned in another direction. He never looked back.

Paul saw a huge world to win for Christ, but Paul was only one person. He knew that, at best, all he could do was plant the seed of a church. He had to depend on others to make the church grow. In some towns, such as Lystra, he stayed for only a short time; in others he stayed several years. When the time came to move on, Paul hoped the training he had given the church members was sufficient to sustain the church.

Paul was a person who was willing to move out of the spotlight so that others could carry on. "I planted the seed, Apollos watered the plant, but it was God who made the plant grow" (1 Cor. 3:6, TEV).

We need to bear Paul's words in relation to our churches.

The church is not our property. As Christians, we are participants with God in helping the church flourish. In a day of declining or plateauing membership, we cannot afford to present a feuding face to the world. We must rise above our tiny areas of interest to see the larger scope of the church. We may sow the seed. We may water the plant. But it is God who gives the growth.

Prayer: *Help us, creator God, to work with you without thought of merit or recognition. May we see the larger view of the church, from local congregation to worldwide presence, and be willing to spend our energies to further that view. Amen.*

Friday, February 20   Read 1 Corinthians 3:16-23.

From dignity to foolishness

Thank God for clowns! The world would be less bright without them. As we watch clowns perform, we could miss the theological meaning of their actions as they convulse us with laughter.

Every motion the clown makes tells a story. As the actor puts on white-face, the paint becomes a symbol of death. In becoming the clown the actor is able, through the death of self and the resurrection of the clown personality, to be transformed and to transform others. On top of the white-face, color is added—a symbol of new life that appears in large outlined eyes, full red lips, and cheeks painted with hearts or flowers.

A clown performs in silence, thus freeing the audience from dependence upon words. In the routine that follows, small things become important—a flower, a smile—while dignity and pride are punctured like balloons.

The clown approaches the audience gently—aware of tender feelings, yet trying to confront with new truth. The world we have grown accustomed to seeing suddenly turns upside down. We laugh at the incongruity. Also, we are given a chance to see the world from another perspective.

Many churches have become aware of the value of clown ministry. In a world too filled with words, clowns offer silence. In a world dominated by power, clowns show through their actions that small things can become great and great things are of small importance. The wisdom of this world is overturned by the foolishness of God.

Prayer: *O God, who always makes things new, give us a clown's ability to see the other side of life. Amen .*

Saturday, February 21   Read Matthew 5:27-30.

From fickleness to fidelity

We live in an age of sexual permissiveness, and we are paying a great price for it. As our society becomes more depersonalized, sexual affairs become easier to arrange. After a while the occasional thrill turns into a game in which people share with their friends the times they have "scored." But what happens when a person who has lived this kind of lifestyle for years begins to age? That person is no longer the attractive lover of before. When a person builds a life on sexuality, the loss of it can become a hell.

In an anonymous society we no longer worry about "what the neighbors will say." Some of us do not even know our neighbors, or they us. To be faithful to one's partner needs a stronger motivation than community disapproval—or even approval.

When commitments are kept and fidelity rules in a relationship, God honors these commitments. The result is a peaceful, productive relationship which brings out the best in both partners. Trust between partners is essential for this fidelity to work. It must be a trust deeper than just vows spoken to one another. Then, instead of the years holding less and less of promise, the richness of relationship grows progressively deeper with fidelity and love.

Prayer: *Lover of all people, we pray for fidelity to those with whom we live and with you. Amen.*

Sunday, February 22   Read Matthew 5:31-37.

From privilege to partnership

Marriage used to be the glue which held the society together. This is no longer true. Several factors are at work which contribute to this change: the economic reasons for marriages are not as strong as formerly; society is not shocked when couples "live together"; and the divorce rate ends approximately one of every two marriages.

In Jewish law the woman had no real rights. The husband was the privileged partner. He could simply speak a word and the marriage was dissolved.

Now that we are in a generation of equality between men and women, the pressure to become someone by marrying has diminished. Couples often cannot see the need to marry at all. If marriage is going to reflect the quality of life with God, a new foundation must be laid. In partnership, each member of the couple is truly equal, though not having the same gifts. There is room for growth. Each member brings special gifts to the partnership—gifts not based on sex roles but on talents and commitments. The couple chooses to marry not to find a hiding place from a cruel world but to be ministers to a hurting world. Together they have more to give than separately. Their commitment is to God first and to each other second.

Prayer: *Ever-loving God, help us see new possibilities in our commitments to others. Help us realize that our first and foremost commitment is to you—that our relationship with you guides and strengthens all our relationships with the people who become a part of our lives. In Jesus' name. Amen.*

SOME ACTIVITIES OF GOD

February 23–March 1, 1987 **Hugh Irwin†**
Monday, February 23 Read Exodus 24:12-18.

One activity of God is communion and contact with believers.

In our reading today we see two very important events. First, in answer to God's invitation, Moses went up to the mountain to be in communion with God. What a great enrichment of soul that would be.

We can hardly imagine all that happened during that inspiring time, but we can be certain that the time with God shaped Moses' life and future.

Like Moses we, too, are invited into God's presence. That reality should hearten and encourage us always. Being with God, *our* lives and *our* future can be shaped. Surely that is the core meaning of prayer—communing with God, not for forty days or nights but throughout our lives.

Being alone with God greatly strengthens our ability to live with others, no matter what their creed or color. All are God's children.

Prayer: *Help us, O God, to know the joy of thy continuing presence. May we ever be ready to accept thy invitation to come into communion with thee. Amen.*

---

†Retired minister and missionary, The United Church of Canada, White Rock, British Columbia, Canada.

Tuesday, February 24   Read Exodus 24:12-18;
                                              31:18; 32:15-16.

One activity of God is to give practical, helpful advice and laws.

Since God had chosen Moses to lead the people out of bondage and darkness, Moses must have sought and received help from God during the spiritual experience of high communion. Part of this help was indicated in the tablets of stone written with the finger of God. These instructions, given directly by God, expressed God's character.

We inevitably think of the Ten Commandments not primarily as a legal document but as a code of conduct to be followed in order for us to live as children of God. These and other codes and documents were permanent reminders of God's law and God's instructions for real freedom. They reminded the Jewish people that God's Holy Spirit teaches them, and us, many of the secrets of eternal life. Today, these secrets have been fulfilled for us in our fellowship with Jesus Christ, our Lord and Savior.

The Ten Commandments and others of God's laws direct us to a spiritual climate in which social order can exist and even flourish. They are a practical recipe of how to live a decent life.

These words were said to have been spoken directly to the people by God through Moses. Since they were intended for instruction and meant to be always remembered, Moses was summoned to Mount Sinai to receive the written tablets.

Prayer: *O God, creator, preserver, redeemer, may thy precepts and commandments be ever written on our hearts and followed in our lives. Amen.*

Wednesday, February 25 Read Psalm 2:6-11.

God demands responsibility with power.

This psalm was apparently written for the purpose of giving confidence to a king on his enthronement. Appointed by the Lord, the king would be given power to control revolts and to spread his favors worldwide. Along with such power, God demanded that the king be wise and that he worship God reverently.

We remember the old understanding of the divine right of kings, the belief that kings were chosen by God. All too often this idea was used to introduce laws that hurt the people. Tyrants too often forgot that with great power comes great responsibility.

Whatever king the psalm was meant for, the image is that of an ideal king—the Messiah, the Sent One of God. The final commentary on this image of the king is found in the New Testament. In real life it is only in Jesus Christ that we find the king who is King of kings and Lord of lords. He alone shall reign forever and ever.

No matter what kings or powers there are and ever will be in this world, powers that strive against each other with the fear of the atomic bomb and weapons in space, we ask, "Will the Lord, who has given us freedom to accept or deny God and God's laws, permit us to destroy ourselves and all of life, or will God intervene?" In it all we should remember that God is the ruler now and will so continue to be—forever.

Prayer: *Help us, our Creator, to remember always that we are thy children and so we live by thy power. Amen.*

Thursday, February 26   Read Matthew 17:1-9.

The Transfiguration, in which God revealed the purpose of Christ, is one of the most dramatic events in the New Testament. On the mountainside, two great figures appeared to Jesus and the three disciples: Moses and Elijah, the greatest of the lawgivers and the prophets. These were men who had seemed too great to die. It was as though these two great figures from Israel's history came to assure Jesus that it was right for him to continue in his great ministry. They would continue with him in spirit.

Was this assurance enough for Jesus? Was it for such assurance that he had come? Grateful as he was for their understanding and approval, there was one great question in his mind which had to be satisfactorily answered. He was certain there was a cross awaiting him. Strengthened by the knowledge that his disciples knew his true identity as God's special and well-pleasing Son, he wished to be assured that his death on the cross was in God's will. Jesus received that assurance, and he received new courage to go on even to the cross, assured that God was with him all the way.

We can never do better than to seek God's will for us individually. We strive to be certain that we are living in God's will. Surely this is one of the great uses of prayer—seeking God's will for us in all areas of our living. Sometimes, as in Jesus' case, it may lead to lonely places, but we can know that God will accompany us.

Prayer: *O God, help us individually and collectively always to seek thy will and to do it. Guide us always by the Holy Spirit. Amen.*

Friday, February 27　　　　　　Read Matthew 25:31-40.

God's vision entails action.

The Transfiguration did something for the disciples. Knowing that Jesus was determined to go to Jerusalem, which they felt would bring shame and humiliation, they now saw the crown beyond. They now saw that instead of humiliation, the trip to Jerusalem would be tinged with glory because of God's presence in it.

Seeing the transfiguration, Peter's reaction was his usual one. He said, "Let us make here three tabernacles; one for thee, and one for Moses, and one for Elias" (Matt. 17:4, KJV). Peter wished to remain on the mountain, to prolong their great experience. We can all sympathize with Peter for we, too, wish to perpetuate our high moments, our great experiences. But as Mary knew, and Peter discovered, there are times to be silent, to listen, to wonder, to adore in the presence of God and Jesus Christ. Afterwards, strengthened by God's might, instead of building tabernacles or other monuments we are to go back to the plain, to the daily ministry in Christ's name and spirit.

Perhaps our greatest moments are not chiefly for themselves but as means to an end. That end is to serve our brothers and sisters in Christ's name and spirit regardless of race, creed, or color. Wherever we go, whatever we do, we can still be in Christ's presence.

So it is *in* worship, *out* to serve; *up* to the mountain for inspiration, courage, assurance, and strength, *down* to the valley for serving the sick, suffering, and sorrowing.

Prayer: *Through the Holy Spirit, O God, fill me with thy love of humankind and make me thy servant. Amen.*

Saturday, February 28   Read 2 Peter 1:16-21.

In our passage today, the writer comes to what seems to be a central message to the people. This concerns the power and the return of Jesus Christ. At the time this was written, many no longer believed in the Second Coming. After all, it had been so long delayed after having been promised as imminent. The writer, in trying to recall the people to a living belief in the Second Coming of Christ, reminds them of the experience of the Mount of Transfiguration, where Christ's honor and glory were seen and God's voice was heard. The writer used the transfiguration story not as a foretaste of the resurrection of Jesus, as it is customarily regarded, but as a foretaste of the glory of the Second Coming.

Adding to this experience, the writer declares that the vision of the prophets, which was a revelation from God interpreted by the help of the Holy Spirit, continues to affirm that the Second Coming of our Lord is a living reality. We must both expect it and prepare for it.

The writer goes on to say that the glory of Jesus on the Mount of Transfiguration guarantees that the prophets were correct when they foretold the Second Coming of the Lord. Many of those who heard this message believed that the strongest argument for the Second Coming was that it was foretold by prophets who were declaring a revelation from God. Hence the writer suggests that no one can interpret scripture or prophecy privately as it suits oneself, but only with the help of the Holy Spirit.

Prayer: *We marvel at the various ways thou dost speak to us, O God. May we be not only hearers of thy word but doers also. Amen.*

Sunday, March 1   Read 2 Peter 3:10-15;
                                                       Philippians 4:4-9.

God acts constantly in life.

The writer of Second Peter does not provide details concerning how or when the Second Coming of our Lord will occur. Instead, he speaks throughout of how we should live in looking forward to the Second Coming. We are to become sharers in the divine nature by growing in grace.

Our expectation of the Second Coming should not be as it so often is: In spite of frequent warnings in the Bible against seeing signs and making assumptions about the time, place, and conditions of the Coming, we still do so. Many people have set even the hour and day of Christ's Second Coming, have sold their homes and businesses at great sacrifice, and have even journeyed to a certain place for that event. When nothing spectacular has happened, all it meant, they say, is that their calculations were incorrect. So they have refigured and set another definite date. These people have given up their everyday life rather than living it guided by the Holy Spirit.

In our preparation for the Second Coming, we should strive always to live in a constant fellowship with the living Christ. We should live with the constant expectation of Christ's return to earth, but not at the cost of missing his living presence with us always, the fulfillment of his promise. We prepare ourselves by walking in his companionship each day and by becoming servants with him of those in need. In this way we are most ready to experience his coming again.

Prayer: *Thou, O Lord, art with us forevermore. We are not alone. Thanks be to thee. Amen.*

CHOICES FOR LIFE

March 2-8, 1987 **Cathy Burkhardt†**
Monday, March 2 Read Matthew 4:1-4.

What if Jesus *had* turned the stones into bread? That sounds like it would have been a harmless action. The devil was not asking Jesus to hurt another person, or steal, or do something we would call drastic. But maybe that is part of the message here.

Are *our* daily temptations usually connected with life-and-death results? Maybe not. Maybe they are more subtle than that. We may experience the temptation to speak up to correct another person's mistake. We may be tempted to alter facts a little when we tell a story in order to make ourselves sound better. But in each of these cases, if we do give in to temptation, we are allowing a force other than God to control our lives.

When Jesus refused to prove himself, he was aware that his worth came from God alone and that he had no need to prove his worth to anyone else.

Suggestion for meditation: *Silently pledge to yourself that this day you will be especially aware of times when the subtle temptation to prove your worth to others comes along. Plan to take a deep breath at those times and realize that your intrinsic worth comes from God.*

Prayer: *Fill me, dear God, with a powerful sense of your image in my life. May I find my worth as I find you. And may I come to believe I need none other than you to mark my worth. In Jesus' name. Amen.*

---

†Free-lance writer, Nashville, Tennessee.

Tuesday, March 3   Read Matthew 4:5-7.

Sometimes a thing's value can best be determined by imagining what life would be like without it. Consider Jesus' temptations as recorded in the Bible. Imagine the character of Jesus without them. If Jesus had never been tempted, would we be convinced deep down that he was human? If Jesus had never been tempted, would we sense the importance of his being without sin? If Jesus had never been tempted, would he have been in a position to make up for all the sins that result when *we* give in to *our* temptations?

We are not often tempted to throw ourselves from the top of a temple. The devil does not show up in full costume to tempt us. But we do encounter situations every day that tempt us. We find behavior appealing that, if we engaged in it, would surely lead to alienation from God.

Temptation will always be real for us. Jesus' humanity shines through when we read that temptation was real for him as well.

Suggestion for meditation: *Identify one temptation you have given in to recently that has required God's forgiveness. Ponder the sacrifice of Jesus that makes forgiveness possible.*

Prayer: *Ever-forgiving God, you know how often temptation invades my life. Keep a strong hand on me, lest I stumble and fall. I know that I have strength of my own, but somehow I am infinitely stronger when I call on you for support. I never want to try to go it alone, dear God. Amen.*

March 4 (Ash Wednesday)
Read Matthew 4:8-11.

If we want to resist temptation as Jesus did, we must look at his secret. How did he refuse the encouragement of the tempter? Jesus kept his mind fixed firmly on his priorities. He didn't say, "Well, I could fall down and worship you, but you really aren't worth it." Instead he stated positively, "You shall worship the Lord your God and him only shall you serve." His positive beliefs ruled out the temptation he was presented with. Jesus didn't need to agonize over the particulars; he always kept clearly before him his highest priority—to worship and serve God.

It is easy for us to face temptations in our lives by trying to reason out the possible consequences instead of standing by our priorities and letting them rule out sin. Believing strongly in and acting strongly on what we profess to believe will help us resist temptation.

Suggestion for meditation: *Visualize yourself responding today to a temptation by saying aloud what Jesus said: You shall worship and serve the Lord your God only. Feel the power that this statement gives you over the temptation. Try to face a temptation today with this approach.*

Prayer: *Sometimes I forget, dear God, the very beliefs that have been my strength in the past. Make clear before me those events and faith-full decisions in days past that have kept me strong, that I may be strong · in the days ahead. Stay with me. Amen.*

Thursday, March 5 Read Romans 5:18-19.

A pessimist would say, "One person's sin has caused all of us lots of trouble." An optimist would say, "One person's righteousness has rescued all of us from sin." Both sides are presented in the Bible.

Without the good news, the bad news would make life hopeless. Without the bad news, God's mercy (Jesus' sacrifice) would have no meaning.

Jesus' sinlessness is presented as the sole reason for our hope. We are reminded of the grim spot we would be in if God had not sent us Jesus Christ. At the same time that we are confronted with our condemnation, we are confronted with our redemption.

Suggestion for meditation: *Think of ways you can adopt an attitude of gratefulness for God's gift during this day. Plan to respond to each individual you come into contact with today as a person who would have faced condemnation because of sin but who instead is saved because of Jesus. Think about God's gift to each of these persons, and to you yourself, another human being for whom life would have been hopeless without God's merciful intervention.*

Prayer: *Thank you, God, for showing me who you are in Jesus. And thank you for letting me know the joy that life holds when I can live as Jesus lived—loving, accepting, forgiving others and myself. I will forever need you, my God. Amen.*

Friday, March 6   Read Psalm 130:1-4.

> From the depths I cry to you;
>   Lord, listen to my voice.
> Let your ear be open
>   To the sound of my plea for pardon.
>
> Lord, if you keep account of wrongs,
>   Who will be able to stand?
> But you are prepared to forgive us,
>   That we may worship you.*

The psalmist presents the dichotomy of our predicament beautifully. We must cry out to the Lord that we have failed. We have sinned. We have wronged our God. As we cry out, we know that by all accounts we are lost. There is no hope.

But God miraculously does not hold our sins against us. God does not measure our sins with a ruler of logic. Instead, we find ourselves forgiven. Past the point of any hope, we have been saved.

Suggestion for meditation: *Where have you most deeply wronged God over the past few weeks? How do you know God has forgiven you?*

Prayer: *Lord, in the midst of busy and hectic lives, we ask you to give us strength to remember that you inhabit the fiber of our being. We are not of the world. We are yours because you have seized us from the most hopeless darkness. Keep us in constant wonder of this miracle. Amen.*

The Psalms: A New Translation for Prayer and Worship, translated by Gary Chamberlain (Nashville: The Upper Room, 1984), page 166.

Saturday, March 7   Read Psalm 130:5-6.

> My inmost self longs for the Lord;
>   I wait for the word of God.
> I tell myself, "Wait for the Lord
>   As a sentry watches for morning."
> As a sentry watches for morning. . . .*

Who can describe longing? It is a hunger, a thirst, an emptiness that must be filled. A missing part.

God is our missing part. When we are separated from God, we experience a dreadful emptiness. Waiting and watching for the one Being who can fill our void, we are alert for any movement. If we were watching and waiting for the Lord all of the time, we would be alert to God's filling us constantly.

Suggestion for meditation: *Think about an experience of waiting for someone you love very much when you had not seen him or her in a long time. Describe the feeling. What does it feel like to wait for God?*

Prayer: *Lord, my inmost self longs for you. Help me to know you are with me even when I feel farthest from you, when I feel most empty and most lost. As a sentry watches for morning, help me watch constantly for your care. Amen.*

---

*The Psalms: A New Translation for Prayer and Worship, translated by Gary Chamberlain (Nashville: The Upper Room, 1984), page 166.

Sunday, March 8   Read Psalm 130:7-8.

> Surely the Lord will be faithful,
>   And redeem us again and again.
> God will redeem Israel
>   From all our guilty deeds.*

Redeem us again and again. This is the meaning of steadfast love. God rescues us over and over. As we do guilty deeds again and again, God is being faithful. The love of God knows no bounds.

We humans have a narrow concept of time. We can't quite imagine what forever feels like or what infinity looks like. But we can look backward in time and see how we have repeated our mistakes with alarming frequency. To imagine God forgiving us each and every time gives us a hint of what our future looks like. A hint of what God's love is like, withstanding a constant onslaught of disobedience. An inkling of what it will be like to be part of this love forever.

Suggestion for meditation: *What sin of omission or commission have you often repeated, only to ask God's forgiveness again and again? What thoughts do you have about God's response to you at those times?*

Prayer: *Eternally faithful Lord, your steadfastness surpasses our wildest imaginings. Your love breaks the boundaries of our limited understanding. Your redemption surpasses all the guilty deeds we continue to repeat. We praise you, we wait for you, and our souls hope. Amen.*

---

*The Psalms: A New Translation for Prayer and Worship, translated by Gary Chamberlain (Nashville: The Upper Room, 1984), page 166.

THE PRIMACY OF FAITH

March 9-15, 1987   **Robert M. Holmes†**
Monday, March 9   Read Psalm 33:18-22.

The heart of our religion is trust, for it is only as we trust that we can manage to believe and dare to love.

As we think about the primacy of faith this week, we are aware that faith has many ingredients. It includes believing certain things to be true. It includes acting out our faith in daring and loving ways. But it also includes such trust as to rely utterly upon God. There is a difference between believing and trusting. If I told you I could hold your rope while you climbed over the edge of a precipice, you might believe me. If you climbed down the rope, you would be trusting me.

The psalmist in our reading trusts God completely. To trust in God's holy name is not just to subscribe to a theological belief but to entrust one's well-being to God as surely as climbing confidently over the edge of a precipice. We all have precipices of various sorts in our lives, and there are points at which, having done what we can to think and prepare, we must finally trust. And that trust is not just a grim and tenacious holding on, for deep in the center of that trust is hope. Hence, the psalmist says that we trust in the Lord and our heart is glad, not only because victory lies at the other end of our trusting, but because trusting itself is exciting.

Prayer: *Dear God, help me to trust you—completely. Amen.*

---

†Pastor, St. Paul's United Methodist Church, Helena, Montana.

Tuesday, March 10   Read John 3:1-8.

About one-fourth of the American population is on the move at any particular time. That is not strange to us. But imagine a seventy-five-year-old man, accustomed to being in the same place all his life, suddenly pulling up stakes, taking his family and all their possessions and moving clear out of his country into another. You might think he has either lost his senses or hears the beat of a different drummer.

Abraham heard a Voice speaking like no other voice he had ever heard, telling him to leave everything familiar and go to strange land where he would become the father of a new nation. As Paul later notes, it was by faith that Abraham left a life of security for an adventure of uncertainty, with nothing but his faith—his trust in God—to sustain him. One can only imagine what hardships and challenges he encountered on the way. This could not have been easy for a seventy-five-year-old man. But despite whatever hardships there were, he concluded his journey with a final act of faith—building an altar and calling on God's name.

We may never be given an assignment like that, but God may be calling us to move out into fresh and unknown territory, unsure of what lies ahead but with the assurance that God precedes us and accompanies us.

Prayer: *Dear God, help me to be open to whatever "marching orders" you are trying to give me, with the assurance of your guidance, your presence, and your care. Amen.*

Wednesday, March 11   Read Romans 4:1-12.

As important as love is in our religion, it is preceded by faith. To be sure, in Paul's famous love chapter in First Corinthians (13), he concluded by saying, "So faith, hope, love abide . . . but the greatest of these is love" (13:13). H. Richard Niebuhr adds that the *first* of these is faith. It is by faith that we do anything loving. What we do depends upon what we believe.

Another way to say that faith precedes works is to say that works express and act out our faith. Paul says it is not what Abraham did but why he did it that matters most. He undertook that long and dangerous trek as a faithful response to God's directive. What he did, therefore, he did faithfully! His works were an expression of his faith. Paul says the same thing about circumcision. The physical ritual was never as important as the reason behind it, which is why circumcision *per se* is not important for the Christian, but rather the faith that lies behind circumcision.

For a lover to say "I love you" and not demonstrate it in some way would be an idle feeling and empty language. Yet it would not be the deed but the love that motivated it that made the difference to the beloved. So with our faith in God. If it is genuine, it will be expressed in works. But it is not works that save us or matter most to God, but the faith that motivates them. So faith and works are not opposites; we cannot choose between them. The Christian carries out works faithfully.

Prayer: *Dear God, I pray that my faith in you will motivate me in everything I do. Amen.*

Thursday, March 12   Read Romans 4:13-18.

The word *promise* in today's scripture is an extremely important word in our religion. God's promise to Abraham is one of a long string of promises God is reported in the Bible to have made. Our God is a God who makes promises. The reason our faith is the most important factor in our religion is that we bank on God's promises. We believe God means what God has promised. We trust that God will keep promises. And God does. God promised to make Abraham a father of nations and did. God promised to liberate Israel from the oppressive rule of the Egyptians and did. God promised to send a deliverer, the Messiah, and did.

God has promised to be with us always, even to the end of the world. God has promised to bring a new heaven and a new earth. God has promised to vindicate the faithful. We have already seen glimpses of the fulfillment of God's promises from time to time. For what we have not yet seen, we trust. We cannot prove God's trustworthiness. That is why it is called faith, for faith cannot be proven. And sometimes the evidence appears to be mixed, as it did to Israel time and time again. Nevertheless the people of the Bible chose to trust God, even in the midst of uncertainty, much as today's physical scientists choose to trust the knowable orderliness of the universe, even in the face of evidence they may not yet understand.

Our lives confront mixed evidence as well. We often face problems that appear insoluble. We have hopes that seem impossible. Yet we choose, like that endless line of biblical witnesses, from Abraham to Paul, to stand on the promises of God, "who gives life to the dead and calls into existence the things that do not exist."

Prayer: *Dear God, I believe. Help my unbelief. Amen.*

Friday, March 13   Read John 3:8-15.

As you may have noticed, this is Friday the thirteenth. Certain people are superstitious about the number thirteen. Hotels have been built without a thirteenth floor for this reason. Interestingly, one theory states that the fear of Friday the thirteenth has a Christian origin: there were thirteen people seated around the table at the Last Supper, and Christ was crucified on a Friday.

A superstition can be a kind of faith. If one believes that Friday the thirteenth is unlucky, it will influence the person's behavior and that person will probably make it a point to remember everything bad that happens that day. But there is a difference between superstition and a sound and rational faith. Superstitions are grounded in the conviction that one must guard against evil spirits by all sorts of false maneuvers, like not walking on cracks in the sidewalk.

Our faith, on the other hand, is based on the conviction that the universe is in God's hands, that God's spirit is as invisible and mysterious as the wind, but that its effects are just as evident. The sovereignty and love of God, which we can trust absolutely, is nevertheless so mysterious that it can often be described by only the most obscure language, like that in today's reading. It is hard for us to believe "heavenly things," which is to say, things that transcend our limited, time-and-space-bound minds. At those points, all we can do is trust the One who shares these heavenly things with us, who "speak of what we know, and bear witness to what we have seen."

To trust that they, especially Jesus, are telling us the truth, is our faith. Such trust comes before everything else.

Prayer: *O God, help me replace my superstitions with faith and trust in you. Amen.*

Saturday, March 14   Read John 3:1-15.

One thing that makes the Bible a difficult book to read is that it contains two kinds of truth. There is literal, historical truth, such as that Jesus was crucified between two thieves, and there is poetic, metaphorical truth, such as the image of Jesus returning on a cloud. If we are not to be misled by a misreading of scripture, we must be clear about which kind of truth we are reading at each point.

In the incident in today's scripture, Nicodemus failed to make the distinction. When Jesus said everyone must be "born anew," Nicodemus failed to see the poetry and interpreted his words literally. It seems absurd that he would try to visualize himself emerging from his mother's womb a second time. That is what happens when we insist on interpreting the Bible literally at every point. What Jesus meant was something much more profound—so profound that ordinary language could not describe it. So Jesus chose the image of rebirth.

Faith must know how to appreciate the poetic and metaphorical. Jesus will return not on a cloud such as we see in the air but in a way no language can describe. Rebirth is an experience that cannot be easily described, but the image of new birth is a good one. It means a new beginning, a starting over, a coming to life in a new way. Only as we are reborn will we begin to see things differently, see things we never saw before, and understand them. Our faith tells us not only that this rebirth can happen; it also tells us that it must.

Prayer: *Gracious God, open to me the possibility of becoming a new person, perhaps even becoming myself for the first time. Amen.*

Sunday, March 15   Read John 3:16-17.

The first verse of today's reading has often been called "the gospel in a nutshell." It says it all. It tells about God's love for us that is so deep and far-reaching that nothing can diminish it. We may diminish God's pleasure in us but never God's love. God expressed that love in the ultimate way—even as Abraham had once expressed his love for God—by the willingness to give his Son.

Jesus' death appeared to be an ordinary execution. Two others were crucified at the same time. And yet in that crucifixion the community of faith was able to see something extraordinary— namely, the evidence of the depth of God's love for the human family! It was as if God had made a sacrificial offering of the divine Self, "the Lamb of God," in order to bridge the chasm between God and humans and bring about reconciliation. That is love to the highest degree.

Finally, the verse says that all who absorb this understanding of the crucifixion will be so lifted by the knowledge of God's unstoppable love that they will be saved from whatever might have limited, burdened, and defeated them before. In other words, the knowledge of God's certain love liberates us to love ourselves properly and to love others even sacrificially. We are saved from self-recrimination, saved from letting that spill over into unloving behavior to others, saved from being excluded from the kingdom of heaven, the very nature of which is love.

Thus we are saved from perishing, for that was never God's intention. Rather, we are meant to cherish and enjoy and use God's gift of life to the fullest.

Prayer: *Thank you, dear God, for the good news of your love and the freedom we find when we live in your love. Amen.*

UNDESERVED GIFTS

March 16-22, 1987   **Barbara P. Ferguson†**
Monday, March 16   Read Exodus 17:3-7.

This week's scripture readings all touch on a common theme: God's gifts to the undeserving. Exodus 17:3-7 is a prime example.

These Hebrews had only recently escaped Egyptian slavery. God had miraculously brought them through the Red Sea and had fed them with manna in the desert. Now they had struck a spot where there was no water. Did they turn immediately in faith to God? No. They complained. Certainly if anyone was faithless, ungrateful, and undeserving it was these Hebrews.

Yet what did God do? God gave them the water they needed. The gracious Lord gave another life-saving gift to this undeserving people.

Have you ever had that kind of experience? I have. God has given me gift after gift and still, when a new crisis arises, I panic. I find it hard to believe that God will continue to sustain me in the future as in the past. Yet my God does! Every time I come to the end of my rope, God has a solution for me.

Throughout this week, think about the crises of your life and about the gifts God has given in those crises. Through them try to realize just how trustworthy is this God on whom we profess to depend.

Prayer: *Lord, help me to remember and to be grateful and to trust in your future. Amen.*

---
†Research assistant, Department of Religion, Millikin University; free-lance writer, Decatur, Illinois.

Tuesday, March 17   Read John 4:7-15, 25-26.

In today's scripture undeservedness appears because of a lack of knowledge or intimacy with God.

The situation reminds me of handkerchiefs. As a child I received on each birthday a pretty handkerchief from a mysterious woman named Mrs. Moorman. I did not actually know Mrs. Moorman. From my parents I knew only that she was my grandfather's secretary. How wonderfully strange that this woman whom I had never met would send me this annual gift!

The Samaritan woman in our scripture knew something about God, but not a great deal (see John 4:22). She had no special "in" with God. She was not in close spiritual touch. She did not recognize Jesus as Messiah before he actually introduced himself as that. Yet, in her ignorance, she received the gift of "living water." (At first she didn't grasp the gift's meaning; later she understood better.)

Some of us may feel undeserving of God's gifts because we don't feel very close to God. Sure, most of us know something about God. Some may have read the Bible quite thoroughly. Some may hold theological degrees. Still, none of us knows God fully, and many of us lack the deep personal contact we desire with our Lord. We may even wonder in embarrassment if we would recognize Christ standing in the flesh right before us! Still, no matter how little or how well we know the Lord, the gifts keep coming.

Prayer: *Lord, I don't know you as well as I'd like to. But you give me such marvelous gifts! I thank you especially today for the gifts of _____ . Amen.*

Wednesday, March 18   Read John 4:16-26.

One important fact that makes us undeserving of God's gifts is our sinful behavior. John 4:16-26 holds an important message for sinners.

When a little girl whom I know returns from school behaving badly, her mother can usually guess that she didn't eat much lunch. Her stomping, book-slamming, and brother-baiting anger her mother and strain their relationship. Yet when the girl asks for a snack, the mother gladly fixes her one. The child doesn't deserve to be waited on. But she's hungry. What's more, she needs the touch of love that goes with the sandwich and milk.

In today's scripture we learn that the woman at the well has been involved in some rather serious sins. Her sin has alienated her from God. She is certainly not deserving of special gifts. Yet Jesus sees that she is spiritually hungry and thirsty. So he gives the living water of his presence. He feeds her heart with the good news that God's Messiah has come.

You and I, too, become involved in sin. We allow ourselves to go spiritually hungry; we behave in ways that displease God; we grow alienated from our heavenly parent. But God knows that we are hungry. Even though the behavior problems remain to be settled, God is ready at any time to give us the spiritual food and drink we need. All we have to do is to ask and to receive.

Prayer: *Lord, I know that my behavior does not always please you. But I also know that I am hungry and thirsty. I need spiritual nourishment badly. Thank you for giving, even when I am least deserving. Amen.*

Thursday, March 19   Read John 4:39-42.

In our commercial society we often see a phenomenon called the "spin-off." Supporting characters from a popular TV show soon appear in their own new shows; popular dolls or cartoon characters "spin off" into cereals, vitamins, lunch boxes, and so on.

God's gifts create spin-offs, too. Today's scripture is a continuation of Jesus' encounter with the woman at the well. This woman, like all Samaritans, was religiously disreputable in Jewish eyes. Beyond that, she was an obvious sinner. Her words showed her poorly prepared to meet the Messiah. Yet this undeserving woman received the gift of life from Jesus.

All this was wonderful for her. But that is not the end of the story. Verses 39-42 show the spin-offs. The woman told her neighbors about Jesus. These others came to meet him, too. Soon many had found salvation. They had done nothing special to earn it; they just happened to be in the village when the news came. The opportunity of a lifetime was offered, and they took it.

Like the Samaritan woman, we receive undeserved gifts from God. And there can be spin-offs from our being gifted. Other needy persons may encounter the Lord by hearing of our experiences. And aren't two or five or a hundred blessed lives better than just one?

Suggestion for prayer: *Think of the gifts you have received as spin-offs, the blessings you have found through someone else's testimony. Thank God for those gifts.*
Now think of others who have received blessings through you. Ask God to continue the chain on and on.

Friday, March 20   Read Romans 5:6-11.

In this passage our undeserving status appears as helplessness and as sinfulness. The gifts are justification (escape from the penalties of sin), reconciliation with God, and the good life that reconciliation brings.

Patricia had been abandoned. She had been left, a helpless child, in an orphanage in far-off Bogotá, Colombia. She had not—indeed she *could* not have—done a thing for my friends Mike and Arlene.

Mike and Arlene wanted to extend their family in a very special way: by adopting a child from a country where many children are in need. They asked to adopt Patricia. It wasn't easy. There was red tape, there were Spanish lessons, there were international complications. Meanwhile they kept busy buying lacy dresses and pink accessories for Patricia's bedroom. Then one day Patricia came. Patricia had a home! The family was complete!

Like Patricia, we are all born helpless and far from our true home. We are separated from God, not just by geography but by sin. We can do nothing to bring ourselves to God nor to deserve God's attention. Yet God has sought us out. Before we knew God, God was preparing for us. Mike and Arlene gave Patricia a secure family, clean clothes, good food. God has given us a place in a family, an intimate life with our Creator. God has canceled out our sin and has broken through our alienation. But it cost. It cost the death of Christ. What a marvel that God should bear such pain to bring helpless, undeserving people like ourselves to know eternal Love and an eternal home.

Prayer: *Thank you, Lord, for preparing a home for me, even before I knew or could respond to you. Amen.*

Saturday, March 21   Read Romans 5:1-6.

Yesterday we read verse 6 of this passage, plus the five verses that follow it. We noted Paul's emphasis on God's gift of reconciliation, made available to us even while we were still weak, sinful, and far from God.

Today's passage speaks about some further gifts that this reconciliation bestows. And what gifts they are: Peace. Grace. The hope of sharing in the glory of God! But then Paul goes on in a very strange way. He begins to talk about suffering. He does not say that suffering itself is a gift of God. He does say, though, that suffering produces the gifts of endurance, character, and hope. Suffering is an opportunity for God's Spirit to work in us. Suffering opens us up to our need, and God does not disappoint us in that need.

God's nurturing, strengthening love is not restricted to those who have earned it. None of us has done that. But Christ reconciles and God comes, even in our weakness. God comes to the marginal church member dying of cancer. God comes to the alcoholic. God comes to the doubt-ridden pastor grieving a dead son.

The gift of growth through suffering is not an obvious one. It seems very odd to say that we can rejoice while suffering. It's not easy even to trust God when we are hurting. Yet we can take some comfort and peace remembering that God has brought growth through previous times of pain.

Suggestion for prayer: *Give thanks for the growth and strength God has given you through times of suffering.*

Sunday, March 22   Read Psalm 95.

Today's reading brings us full circle in thinking about unde-served gifts from God. You may recall that our first scripture passage, Exodus 17:3-7, told of Israel's ungrateful, faithless complaint over a water shortage at Meribah. Now we hear again of the Meribah incident.

The psalmist uses it to impress upon us an important message. The people at Meribah were obviously wrong. They had not learned from the past that God would indeed care for them. But despite their faithlessness, God did provide the water they needed.

The psalmist says that we have a chance to learn from that earlier experience. Again and again, God has shown trustworthy care for us. We don't have to panic like those early Hebrews did. We don't have to disappoint God and make ourselves miserable. We can go ahead, trust, and praise God in confidence!

Fine! That all makes sense. But just try it the next time your child shows signs of developing a dangerous habit or you your-self come down with a two-week flu. If then you can sing praise to the Lord, you will surely have learned the secret of faith. But if you cannot sing, just remember: God gave the Israelites their water at Meribah anyway!

Prayer: *Lord, when the future is uncertain, songs of thanks don't come easily. Please help me to learn from the past that, undeserving though I be, I can trust you to provide in the future. Then, perhaps, I can sing. Amen.*

March 23-29, 1987   **James W. Holsinger, Jr.†**
Monday, March 23   Read 1 Samuel 16:1-13.

Spirit

God has called Samuel to anoint a new king to reign over God's people Israel! This was no little task that God called Samuel to perform. Should Saul hear of his treason, there would be little that he could do to protect himself.

Samuel looks at several of Jesse's sons, only to be told by God that these are not whom God has chosen. Several look like a king, but God reminds Samuel, as he reminds us, that it is not outward appearance but what is in the heart that matters to God. God simply does not look at people the way that we look at ourselves! The last son, David, is anointed by Samuel to serve as king.

With the anointing by Samuel, the Spirit of the Lord comes upon David in a mighty way and remains with him throughout his life. In the Old Testament, those on whom the Spirit came were set apart either for battle, royal office, or prophecy. What is important is not how this gift is received but that it *is* received. In the New Testament, the Spirit is given to all Christians as a mark of God's grace. It is not a possession to be seized with pride but a gift to be used in the service of others.

Prayer: *God of all ages, teach us that your Spirit comes to us in order that we may serve your people and demonstrate your grace. Amen.*

---

†Medical Center Director, Hunter Holmes McGuire Veterans Administration Medical Center, Richmond, Virginia.

Tuesday, March 24   Read Psalm 23.

Shepherd

The 23rd psalm has long been ascribed to King David. Its imagery is based on the shepherd theme, used to portray the attributes of the ideal king. It was symbolic, then, that God called David from tending sheep into kingship. The king was expected to lead, guide, and care for his people, but in addition the king of Israel was thought to be specially equipped by God for this demanding role. Just as David was called from being a shepherd of sheep to being a shepherd of his people, so the disciples of Jesus were called from being fishers of fish to being fishers of people.

This psalm clearly is the favorite of Protestant, Catholic, Eastern Orthodox, Jew, and agnostic alike. As a psalm of trust, it vividly expresses the individual's private experience of God's grace. It comes alive when sung, expressing what it feels like to find one's way back home to God. David, with all his many imperfections, often strayed from the presence of God; we easily identify with him when he felt the presence of God's grace once more in his life. For King David, as for us, this awareness of God's caring for us as a shepherd—protecting, guiding, and providing for us as only God can do—leads us to the knowledge that God's presence in our world is very real.

Prayer: *O God, we yearn to feel your shepherding hand upon our lives, guiding, protecting, and providing for us each day. Amen.*

Wednesday, March 25   Read Ephesians 5:8-14.

Light

For Paul, the life of the unbeliever is a life lived in darkness, while the Christian life is one lived in the light of Jesus Christ. Paul states that the Christian is a child of the light—the Christian *is* light! The light of the risen Christ produces truth and righteousness, as well as benevolence. This light enables us to discern between that which God finds pleasing and that which is not pleasing to God. All actions and motives in life are tested in the light of Jesus. To determine if flaws exist in an object, we place it in bright light. We will not purchase many things unless they pass the test of light. As Christians, we must test all our worldly actions in the light of Christ.

Light exposes the evil in our world. It is our responsibility to recognize that which is sordid and hidden in ourselves and to open ourselves to the bright light of Christ's love. When evil is pulled out of its depths into the light of Christ, it can be eradicated. We know the cleansing action of light in that certain diseases are destroyed by exposure to it. The light of Christ is similar in that it not only illuminates but it cleanses as well.

Paul quotes an early Christian hymn:
>Awake, O sleeper, and arise from the dead, and Christ shall give you light.

With these powerful words Paul states that the grace of God is ours because Jesus Christ himself shines upon us as we awake in the new life of discipleship.

Prayer: *God of light, shine upon us this day so that we may know that your grace is ours. Amen.*

Thursday, March 26   Read John 9:1-12.

Humanness

Jesus was not only the Christ, the anointed one, but he was one whose humanness we often overlook. In the Synoptic Gospels, we see Jesus as one who is almost always active—one who seems never to be tired. However, in John's Gospel we find a different sort of Jesus—one who becomes tired, needs rest, weeps. Most of all, Jesus was one who made friends, even of tax collectors and sinners.

In this story, Jesus is concerned that this blind man is presumed to have sinned *prior* to his birth! It was actually thought that a person could sin while still in the womb. But if he had not sinned, then his blindness must be due to his parents' sin. This thought occurs throughout the Old Testament—that the sins of the fathers are visited upon the children. As William Barclay says: "It must never be forgotten that no man lives to himself and no man dies to himself. When a man sins, he sets in motion a train of consequences which has no end."

The Jews of Jesus' day connected sin with suffering. But Jesus made no effort to connect the blind man's suffering with either prenatal sin or his parents' sin. Out of his deep humanity, Jesus sees only the suffering and is moved by the blind man's plight. Because of the depth and intensity of the humanness of Jesus, the grace of God came that day to a fellow human being—a fellow sufferer.

Prayer: *Dear Lord, help us today to find in your Son not only the majesty of your divinity but the kindred spirit of another human being. Amen.*

---

*Barclay, William, *The Gospel of John,* vol. 2 (The Westminster Press, Philadelphia, 1975), p. 39.

Friday, March 27   Read John 9:13-34.

Compassion

Throughout the Gospels, the miracles provide numerous examples of the compassion of Jesus. John sees in Jesus' miracles signs of the glory and power of God. In reality the miracles demonstrate both the compassion of God as well as God's glory, for in God's compassion is found God's glory. In healing the man born blind, Jesus is able to show what God is able to accomplish through this man's suffering.

Through the sorrow, pain, affliction, and disappointment of each individual, the grace of God can be demonstrated. The sufferer is allowed to see God in action just as the blind man was able to see the compassion of Jesus as he was healed by Jesus. Thus when life has dealt us an unbearable or devasting blow, the Christian can prove to all observers how sufficient the grace of God can be in our lives.

Also, the Christian can demonstrate the grace of God by aiding those who suffer in our world. We become the path or conduit of the grace of God flowing through us into our suffering neighbor. Indeed, we become a part of the grace of God as we expend ourselves in serving those who are in distress, in physical or spiritual pain, or in sorrow. God uses us as a pathway for his grace in order that it may be a part of the life of another person. To help others is to give to the world an example of the grace of God.

Prayer: *Our God in heaven, help us today and every day to be a pathway through which your grace and power may flow to a suffering human being. Amen.*

Saturday, March 28   Read John 9:35-41.

Power

For the man born blind, God's grace comes through Jesus with power. He confesses that Jesus is Lord by the simple but profound statement "Lord, I believe." He was able to throw off a life of suffering and discover a life filled with the power that can only come from the grace of God. The blind man's confession is no different from that of Peter when he declared, "You are the Christ, the Son of the living God" (Matt. 16:16) or of Thomas who exclaimed, "My Lord and my God!" (John 20:28). All three were making the same confession, with different words and different understandings, perhaps, but with the same meaning. All three had come face-to-face with the power of God through Jesus.

Through the power that God's grace had conferred on the blind man, he was able to accept the abuse which was heaped upon him by the Pharisees. Here was a man who was literally thrown out of the temple. For a Jew to be excommunicated was to be not only shut out of the temple and cut off from his fellow Jews but to be cut off from God as well. But as both the blind man and we discover, when persons are separated from others because of their Christian witness, they are brought nearer to Jesus the Christ. The life that is empowered by the grace of God is a life that is sufficient to meet the trials that life brings to all of us.

Prayer: *Dear Lord, we seek today the power of your all-sufficient grace. Empower us this day to meet the trials that come to each of us. Amen.*

Sunday, March 29   Read John 9.

Grace

(Before we begin today, read John 9 in its entirety.) This beautiful story of the man born blind recaptures the essence of God's grace as it comes into a person's life. Slowly but surely, as the tale unfolds, the blind man's eyes are opened as to who and what Jesus really is. The story symbolizes every person's dawning understanding of Jesus. First, the blind man recognizes Jesus as a man. He sees in Jesus a humanness that reaches out to him in his misery and suffering and treats him as a fellow human being. It is fair to recognize that Jesus is a human being among human beings.

Second, the blind man began to recognize in Jesus a spirituality which encompassed calling him a great prophet. Too many of us today are content only to recognize the great prophet in Jesus. It is easy to see in him one who has brought God's message to us. Clearly, Jesus lived a life that was close to God; he also lived a life which spoke of a clear knowledge of God. Thus we, too, can state, "He is a prophet." But is that all?

As God's grace continued to unfold for the blind man, he came to realize that Jesus was more than a human being, more than a prophet. He realized that human words and notions are simply inadequate to describe Jesus. As God's grace unfolded in the life of this blind man, he discovered the greatness of Jesus. Ultimately he was able to confess that Jesus is Lord! Can we?

Benediction: *"Grace to you and peace from God the Father and the Lord Jesus Christ."* *

---

*Gal. 1:3.

PREREQUISITES FOR RESURRECTION

March 30–April 5, 1987   **Mary Olson†**
Monday, March 30   Read Romans 8:6-11.

With gentle hands the pastor deliberately breaks the communion loaf. When the rough-edged halves no longer touch one another, she says, *"We recognize and give thanks that it is in the most broken and fractured places of our lives that God is present, bringing us resurrection."*

Then the bread is tasted by the community. The challenging memory of Jesus and the comforting Spirit of Christ merge into the gathered experience.

This week, as the pace to the Passion quickens, we ask ourselves what is necessary if that communion bread is truly to be experienced as a sign and presence of resurrection. If resurrection comes at the most dead and broken places of our lives, where could it happen for us? Where are we most dead and broken? How can we prepare ourselves for the miracle within the broken bread: God's great act of resurrection? We list six prerequisites to resurrection readiness:

> Recognizing death
> Knowing our history
> Owning our destiny
> Being assertive with God
> Experiencing intimacy
> Assessing our God-esteem

What would you add to the list? Delete? What might Paul add?

Prayer: *O God, open our hearts to the resurrection of Jesus and to the resurrection you can bring out of the despair of our own lives. Amen.*

---

†Director, D. Min. Program and Continuing Education, United Theological Seminary, Dayton, Ohio.

Tuesday, March 31   Read Ezekiel 37:1-2.

Recognizing death

God wants to be sure Ezekiel knows that those bones are not only dry; they are very dry. They are lifeless, useless, and without breath. Israel had made some haughty mistakes and paid a heavy price. It looked as if the nation's existence was to be only a short phase in human history. And God is not about to deny the sad state of affairs, the suffering, or the condition of the people. Death is real.

It sounds so obvious: God resurrects only that which is dead. We nod agreement. Yet, we want to jump past Good Friday to Easter. We had rather not face Christ's pain or our own. We had rather deny all of it, keeping it hid in the closets of our hearts.

Consider our church attendance. Sparsely filled pews mark Good Friday services. Extra seats in the aisles mark the celebrations of Easter Day. Yet little change is possible until Good Friday is as vivid as Easter.

Consider divorcing couples. Until they can say, "The marriage is dead," God's resurrection for them together or as two people leading two separate lives is denied. When death is recognized, resurrection relationships become possible.

Consider the terminally ill patient. Until death's reality is recognized, there can be no sense of God's eternal care. With the recognition of death comes the possibility of eternal life.

The death in Ezekiel's valley is real. The death of relationships is real. The death of nations and individuals is real. God's first prerequisite is for us to face death's reality and pain.

Prayer: *O God, who both challenges and comforts, help us name specifically the broken, dead places of our lives so you can bring your resurrection. Amen.*

Wednesday, April 1   Read Ezekiel 37:3-12.

Knowing our history

"My people" God calls those dry bones in the valley. The messages of the entire Bible can be summed up in those two words, if we understand our history.

If we do not understand our biblical heritage, those two words make God sound like an absolute fool. God Almighty standing in the middle of nowhere, talking to a bunch of very dry, very lifeless bones. Without a knowledge of our history, stranger still is the fact that God doesn't even say those dead bones *will become* "my people." God flatly insists they were and are God's same people who will be brought back to life.

God's naming those bones "my people" is one more time when God is true to the covenant. Our history is one of God's loving action in the most desolate places and conditions imaginable.

Our biblical history is a history of people and a nation making mistakes and suffering for those mistakes. But it is also a history of God's new life breaking in to make use of even the worst selfish errors. Knowledge of wounds as deep as death becomes a source from which God initiates resurrection.

It is when we know our history as God's history and our story as the story of God working to bring resurrection experiences into the world that we can sing with enthusiasm and joy, in the midst of the good times and the bad:

> O God, our help in ages past, Our hope for years to come,
> Our shelter from the stormy blast, And our eternal home!*

Prayer: *O God in and beyond history, grant us the historical perspective on which to base our belief in you. Amen.*

---

*Isaac Watts, "O God, Our Help in Ages Past," the United Methodist *Book of Hymns*, no. 28.

Thursday, April 2 Read Ezekiel 37:13-14.

Owning our destiny

It would be easier to stay dead and lifeless. God puts spirit and life into these old bones that are the whole house of Israel and makes them an alive people called to the challenge of every age: to know God as Lord of their lives and relationships. It would be easier to stay dead and lifeless.

It would be easier, but it would not be their destiny to remain so powerless and insignificant. For Israel's destiny and ours is a destiny of chosenness—chosen to offer light to the world, to suffer for the sake of others, to bear one another's burdens. Those bones were resurrected to be destined for the same purpose for which they were originally given form: to be God's people in word and deed.

To own that destiny is to say with the hymn writer:

> Lord, speak to me, that I may speak
> In living echoes of thy tone;
> As thou hast sought, so let me seek
> Thine erring children lost and lone.*

It would be easier to stay dead and lifeless. There would be no risk of failure, no angry judgment, no unknown roads. There would be no more crosses to bear, no more pain to take on, no more losses to endure. But neither would there be the joy that lives through pain or the love that transforms. To become ready for resurrection is to own our destiny as God's chosen people.

Prayer: *O God of all of life, we give you thanks for not leading us to the easy way of living but to the meaningful way of living. We give you thanks for giving us joint destiny with you. Amen.*

---

*Frances R. Havergal, "Lord, Speak to Me," the United Methodist *Book of Hymns*, no. 195.

Friday, April 3   Read Psalm 116:1-9.

Being assertive with God

"What do you expect the Lord to do in your life today?" the pastor inquires. The group listens to the question and responds with stony silence.

"If you don't expect the Lord to do much, I wouldn't look for much action," was the pastor's concluding comment.

Unlike the passive group, the psalmist calls to God with bold exclamations and expects action. This psalmist is in trouble—despair-unto-death—and expects God to intervene with quick, powerful change. The writer doesn't even say, "Lord, I don't really want to bother you," or, "It'd be kind of nice if you would listen to me." There's nothing wishy-washy or quiet about this psalmist. He is assertive before God, talking as a person who remembers even when "surrounded by the pangs of Sheol" that he is a child of God. He remembers who he is and Whose he is.

The psalmist's faith is based on the certainty that God is consistent and dependable. In trouble and sorrow, God's actions will be righteous and merciful because that's the way God has always acted before. God can be trusted.

The rainbow couldn't have been far from the mind of this psalmist calling out to God. Genesis 9:15 tells us God put that rainbow in the sky not so much to remind people of the covenant relationship as to remind God of God's responsibility. The psalmist intends to hold God to the promise.

Prayer: *O God, hear us today as you heard the psalmist of old; for we, too, expect you to transform our lives. Amen.*

Saturday, April 4   Read John 11:1-16.

Experiencing intimacy

"You can't be Christian alone," we quip in the church. It is just as accurate to say, "We can't get resurrected alone." We are created to be in relationship with people and with our Lord. When resurrection comes out of death—be it death of the physical, emotional, spiritual, or mental—God's resurrection is an experience among people in God's presence.

Read the Lazarus narrative. Lazarus himself didn't ask for resurrection. It was the people who loved him who wanted that resurrection enough to be assertive with Jesus and seek out Jesus' presence.

Read the Lazarus narrative again. It isn't a story of a group of people expressing deep emotions among themselves at one moment and with Jesus at another. Rather, the account of the events leading up to Lazarus' resurrection shows passionate feelings of people intimate with each other and with Christ.

Resurrection readiness may lead to new life with the same people or with entirely different people. But the relationships must begin in intimacy with God.

A small group of friends joins hands before scattering to various parts of the country. One person interrupts the parting silence to ask, "Please, this week, pray with me wherever you are. Ask God to be with us and our daughter as she comes home from the hospital where she checked herself in to combat depression."

The resurrection hasn't come yet—but preparation is being made for the possibility of God's inbreaking.

Prayer: *O God, we give thanks for the intimate relationships in our lives which channel the power of your resurrection. Amen.*

Sunday, April 5   Read John 11:17-46.

Assessing our God-esteem

Self-esteem is belief in one's own importance and ability. "God-esteem" is belief in God's importance and ability.

We talk a lot about self-esteem today. Some even conclude that development of our full potential as human beings is a God-given top priority. But the top biblical priority is not self-esteem but honoring and glorifying God.

Therefore, God-esteem is at the core of our very existence. We believe in who we are as God's people because we hold God in highest esteem. "To God be the glory," we respond liturgically.

To assess our God-esteem, we look at our faith in God. To have faith in God, we must first of all know God and God's action. God is at the heart of all our relationships, words, and actions. Our belief and trust in God grow into fuller God-esteem as we experience God face-to-face in our lives.

Jesus says to Martha, "Did I not say to you that if you would believe you would see the glory of God?" It is Martha's belief in the power of God, or God-esteem, that is the prerequisite for the resurrection of her brother.

All week we have been thinking about prerequisites for resurrection. Having all the prerequisites in place is no guarantee of resurrection living. The ultimate initiative of the inbreaking is God's. We await God's enthusiastic vision and action. We are as clay, ready to be remolded by the God of love and mercy.

Prayer: *O God, remold us as you will, for we are your people and the sheep of your pasture. Amen.*

HOSANNA: SAVE NOW!

April 6-12, 1987   **Evelyn Laycock**†
Monday, April 6   Read Psalm 31:9-16.

A unique thread is woven through the scripture passages of this week. It is the cry, "Save now!" *Salvation* is a word that is common to our language, but if we tried to define it, there would be as many definitions as individuals who were given the task. So it is in our scripture passages. Salvation, in a variety of forms, is yearned for; it is desperately sought.

Studying Psalm 31, we become very much aware that verses 9 through 11 are a long lament. The writer leaves nothing unsaid. The writer's life is in utter turmoil: "My eye is wasted from grief . . ."; "I have passed out of mind like one who is dead . . ."; and "I have become like a broken vessel."

Notice, however, in spite of this condition, in verse 14 the psalmist takes the first step to recovery: "I trust in thee, O Lord." This is a response to the psalmist's realization of what God is really like. Even though life has "closed in," there can still be purpose and meaning when trust is placed in God.

With such a commitment, the psalmist is then able to affirm, "Thou art my God." Such a declaration confirms that God is not just the God of the universe or of Abraham or of Moses. This God is one who desires a personal relationship with each of us. Salvation came for the psalmist in the experience of an encounter with the living God.

Prayer: *Dear God, help me open my life so I may experience you in all situations. Amen.*

---

†Professor of Religion, Hiwassee College, Madisonville, Tennessee.

Tuesday, April 7   Read Psalm 118:19-29.

There is a company of pilgrims marching toward the Temple on Zion's hill. As they march, they sing. A tuneful, solitary voice announces the theme of the song, "O give thanks to the Lord, for he is good!" To this statement other pilgrims respond, "His steadfast love endures for ever." This antiphonal theme continues as the pilgrims make their way to the Temple.

By the time the procession has reached the precincts of the Temple, the gatekeeper is hailed, "Open to me the gates of righteousness, that I may enter through them and give thanks to the Lord." These gates give entrance to the Temple court. They are righteous because persons believed them to lead to the earthly dwelling place of a righteous God. The psalmist wants to go through the gates in order to praise God for God's mighty work.

What mighty work has God done for this pilgrim? The writer of the psalm has suffered greatly and has been released from many distresses. Exactly what the suffering was is not revealed, but what is clear is that it was severe enough to try the pilgrim's soul to the uttermost. The pilgrim called upon the Lord, who heard the cry of distress and gave deliverance (salvation). Now, the psalmist wants to give praise for the fact that God's steadfast love *does* endure forever. The psalmist knows—the psalmist has experienced it!

Suggestion for meditation: *Think of times in your life when you have experienced God's mercy—God's steadfast love. Give thanks for these times. Think of the future. Can you in faith affirm that God's love and mercy endure forever?*

Wednesday, April 8   Read Philippians 2:5-11.

The letter to the church at Philippi is thought by some to be Paul's last letter from prison before his death. But regardless of when Paul wrote it, one senses in his writing an urgency to give to the Philippians the heart of the teachings of Jesus Christ. When one is facing death, he or she does not deal in trivia but, rather, in what is extremely important and meaningful.

Paul tells the Philippians, "Have this mind among yourselves, which is yours in Christ Jesus." What a teaching! It is easy to imagine the questions this statement generated, because they are the questions of every person: "I am human. How can I have the mind of Christ?" or "What does one do to have the mind of Christ?"

What does Paul mean when he makes such a bold statement? Because we are created in the image of God, Paul felt this gave us unlimited possibilities to grow in Godlike qualities. For example, we have the ability to love and be loved, the ability to conceive of justice and pursue it, the ability to know God and enter into a personal relationship with God. In Jesus we fully see these Godlike qualities. Therefore, to have these qualities is to become fully human—that which we were created to be.

It is easy to excuse our mediocre living by saying, "I'm only human," when in reality being human is one of the greatest gifts of God to us.

Is it possible to have this mind in us which was also in Christ Jesus? According to Paul, it is a normal happening as one follows Christ.

Prayer: *O God, save me now from smallness of vision of what it means to be created in your image. I ask that the mind of Christ may be in me this day. Amen.*

110

Thursday, April 9   Read John 12:12-13.

During the next four days our thoughts will focus on the events surrounding Palm Sunday. In these hours again we will see God taking the initiative on behalf of humanity.

It is the time of the Passover in Jerusalem! During that season, Jews came great distances to celebrate.

News and rumor had gone out that the man who had raised Lazarus from the dead was on his way to Jerusalem. A crowd was waiting in Jerusalem, and a crowd journeyed with Jesus from Bethany. In Jerusalem, both groups united into one voice and cried, "Hosanna! Blessed is he who comes in the name of the Lord, even the King of Israel!" The word *Hosanna* is the Hebrew for "Save now!" Jesus is regarded as a conqueror.

The words with which the people greeted Jesus are a quotation from Psalm 118:25-26. That psalm had great significance in the minds of the Jews. It was the last psalm of a group known as the *Hallel*, which means "Praise God!" The *Hallel* was part of the first memory work every Jewish boy had to learn, and psalms from the *Hallel* were sung in the Temple. Psalms from the *Hallel* were and still are an integral part of the feasts of Passover and Tabernacles, and Psalm 118:25-26 was used to welcome back victorious leaders who had been engaged in battle.

This was a psalm for a great occasion. There is no doubt that they were looking on Jesus as the Messiah, God's Anointed One; the Conqueror, the one who would save them from their oppressors.

Suggestion for meditation: *Picture yourself among that crowd in Jerusalem. Imagine the thrill you will experience as the realization comes to you that this Jesus, whom you are seeing, is truly the Son of God and your Savior.*

Hosanna: Save Now!

Friday, April 10   Read John 12:14-15.

It must have hurt Jesus deeply to know the expectations the people held of the Messiah and how these differed with his life and teachings. The crowd looked for the Messiah of their own dreams and their own wishful thinking. They did not look for the Messiah whom God had sent.

In this situation, Jesus chose to "live out" his message for all to see. In a deliberate claim to be the Messiah, Jesus rode into Jerusalem on a donkey. This act is the fulfillment of the prophecy about the Messiah found in Zechariah 9:9, "Rejoice greatly, O daughter of Zion! Shout aloud, O daughter of Jerusalem! Lo, your king comes to you; triumphant and victorious is he, humble and riding on an ass, on a colt the foal of an ass." Jesus is saying by this action, "I am the one about whom Zechariah spoke so many centuries ago. I am the long-awaited Messiah."

People in the crowd had heard the words of Zechariah many, many times. The greatest longing in the hearts of the Jews was for the Messiah to come and usher in the kingdom of God. This act of Jesus was more than a proclamation about the kingdom; it proclaimed the kingdom had already broken into the world.

Prayer: *Loving God, save me now from my blindness to your mighty work that is going on right in the arena in which I live. May I accept your gift of your kingdom. Amen.*

Saturday, April 11   Read Zechariah 9:9-10.

There is another interesting reason for Jesus' riding into Jerusalem on a donkey. Jesus, by this very act, is describing the nature of the kingdom of God. In the United States the donkey is thought to be a lowly and rather useless animal, but not so in the East, where it is regarded as a noble animal. Jair, a judge of Israel, had thirty sons who rode donkeys (see Judg. 10:4). The royal prince, Mephibosheth, came to David riding on a donkey (see 2 Sam. 19:26).

The kind of animal on which a king rode indicated the nature of the king's reign. If a king came riding on a horse, he was bent on war. If he rode a donkey, he was coming in peace. The action of Jesus told the crowd that he was not the mighty warrior that so many Jews dreamed of, but he was the Prince of Peace.

The triumphal entry of Jesus into Jerusalem was an act of great courage. Jesus was being sought by the authorities. It was dangerous for him to be in the city. If he had to come to Jerusalem, then the best way would have been to slip in and out. But Jesus did not choose that way. Instead, he fulfilled the prophecy of Zechariah right in front of the eyes of the entire crowd, with the hope that they might truly see God's Anointed One, the Prince of Peace.

Suggestion for meditation: *The teachings of Jesus are the road to true peace. When Jesus is experienced as Messiah in my life, then I become a peacemaker. Is this my position? How can I fulfill this?*

April 12 (Palm Sunday)

Read John 12:16.

Even though the disciples of Jesus had been with him for three years, they did not grasp the great significance of what was being proclaimed in their midst. The theme of all the teachings of Jesus had been, "Repent, for the kingdom of heaven is at hand" (Matt. 4:17). But they had difficulty in connecting the life of Jesus with the inbreaking of this kingdom. Is it the same with us today?

One of the most misunderstood and misused phrases in the Bible is "the kingdom of God." A recent survey was made among church folk. One of the questions asked was, "What do you believe the kingdom of God to be?" Eighty-two percent said that it was a place where souls go after death. This is not consistent with the teachings of Jesus! Jesus proclaimed the kingdom to be the activity of God. Or, to put it another way, the divine rule of God over human life now and in the age to come. It means becoming a member of a new kingdom *now*, having a new citizenship, and participating now in the life of this kingdom.

The parabolic teaching method of Jesus contained many stories that began, "The kingdom of God is like . . ." From these comes a picture of God who is active now in the hearts of people and in the shaping of a new world. Jesus also taught that to participate in this kingdom is to experience the greatest treasure of the universe.

How does one come into such a relationship? "Repent," said Jesus, "for the kingdom of heaven is at hand."

Prayer: *Hosanna! O God, may your kingdom come and your will be done on earth as it is in heaven. Amen.*

114

April 13-19, 1987   **Russell T. Montfort†**
Monday, April 13   Read John 12:1-11.

. . . Also to see Lazarus

Judas missed the point, of course. What he saw and smelled was the expensive ointment that Mary put on Jesus' feet. He missed the complete devotion of the donor, so deep that she loosed her hair and used it to wipe Jesus' feet.

The imagery is rich. The gathered group in the house of the sister of Lazarus. Lazarus has been raised from the dead. Joy and wonder combined in a kind of ecstasy. But Judas missed it because he was still operating out of the world's economy.

And to add to Jesus' disappointment, at least part of the crowd had come not first to see the Son of God, they came "also to see Lazarus." Not to wonder at the power of Jesus, but to see how a dead man looks who suddenly isn't dead.

We spend much of our time reducing great life truths to manageable proportions. The citizens of Bethany could not cope with the idea of God's power made manifest in a man. They didn't want to deal with the possibilities for their own lives. And Judas reduced an act of devotion to the price of perfume.

Jesus represented enlargement of life with its infinite possibilities. They preferred to look at life as they understood it—with its limitations and, of course, its security. If they didn't allow that same Spirit in their lives, then they didn't have to risk anything. So they came "to see Lazarus."

Prayer: *Dear Christ, we want your Spirit to open us to the infinite joy of abundant life. Help us. Amen.*

---

†Senior minister, West End United Methodist Church, Nashville, Tennessee.

Tuesday, April 14   Read John 12:37-50.

Maybe

Jesus wasn't in the judging business. He said it plainly, but still it wasn't understood: "If any one hears my sayings and does not heed them, I do not judge him; for I did not come to judge the world but to save the world."

Jesus wasn't the judge. The Word was the judge. Truth is the judge. As it always is. Jesus' life was the perfect, the fulfilled, the complete life. Therefore, any lesser life is automatically judged in that presence.

Jesus wanted it understood that he accepted all people, and that if coming to him they felt discomfort or rejection, such feelings welled up from inside them. He didn't apply such criteria. He just happened to *be* the criteria.

And misunderstanding that, those who opposed him made the mistake of thinking that by stopping his mouth or taking his life they could rid themselves of his words—of the unsettling witness of his life. All they could do, of course, was kill him. But the Truth lived on. Lives on. To judge. To make uncomfortable.

It is an irony that those who opposed Jesus did so for the wrong reasons. They thought he was a blasphemer. His truths were simply too big for their limited imagination. So the healer's hands were crushed and love was entombed. If hope should ever get out in the world, it might be catching. Maybe people would become healers of one another. Maybe people would give things away instead of acquiring them. Maybe wars would stop. Maybe there would be enough for everybody.

It was too big a risk. So they destroyed him.

Prayer: *Help us, O God, to measure our lives against the life of your Son, the Savior of the world. Amen.*

Wednesday, April 15   Read Matthew 26:14-25.

Scared to death

Serious Christians have wondered about the treachery of Judas Iscariot. Why would someone from the inner circle of Jesus' friends betray him? Had he plotted this perfidy from the beginning? If not, when did he become disenchanted? Why?

We have such spare details that much of the story has to be imagined. It begins with Judas' offer to betray Jesus. We know that there was resentment abroad, enough to let Judas think there were those who would purchase his knowledge. And why did he ask for money? It was no significant ransom.

Some have thought that perhaps, at first, he truly thought Jesus was the Messiah, but that as time went on, and he listened carefully to the Master, he realized that the things he was hearing were quite revolutionary. Judas knew how upset those in power must be. He knew how disturbing he found it himself. It was an entirely new way of looking at life and of living it. It was based on grace rather than regulation.

Judas could not give up a lifetime habit of thinking of his relationship with God in terms of "tit for tat." That is, so many good deeds on his part elicited so many rewards from God. Jesus said, "Not so!" God is good to whomever God wishes.

Judas saw it coming to an end. The time to move had come. He arranged Jesus' arrest. But afterward, in despair, Judas killed himself. They found his body, hanging from a tree, swaying in the same breeze that moved across Golgotha.

Judas, unable to understand the nature of the new life, forfeited his life without ever finding it. He was scared to death.

Prayer: *Free us, O God, to follow the way of the Master without reservation. Amen.*

April 16 (Maundy Thursday)

Read John 13:1-15.

They all ran away

At the supper which we call the "last," Jesus took a pan of water and a towel and went about the room washing the feet of his friends. Peter protested. He was embarrassed by this humility, scandalized that the Holy One should be a servant.

What agony Jesus must have experienced! He had been with them so long, yet they still didn't understand who he was or the source of his authority. So he acted it out in the most dramatic way possible. Then he explained what he had done. "If I then," he said, "your Lord and Teacher, have washed your feet, you also ought to wash one another's feet."

I once found it difficult that Jesus commanded that we are to love one another. It seemed to me that real love should always have a spontaneity about it. But the more I thought, the better I understood. Jesus was speaking to a people whose lives were hedged about and held up by the law. Jesus reduced the laws to two: love God and love one another.

Jesus also knew that we may not always feel spontaneous about loving. He knew we might say in all sincerity that we didn't feel like loving, failing then to do what was required. But sincerity is actually a second-rate virtue. Loving service requires, first, obedience—obedience to the law of love. We serve one another whether we feel like it or not.

Jesus' words that they should eat his flesh and drink his blood were only part of the disciples' shock that night. The other was Jesus' directive that they should serve one another. So before the night was over, they all ran away.

Prayer: *Teach us, O God, to be servants and to respond to Jesus' command to love, because only then will we find our lives. Amen.*

April 17 (Good Friday)

Read John 18:1–19:42.

. . . To be continued

We are violent people—not just Americans, the human race. In spite of all the nice things one hears about crimelessness in Japan, low street crime in Germany, the gunless London bobby, we are violent people.

In "wonderful, wonderful Copenhagen," where it used to be said one could drop a wallet and return three days later to find a policeman standing over it, I was elbowed out of line by some aggressive great Danes. At Versailles, outside Paris, (that oh-so-sophisticated "city of light"), a lady punched me out with her umbrella because I zigged when she meant for me to zag. I have heard of drunken fights where people have split one another's heads open with machetes. We are violent people.

Love once came among us to show us a better way and to empower us to live it. Love entreats us to give rather than expect; to speak softly, rather than with rancor; to sing rather than sigh; to do good to those who misuse and abuse us.

One Friday we took Love out to the edge of town and nailed it up where everybody could watch it die. It writhed, muttered, cried, and died. Darkness spread over the earth. The what-might-have-been became the no-longer-possible. How sad!

There is a word passing among some people, however, that is almost too incredible to believe. I can't tell you about it now, but I'll pass it on to you Sunday.

I think we violent people need to hear this.

Prayer: *O God, we know that we continue to crucify Jesus when we say no to love and yes to hate. Take away our violent nature so that peace can come to the world. In Jesus' name. Amen.*

Saturday, April 18 Read Matthew 27:57-66.

The saddest day

Saturday was probably the most difficult day of all. The shoving and shouting were over. By Friday afternoon Jesus was dead. His body was taken down and stashed in a borrowed tomb until the Sabbath was over. Then they could properly prepare it for burial.

It was a chaotic time. Things happened so fast after Sunday that there was a kind of inevitability about it, now that they had time to think it over. Those who had been afraid they might be accused with Jesus had run away or lied. And now they had to live with their consciences.

The week past we call Holy. It was hard for those close to it to see God in the events of the previous six days. On Sunday a few opportunists, some children, and some naive souls who thought Jesus could do something for them were among those who greeted him. Now on Saturday the dreamers and hopers were in despair, trying to get their lives back together. It was hard to see God in that figure stretched out on the wood between the thieves. It was hard to see God in the broken body of a man who refused to talk his way out of a spot and went to a shameful death.

Later we came to call the week Holy because it packed power. The whole story was edited down to one week. All the components were there. Love incarnate took on worldly power. They stood eyeball to eyeball, and Love was destroyed. Apparently.

We know why the week is called Holy. It is called that because it wasn't the last one.

Prayer: *Stay with us, dear God, through our sadness to the new day you have for us. We trust in you alone. Amen.*

Sunday, April 19 (Easter)

Read John 20:1-18.

As it began to dawn

It was just before daylight one Easter morning. We had gone to a small village in the country about ten miles away to worship at daybreak. We stood around in the half-dark, moving our feet to stay warm and only half-whispering while the crowd assembled in the churchyard.

At the precise hour, the door of the church opened. The pastor stepped out and declared, "The Lord is risen!" We answered, "The Lord is risen indeed!"

Then we trekked up the steep hill behind the church to the cemetery on top, through an avenue of huge ancient cedar trees. A brass ensemble played along our way: "Sleepers wake, the night is over!" We kept our silence and moved steadily to the top.

Just as we passed through the gates into the cemetery where the service was to continue, a bird high up in one of the cedars sang a succession of notes so high and so beautiful that it was beyond description. It was like a choirmaster's signal. Other birds took up the melody until there was an entire chorus singing unseen in the cedars along with the brass ensemble.

It was as if all the world were declaring what we travelers had come to hear: Life had been renewed. The night was over. The storms were past. Death itself was overcome. A new way of being was possible. Available. We could hardly wait to get back to town and tell it.

Prayer: *We thank you, O God, that you overcome death with life, despair with hope, darkness with light. May we live in your light— always. In the name of the risen Christ, we pray. Amen.*

FAITH, PEACE, AND COURAGE

April 20-26, 1987   **David Maldonado†**
Monday, April 20   Read Psalm 16:5-11.

The search for peace seems to be at the core of the human experience; it is a natural and admirable desire for the individual, as it is for societies and nations. Yet for most of us, peace continues to be elusive and difficult to understand. The psalmist provides us an insight into the nature of the peaceful experience and of peace itself.

First of all, while it is a human desire, peace is not totally the product of human action. Peace is, foremost, a gift from God. It is that portion and cup that is freely given to humanity. However, human responsibility is involved. God's gift must be accepted or rejected.

The psalmist shares the joy that comes to the heart and soul. Yet peace is not restricted to the spiritual aspects of the human experience. Peace makes us whole and touches all parts of our lives, freeing us from fear, loneliness, oppression, and all those forces that threaten our wholeness. Indeed, peace becomes a liberating experience.

The psalmist is also a realist. Peace cannot be taken for granted; it must remain our constant task. The Lord gives counsel and shows the path of life. The Lord is on our right hand and before us; our task is to keep the Lord before us, conscious of that which is freely given and daring to accept our cup.

Prayer: *God of peace, open our eyes that we may see your presence, and give us courage to accept your offer of peace and wholeness. Amen.*

---

†Associate Professor of Church and Society, Perkins School of Theology (SMU), Dallas, Texas.

Tuesday, April 21   Read John 20:19-23.

Most of us have experienced fear sometime in our lives. It is a common human emotion in response to a perceived threat. In fact, the anticipation of danger can be an important step in overcoming the danger. However, many times fear can have opposite results. Fear can be overwhelming and lead to immobilization, flight, and alienation.

The disciples had become closely identified with Jesus. Thus, it was natural for them to be threatened by the prosecution and crucifixion of Jesus.

Fear can be immobilizing. Humans often freeze in the presence of immediate danger. Peter's denial was an immediate response to fear. The disciples, frozen and paralyzed, immediately ceased their daily routines.

Fear can lead to flight. To run away from danger is one form of survival. The disciples went into hiding. By shutting their door, they hid from their threatening world.

Fear can be alienating. The perception of danger can produce barriers between individuals and between groups of people. The disciples became afraid of the Jews. Immediately, a whole group of people was blamed for the crucifixion of Jesus and thus became a source of fear.

Fear for our security and welfare immobilizes us from action. Fear of harm causes us to become prisoners in our homes, churches, and other social structures. Fear of others who are different leads to alienation. Jesus shattered the fear of the disciples. He penetrated their immobilization and isolation and sent them out into the world.

Prayer: *O God, grant us your peace that we may overcome the fear that immobilizes us and keeps us apart. Amen.*

Wednesday, April 22   Read John 20:24-31.

Uncertainty and doubt can lead to a restless heart, especially for one who once had believed. Having known and been a witness to Jesus' ministry, Thomas found himself in a state of skepticism. He had not been present when the resurrected Christ first appeared to the disciples. Why had he been excluded? Was it a matter of coincidence? Had Jesus chosen a time when Thomas would not be there? Was it something Thomas had done? So many questions! Under the stress of so many questions, faith turned to doubt.

To not know what we believe can be unsettling and disruptive. Thomas had been certain of Jesus' ministry and had believed. Yet, now he found himself in a state of confusion. Here he was with the disciples again. He identified with them and felt a part of them. However, he also felt that he could not share with them; he was surrounded by believers and he had doubt in his heart. The peace and harmony he had once known were gone.

Perhaps Thomas had not been a model for the faithful. However, it is worth noting that even in doubt, Thomas remained true to himself and to his fellow believers. He shared his doubt and questions. He did not hide his concerns or run away from the fellowship of believers. He stayed and confronted his own disbelief.

Jesus' greetings of peace come to those whose hearts are uncertain as well as to those with faith in their hearts. Peace comes to those whose faith is restored, as it did to Thomas.

Prayer: *O God, grant us the peace that comes through faith. Amen.*

Thursday, April 23   Read Acts 2:14-21.

The early days of the post-resurrection period were crucial for the disciples. They had experienced great pain witnessing the crucifixion, and they remembered well their fear and hiding. They had been awed by the ascension and now were overwhelmed by the Holy Spirit. So much had occurred in a short period of time for this struggling group. Just trying to make sense of these events was a challenge to them as believers. How were they ever to be "witnesses in Jerusalem and in all Judea and Samaria and to the end of the earth"? (Acts 1:8) How would they be received? Would they also be persecuted? Would people listen?

"But Peter, standing with the eleven, lifted up his voice and addressed them." At last, fear, doubt, and uncertainty had been overcome! The disciples had responded in faith and action. They had accepted God's offer of the Holy Spirit and Jesus' command to take the gospel to the end of the earth. The disciples took a stand of faith in an uncertain and potentially hostile environment. No longer were they constrained by fear and driven into hiding. They proclaimed their faith publicly.

Faith has the power to transform people. Faith took a frightened group of followers, whose leader had been crucified, and transformed them into believers who boldly proclaimed the gospel. God's Spirit through our faithful response continues to transform women and men today. Our doubts and fears are real. The issues and challenges in the world are likewise immense. However, as we respond to God's Spirit through faith, we can take a stand and lift up our voices in the name of Christ.

Prayer: *O God, grant that we may receive your Holy Spirit and respond in faith. Liberate us from our fears and doubts and give us the courage to stand and speak in your name again. Amen.*

Friday, April 24   Read Acts 2:22-32.

The time had come. Jesus had personally selected the disciples and patiently taught them. They had been prepared by the Master himself. The crucifixion had tested their faith, and the Holy Spirit had been sent upon them. God had acted. Now it was time for the disciples to take action. It was time for faith to be made known through faithful witness.

It was a bold and decisive step, but it could not have been otherwise. The first step was to proclaim that indeed Jesus was the Christ resurrected. This was not an easy message to deliver to a world that had just crucified him. This was the world that would rather release a known criminal than allow Jesus to live. But Peter stood before the mocking crowd, mustered his courage, and gave witness that the man his listeners had crucified was the long-awaited Christ.

Christian faithfulness is grounded in the belief that Jesus is indeed the Christ. Believing in Jesus Christ is the essential item of faith. However, it is not all that is expected. Faithfulness involves maintaining loyalty to Christ's ministry and God's work. Witness must be given even in the most difficult situations. Just as Peter proclaimed what God was doing in the world two thousand years ago, so does faithfulness call us to muster our courage and proclaim God's work in our world today.

Prayer: *O God, grant us the courage that comes through faith, that our words and deeds may be loyal to your task. Amen.*

Saturday, April 25   Read 1 Peter 1:3-5.

As the belief in the risen Christ spread beyond those who had known him and had been witnesses to his life and ministry, it was important to communicate the nature of the Christian faith and experience. Converts were now scattered and in need of instruction and nurturing. But who was to do it? The disciples were not called by Jesus necessarily because of their skills or other abilities. They had responded to a call to follow. Now they were facing a need to lead, to take the initiative, to address the needs of the church in the world.

Peter had been a fisherman. He had prepared himself for a life on the sea. Yet, here he was writing as an apostle to Christians dispersed throughout the world. Christ had changed his life and transformed it in a way he probably had never envisioned! Thus, it is not surprising that in writing this general letter, Peter refers to the Christian experience as that of renewal. However, it is not a narrow self-renewal or a product of self-help. Rather, the Christian experience of renewal is known as a gift from God made possible through God's mercy.

To accept this gift is to accept God's vision for us. Thus, it is taken in faith, not knowing exactly where it will take us or how we shall be used. Our new lives are in Christ and subject to the needs of his ministry.

The Christian church has become a worldwide community. Its faithfulness to Christ's ministry takes us to all parts and situations in the world. As God calls women and men today, we are called to be born again into a life of faithful service.

Prayer: *O God, grant to us faith that transforms our lives, that we may be renewed to powerful service. Amen.*

Sunday, April 26

Read 1 Peter 1:6-9;
John 20:24-29.

Thomas had doubted the good news of the resurrected Christ. Even though the good news came from those whom he knew and trusted and who had seen the risen Christ themselves, doubt weighed heavily in Thomas' heart. Certainly he could not be a happy man. To be surrounded by the living hope of the resurrection, yet not being able to enjoy its taste, must have been disheartening for the disciple. Peter describes faith as believing and rejoicing with unutterable and exalted joy. The Christian rejoices and celebrates the revelation of Jesus Christ. Fortunately Thomas' doubt was transformed to a faith that proclaimed Christ as "my Lord and my God."

To rejoice through faith, however, is not to suggest that the faithful are free from challenges, temptations, and difficulties. On the contrary, Peter reminds the early church and us today that serious challenges confront the community of believers. The early church faced persecutions because of their faith. Today in many parts of the world persecution takes the form of social oppression, political control, and even ridicule. In some parts of the Western world the challenge is that of not being taken seriously by a society that ignores the church as an irrelevant, social institution.

In the midst of such testing and trials, it would not be surprising to find ourselves saddened at times with a heavy heart. However, Christians are called upon not merely to suffer such trials for a little while but indeed to overcome and join in the rejoicing of the faithful.

Prayer: *O God, grant us the joy that comes through faith, that we may celebrate new lives in the risen Christ. Amen.*

ON THE ROAD TO EMMAUS

April 27–May 3, 1987   **Marjorie J. Williams†**
Monday, April 27   Read Luke 24:13-16.

Emmaus was a small village about seven miles from Jerusalem. The journey took two hours if a traveler walked at a steady pace.

On the afternoon of resurrection day, two of Jesus' disciples started down the Emmaus road, apparently on their way home. Their whole attitude and appearance was one of sadness and desolation.

Luke does not tell us what they were saying to each other but "all these things" must have referred to the perplexing reports about the empty tomb and the absent body of Christ. The situation had left the two disciples in a state of bewilderment.

They were so deeply immersed in their conversation that they hardly noticed when Jesus overtook them and began traveling with them. "Their eyes were kept from recognizing him." Mark 16:12 states that Jesus "appeared in another form." In the forty days after the resurrection, each appearance was made to fit the time, place, and persons concerned. As Jesus joined the two disciples, he must have looked like just another traveler.

Often Jesus is nearest when it seems all hope is gone. He hears and responds to us when we earnestly seek him.

Prayer: *Ever-present God, help us remember that you are the silent listener to all of our conversations and that you will help us when we are perplexed and troubled. Amen.*

---

†Free-lance writer, member of First Assembly of God Church, Colorado Springs, Colorado.

Tuesday, April 28   Read Luke 24:17-18.

Jesus was a master when it came to asking questions. Often he used them to silence his enemies, but frequently it was for the simple purpose of making people state their problems.

This was the case with the two disciples. Luke 24:15 says that Jesus began traveling with them. This implies that Jesus listened to their discussion for a while. Since the scripture states that there was a discussion between the two disciples, it may be that they were asking each other questions which neither could answer.

It was at this point that Jesus said to them, "What are you talking about to each other, as you walk along?" (TEV) The effect of the question stopped the two disciples in their tracks. "They stood still, with sad faces" (TEV). The word *sad* should be interpreted in much stronger language. It means with darkened faces and suggests astonishment and displeasure.

Cleopas is now identified as one of the two. His question in verse 18 tells us that the arrest and crucifixion of Jesus had stirred all Jerusalem. Cleopas and his companion could not believe that even a stranger in the city would have lived so alone that he did not know of the recent events that had taken place. Since Cleopas assumed that Jesus was not a native of Jerusalem, it is possible that Jesus used the dialect of Galilee when he spoke.

Suggestion for meditation: *Remember that Jesus has the answer to all of the questions in your life.*

Wednesday, April 29   Read Luke 24:19-24.

In John 2:25 the scripture reminds us that Jesus knew human nature. He "knew what was in [people's] hearts" (TEV). He seemed unsympathetic when he asked Cleopas another question, yet it accomplished his purpose. He wanted the two disciples to talk, to express what they were feeling. This opened the way for him to explain the meaning of the very things they did not understand.

The theme of their story was "the things concerning Jesus of Nazareth." The Jews frequently used the name "Jesus," and they distinguished whom they meant by naming the town he came from.

They saw Jesus as a prophet—a teacher sent by God. He was mighty in deed before God and all the people. His word was regarded as supernatural eloquence. When guards were sent to arrest him at the Jewish Feast of Tabernacles, they returned empty-handed with the testimony, "Nobody has ever talked the way this man does!" (John 7:46, TEV) The disciples had seen Jesus as the promised Deliverer, but now he was dead. Their own rulers had given him up to be crucified.

The report of the women and their vision of angels was overshadowed by the fact that "they did not see [Jesus]" (TEV). The disciples' reasoning was that they had trusted and hoped that Jesus would free Israel, but this was the third day and they had not seen him.

The third day had not yet ended, but they had given up hope and started home.

Suggestion for meditation: *Read the parable in Luke 18:1-9. What does it say about giving up?*

Thursday, April 30   Read Luke 24:25-27.

When Jesus finally began to talk to the two disciples, he rebuked them. The words *fools* is perhaps too strong a word. The *New English Bible* conveys the thought of "dullness" and emphasizes their lack of faith in the word of God. Jesus could have shown them the scars in his hands and feet, but he chose rather to point them to the scripture.

Cleopas and his friend were "slow of heart to believe" and had not grasped all that the prophets had plainly spoken. The word *all* is important. They believed that the Messiah would come and establish his kingdom, but they did not believe in a suffering Savior.

Jesus then began a systematic Bible study. He diverted their attention from rumors and visions to the solid foundation of the teaching of the prophets. Luke does not indicate which passages Jesus chose, but it is clear throughout the Old Testament that there was a consistent divine purpose which made Calvary inevitable. All that was written concerning the Messiah applied to Jesus. Since the two had wrong ideas of what Moses and the prophets taught, they had wrong ideas about the cross.

Can you imagine what it must have been like to listen to Jesus himself interpreting scripture? We cannot literally walk with Jesus as the two disciples did, but we can search the scripture daily and allow Jesus to open our eyes to the truth of his word (see John 5:39).

Prayer: *Lord, help me to grow in wisdom and knowledge as I study your word. Amen.*

Friday, May 1   Read Luke 24:28-29.

As Jesus expounded scripture to the two disciples, they soon drew near to the village of Emmaus where they lived.

Jesus did not ask if he could spend the night with them or even hint that he needed to find lodging. He started to walk on down the road. But Cleopas and his friend had been so impressed with his exposition that they constrained him to stay with them.

In the Greek, *constrained* means to "press with urgent entreaties." They did not yet know it was Jesus, but they did not want to part with this gracious stranger. They pointed out that the day was far spent and it would soon be dark. Besides this, robbers and wild beasts might hide in the darkness, and it would not be safe to continue.

Now we see the courtesy of Jesus. He comes in to dwell with those who offer him an invitation. The disciples made time for him and, at their insistence, "he went in to stay with them."

Revelation 3:20 says, "I stand at the door and knock; if any one hears my voice and opens the door, I will come in to him and eat with him, and he with me."

Jesus rewards the constraint of persistent faith (see Matt. 15:22-28). If we want the Lord to fellowship with us, our love must be great enough to detain him. Matthew tells us that the kingdom of heaven suffers violence, and the violent take it by force (11:12). Seek the abiding presence of Christ, even if you must wrestle to secure it.

Prayer: *Lord, help me to be like Jacob who said, "I will not let you go, unless you bless me."* * *Amen.*

---

*Gen. 32:26.

Saturday, May 2   Read Luke 24:30-31.

Hospitality has almost become a lost art. Yet the Bible addresses this issue many times. In Hebrews 13:2 there is a classic example: "Do not neglect to show hospitality to strangers, for thereby some have entertained angels unawares."

The two disciples shared their home and perhaps frugal meal with the stranger who had joined them on the road to Emmaus. In Jewish fashion, they reclined at the table. Neither of the two thought it strange when Jesus took the bread, blessed and broke it, and gave it to them. Since Jesus had acted as a teacher on their journey, they saw this as a natural gesture because of that relationship.

Verse 31 tells us that as Jesus handed them the bread, "their eyes were opened and they recognized him." They may have seen the scars left by the nails, or there may have been something unusual in the way he broke the bread. But their recognition was sudden and unexpected. Then, because he had accomplished his purpose, Jesus vanished out of their sight. They had seen the risen Lord! Their hospitality was richly rewarded.

Prayer: *Lord, even though my home may be small and my food common, help me to share them with someone in need. Amen.*

Sunday, May 3   Read Luke 24:32-35.

In Psalm 39:3, the psalmist says, "My heart became hot within me. As I mused, the fire burned; then I spoke with my tongue."

The exposition of Jesus on the Emmaus road so affected the two disciples that their hearts glowed within them. The opening of the scripture had brought new faith and assurance. The words reinforced what they had just seen—Jesus was alive!

In effect, they said, "We should have known who our companion on the road was." The word *burn* expresses unusual emotion. The disciples were so inflamed with the love of God that they didn't even finish their meal. The scripture implies that they immediately left their home to return to Jerusalem. There was no fear now of a night journey. Their Lord had risen and, like the psalmist, they had to tell others of their experience.

The incident that took place on the road to Emmaus shows that Jesus will reveal himself to us in the privacy of our own life, in daily affairs. How pathetic that our eyes are often dimmed by unbelief and we fail to recognize his presence. We walk along sad and discouraged when we should be rejoicing in his companionship.

When we really *see* Jesus, it will change us, just as it changed Cleopas and his friend. We will find a way to go and tell others, "He lives!"

Prayer: *God of comfort, may we never forget that you are with us on our journey—our Emmaus road. We have faith that "what we see now is like a dim image in a mirror; then we shall see face-to-face."* * Amen.

---

*1 Cor. 13:12, TEV.

PORTRAIT OF THE FIRST CHRISTIANS

May 4-10, 1987   **Dan B. Genung†**
Monday, May 4   Read Acts 2:42-47.

In these verses, Luke, with his physician's concern for detail, presents a composite photo of Jesus' followers in the weeks after Pentecost. Sense their excitement, their tension and hope, and their fear, as they devoted themselves to study and prayer.

Most of their gatherings were in homes. I wish Luke had told us how they organized. The 3,000 converts at Pentecost must have been divided into class-size groups. Did the Twelve visit each home? Did they go to a different house night after night? Luke fails to say, even though he tells us much.

Mentally let us join them in study at a first-century home. Still responding to the thrill of the Resurrection and of Pentecost, let us question Peter.

"Tell us once more about your call. Describe the supper in the upper room, please. What scriptures besides those of Joel predict these last days and prove that Jesus was the Messiah?"

"Andrew, when did John the Baptist first know that his cousin Jesus was the Messiah? Did John quote Isaiah to you, about the Wonderful Counselor, the Prince of Peace?"

Let us be as eager and determined as they to grow in understanding the meaning of Christ Jesus for our lives.

Devotional exercise: *Choose two of the early church leaders, either man or woman, and think of questions you would ask.*

---

†Pastor Emeritus, Mount Hollywood Congregational Church, Hollywood, California; founding pastor, All Peoples Christian Church and Center (Los Angeles); Los Angeles, California.

Tuesday, May 5   Read Acts 2:42.

Devoted in prayer, serious in study, those early believers knew a rare depth of fellowship. This was true when they united to worship in the temple, but even more so as they broke bread in individual homes. The Lord's Supper was served, but Luke makes clear that these were "potluck" suppers, the "well-to-do" sharing with the less privileged.

That spirit of oneness, of *koinonia*, bound them "with one accord" (KJV). It is difficult for us to achieve that sense of unity in our rushing world. Young people share it when they have labored together in Christian workcamps. Missionaries in isolated fields know it with co-laborers. Groups who have endured times of suffering experience this bond. And sometimes we are aware of it in our church life. I felt its power when eighteen of us came together spontaneously the evening of Pearl Harbor. We were seminary students, two from Japan, the rest U.S. citizens—men and women, white and black. Silently we sat, then began to pray. Our hearts reached out with a yearning love to the two praying in Japanese. Even today I cannot describe the unity we experienced that night. We were *one* in Christ Jesus.

Prayer: *O God, bind us in close and loving unity not only with fellow Christians but with your children of every race and nation. Amen.*

Wednesday, May 6   Read Acts 2:43; Psalm 8.

Can you sense the chills that went up and down the spines of those early followers? "And fear came upon every soul." The shocking events of the crucifixion, the resurrection, the continuing presence of Christ, and then Pentecost, were beyond their understanding. Are they beyond ours?

We object to the word *fear*. If this is because we have an intimate personal relationship with a loving God, fine. Or is it because we are involved in discussions of the feminine and masculine qualities of God? Or when our astronauts dance jigs on the moon and build structures in outer space, do we forget the God "who has measured the waters in the hollow of his hand and marked off the heavens with a span"? (Isa. 40:12)

In California cars display the sticker "Prosperity is your divine right." One movie star has described the Lord as "a living doll." Television programs assure us that if we "get right with God" we will have a new home, a new job, and a new car. What would the apostle Paul say of such theology?

Rather than "fear," I prefer the *New English Bible* translation, "a sense of awe." Yet as I gaze into the Grand Canyon or stare at Mount McKinley; as I see God's continuing creation in volcanic eruptions and hear it in the thunder of ice calves at Mendenhall Glacier; or as I marvel at the birth of a new grandchild, I experience both awe and fear. "Sometimes it causes me to tremble, tremble . . ."* at a Creator God who loved and still loves this world.

Prayer: *O God, never let me lose a trembling sense of awe at the miracle of your love. Amen.*

---

* "I Wonder as I Wander," Appalachian folk song.

Thursday, May 7 Read Acts 2:44; 4:32-35; 5:1-16;
1 Chronicles 29:11, 16.

How great was their joy in giving! The early Christians accepted responsibility for one another, not as a burden but "with glad and generous hearts."

I have often been troubled by the story of Ananias and Sapphira. I believe Luke intends for us to see how seriously followers of the Way took the obligation of sharing. This couple sought to avoid the demand for complete honesty in using possessions. They refused to recognize that all belongs to God, the Divine Provider. This is just as difficult for us today.

My own son shames me. He, his fiancée, and a young ministerial friend served with the Catholic Workers on skid row in Los Angeles. They lived in cell-like rooms on a stipend of five dollars a week, provided food daily for 500 to 1,000 persons, gave out clothing, and arranged for legal and medical help. They were always on guard, because several friends had been murdered by the "skid row stabber."

Members of a church I served in Oceanside, California, recall with joy the "bean-feeds" preceding their mid-week prayer meetings during the depression. This was the main meal of the week for many as they united in a deep spirit of love and fellowship.

Earthquakes in Mexico, famines in Ethiopia, volcanoes in Colombia, recently stirred citizens of the United States to generosity. But true followers of Christ do not wait for tragedy before they donate; they know the sheer joy of constant and faithful sharing.

Prayer: *O God, teach me the discipline of giving so grandly that I will know its true joy. Amen.*

Portrait of the First Christians

Friday, May 8   Read Acts 2:45.

The stewardship example of the early Christians stirs many questions in me. Am I doing my share? Is my congregation truly committed?

Our church of 150 members maintains a food pantry, gives faithfully to local food agencies, and this very day provided temporary work for seven Central American refugees while trying to find housing for them. We are purchasing 1,000 blankets for a village in Nicaragua. Some of our members keep track of their expenditures for holiday dinners and give an equal amount to charity. Yet we wonder if we are living up to that first-century challenge.

A few years after the death of the apostle Paul, 250 Christians in Rome were reported to be feeding 1500 needy persons. Later the *Didache*, or "Teachings," written about 100 A.D., commanded Christians never to turn the hungry away. About A.D. 125 a Christian philosopher named Aristides instructed church members that when they were short of food themselves they should fast two or three days in order to supply others. Even an avowed enemy of the church, Julian the Apostate, wrote that "the godless Galileans" cared for the poor among their own membership and fed the other destitute of the community.

The *New English Bible* translates verse 46 this way: they "shared their meals with unaffected joy." Early history proves that this joy continued.

Prayer: *I am humbled, Lord, by the abundant blessings you have poured upon me. I thank you for the happy privilege of sharing. Amen.*

Saturday, May 9   Read Acts 2:47.

Phillips' translation says, "They praised God continually and all the people respected them." We know that before many weeks had passed, the authorities stirred up hostility against them, but this verse suggests that their sheer goodness, their joyousness, endeared them to all who knew them.

Growing up on Arizona ranches and in mining camps, my older brother and I knew little of churches. Occasionally we visited evangelistic services in town. We were repulsed by the lurid pictures of hell painted on the walls and described angrily by the preacher.

When we were in college, we rather casually attended a worship service. The sermon challenged our minds, but most of all, the people were happy and friendly. One man puzzled us. His sparkling smile beamed love and goodwill at the youth and young adults who gathered around him. Could he be real? We wanted to know.

This man did prove to be real. He had come to Arizona for his health after losing his wife to tuberculosis. But his faith was unshakeable. His closeness to Christ gave him a contagious joyousness. We decided that we, too, would seek that faith in Christ.

Those early Christians, soon to be in danger of martyrdom and always suspected by the Romans, radiated a winsome spirit of joy and love. With God's help, may we also show this spirit of joy.

Prayer: *Lord, young people at camp sing "Let the beauty of Jesus be seen in me." May it be so in me throughout this day. Amen.*

Sunday, May 10   Read Acts 2:42-47.

When those early Christians came together, something happened. They studied, they prayed, they shared, they praised, they loved, they radiated goodwill, they stood awestruck at the greatness of God—and something happened! "Many wonders and signs were done through the apostles . . . and the Lord added to their number day by day."

The unity and dedication of the total group were indispensable requirements before miracles could take place. Even our Lord Jesus did not perform many miracles in his own country because of unbelief (see Matt. 13:58).

On a monument in Orange, California, is a bronze tablet which reads, "On this site in 1897 nothing happened." How often could that plaque be placed on some of our churches? How often does a carefully prepared service or a well-thought-out sermon fall flat because of late arrivals or of the obvious indifference of a few? How many programs are weakened or blocked by lackadaisical church members?

And then, praise God, there are times when an enthusiastic committee and a praying, loving, praising, expectant congregation join with the power of God to accomplish signs and wonders—miracles!

Prayer: *Today, O Lord, I resolve that my entire attitude will inspire others so that miracles of love and service may take place. Amen.*

STONES OF REMEMBRANCE

May 11-17, 1987
Monday, May 11

Thomas P. Harp†
Read 1 Peter 2:2-5;
Joshua 4:19-24.

I remember as a child finding fossils in my back yard. I marveled that once they had been alive. I could pick one up and with absolutely no effort be swimming in ancient seas looking for a familiar "stone." Funny how our minds can leap across the ages! It is even more strange that a mere stone can trigger such experiences.

Now read these scriptures with new thoughts about living stones. Think back to Joshua's having twelve stones from the Jordan river built into a monument. Those stones of remembrance were keys to identity. Curious children asking about the monument heard the story of God's leading their people into the promised land. Like a child searching an ancient sea for fossils, the children likely were wide-eyed, envisioning themselves following Joshua and the ark through the river. Their remembrance walk into the promised land firmly linked them with the people of Israel.

Peter invites us to be living stones, built into a spiritual temple. People asking us about this monument hear the stories of Jesus. Like little children they may walk with Jesus, catching the excitement of the crowds. Remembrance walks with Jesus bring hope and transform lives.

Prayer: *How marvelous you are, O God. Thank you for giving us stones of remembrance. Remind us of our walks with Joshua and with Jesus. Amen.*

---

†Pastor, Kenmore Presbyterian Church, Kenmore, New York.

Tuesday, May 12   Read Acts 7:55-60;
                                        Hebrews 12:1-2.

The Vietnam Veterans Memorial in Washington, D.C., is a new stone of remembrance. The engraved names include our children, playmates, high school friends, college classmates, and military comrades. Just writing about it is a moving experience. It seems ironic that a monument can be both a reminder of pain and an agent of hope. Yet just as those Hebrew children remembered wandering with their ancestors, so also we remember our lives with those named. Generations unborn will be able to remember with us. Perhaps, like Paul, whether they approve or disapprove, they will not walk away unchanged. Remembering brings healing and hope.

Consider Stephen's words quoted in Acts. In the midst of mortal pain, Stephen could see himself with Jesus. Remembering that Jesus had placed his Spirit in God's hands and that Jesus had forgiven those who crucified him, Stephen received courage and strength to do the same. Quoting Psalm 31, like touching a memorial stone, united him with Jesus and a host of others in faith, suffering, trust in God, and hope.

Stones of remembrance put us in touch with the cloud of witnesses who have preceded us. We are united not only with their suffering but also with their faith, hope, and love. With Stephen, each of us remembers, "Lord Jesus, receive my spirit!" (TEV)

Prayer: *Lord God, you provide remembrance stones to keep us in touch with you. Forgive our destructive use of the stones you give. Thank you for all stones that bring healing and hope. Amen.*

Wednesday, May 13   Read Psalm 31.

Whose words are these? They are full of fear, grief, and pain. Here is a person in the pit of despair. If we stop reading at verse 8, as the lectionary suggests, we seem to have little hope. We are left in the midst of crisis, though not yet imprisoned by the enemy.

One key for our understanding lies in verses 21-24. Here we learn that the crisis has passed. God heard the psalmist's prayer. And God acted to save the psalm-writer. The psalm invites us to remember particular times of crisis and to praise God who heard our prayers and acted.

Like a stone of remembrance, the psalm renews our minds, calling us beyond the desperation of present circumstances. It puts us in touch with people who have traveled similar paths as we, who have rejoiced in God's faithfulness. It reminds us who we are, people who once wandered despairingly through the wasteland. God, our refuge and defense, led us to safety. Though we weren't there, we remember through God's provision for our remembrance. When you eat this bread, when you drink this cup, *remember!*

How gracious God is, providing for our remembrance and identity through psalms and sacraments. How marvelous are these "stones" that fill us with hope, uniting us with a people, a psalmist, a martyr, and our Lord!

Prayer: *Gracious God, you provide for us in remarkable ways. You fill us with courage and hope by identifying us with faithful people we trust, for they have walked the same paths as we. Their faith is ours. Amen.*

Thursday, May 14   Read 1 Peter 2:6-8.

Some artists specialize in using junk as raw material for their art. Walking through art galleries can be an exercise in amazement. Even those who do not like what they see often marvel at what an artist has done with stuff others have thrown away. Pieces of twisted metal become intricate and strangely attractive sculptures. Nuts and bolts take on peculiar grace when welded into artistic figures.

When particular memories are attached to the raw materials, the piece of art becomes a stone of remembrance. Signatures from our wedding cards were made into a collage of remembrance by a gifted artist. That collage has introduced our children to people they've never met. Every time we look at it we remember the artist, the people, and the places that are so important to us.

Peter reminds us that God is an artist with human lives. People we consider worthless are valuable raw materials to our loving God. God's creative power is supremely demonstrated in the resurrection of Jesus Christ. Good news for all who have been rejected by "experts"! God used the stone that the experts had trashed for the cornerstone of the masterpiece. The world may stumble in disbelief. But those who believe are filled with hope. God has built a living monument to Jesus, using stones the world considers just stones.

Prayer: *How remarkable, O Christ, that your church is built with raw materials such as we! Grant that we may serve you well, reminding the world of your love. Amen.*

Friday, May 15   Read John 14:1-9.

A few years ago a man visited a family with the same surname as his. That family had lost contact with their relatives. They had written to inquire if he might be related to them. Upon seeing him, the woman began to cry. The man resembled her son who had been killed in World War II. That meeting was an occasion for remembering the pain of her past heartbreak, but it also was an occasion for rejoicing. The two families still haven't traced any direct family ties. But an isolated introduction brought hope to one who feared that all family ties had been lost.

Just as seeing that man reminded the woman of her son, reading this passage reminds us of Jesus. In promising a future meeting with Jesus, it also reminds us that Jesus is not physically present with us now. Our knowing Jesus is linked to various stones of remembrance—passages of scripture, images of Jesus we see in others, that monument called the church, built of living stones. The One you and I have known only through stones of remembrance will someday meet us face to face. But rather than despair that we do not know how all this shall take place, we are invited to trust in God and to trust in Jesus.

Jesus said, "I am the way, the truth, and the life. . . . Whoever has seen me has seen the Father." In some mysterious way, stones of remembrance are an aid to knowing Jesus. Likewise, knowing Jesus means knowing God.

Prayer: *How remarkable, O God, that you make yourself known to us in this way. Thank you for everyone who reminds us of Jesus, our Lord. For it is because of Jesus that we can know you. Amen.*

Saturday, May 16   Read John 14:8-14.

How often people look at a child and comment about the child's resemblance to its mother or father! It seems only natural to make those comparisons. Some families have a very strong family resemblance. In this passage Jesus speaks of himself as a "chip off the old block." He says, "Whoever has seen me has seen the Father" (TEV). Jesus is a visible reminder, a living stone of remembrance through whom we know God.

We all have a desire to see God if for no other reason than to satisfy our curiosity. Philip expresses our hunger, saying, "Lord, show us the Father, and we shall be satisfied." Unlike religions that provide exotic images of their gods, Christians claim that God was uniquely present in Jesus: "I am in the Father and the Father in me." In some mysterious way God is present with those who believe. We have already been told that it is God living in Jesus that is doing the work. Thus, God lives also in those who believe in Jesus. "Whoever believes in me will do what I do" (TEV).

We are tempted to ask how this can be. Such a question diverts us from our responsibility. Who knows how stones of remembrance work? Who knows how the sacraments of the Lord's Supper and Baptism work? Thank God that they do! Thank God that they fill us with the remembrance of Jesus among us, encouraging us to do the work that God has given us.

Prayer: *Like Philip, we hunger to see you, O God. Help us to recognize you in people around us who do your work. In Jesus' name. Amen.*

Sunday, May 17   Read 1 Peter 2:9-10.

This is a remarkable key to the church's identity. We learn that the church itself is a stone of remembrance for the world. Just as those who had seen Jesus had seen God, so also those who have seen the church have seen Jesus.

How often we focus on what the church should be doing, forgetting what it already is! We forget that by its very existence the church serves to remind people of God's mighty acts. Even those who claim to be atheists know about Jesus because of the church. People in need turn to the church for help. They remember Jesus' love for all people. They have heard how Jesus healed the sick, fed the hungry, and had compassion on outcasts.

We are invited to remember that once we were not chosen people. Now, by the grace of God, we are. Most of us feel inadequate as living reminders of Jesus. But remember that stones of remembrance are also inadequate. The Vietnam Veterans Memorial can hardly fill the void left by the death of those it memorializes. Yet inadequate as any monument is, it brings remembrance. Inadequate as we are, we remind people of Jesus. And in some mysterious way, Jesus is present in our reminding. Indeed, we are not just remembering. We believe that Jesus is present with us in our remembrance. Remarkable! With Jesus present, we are a royal priesthood, the people of God, a very real presence of God in the world.

Prayer: *Thank you, O God, that inadequate though we may be, by your grace you use us as stones of remembrance, building blocks of love and grace in this world. Amen.*

GOD IS NOT FAR FROM US

May 18-24, 1987   **Pamela Hadsall†**
Monday, May 18   Read Psalm 66:8-20.

The little Ethiopian girl is ten years old. Her dark skin is stretched like a drumskin over matchstick bones and a swollen belly. Her family lays her gently on a mat in a relief center in Ethiopia. Someone holds a bowl of liquid to her immobile lips. The child's owl-wide eyes stare beyond pain as the fluid fills her mouth and overflows down the side of her face. It is too late. Her throat is paralyzed, and she cannot swallow the food. The child dies. The image on the television screen makes us turn our heads numbly away or cry out as we share the horror.

Human beings suffer physical and emotional pain from illness, persecution, violence, neglect, torture, greed, misunderstanding, need. The images of pain flash like red neon signs in the night, and we can't ignore them. How do we find God in this suffering?

The psalmist, like Job, responds out of his own experience of trial and affliction. He recognizes the presence and comfort of an all-powerful God who listens and saves. His awareness leads him to worship, to offer sacrifices, and to proclaim God's sustaining love.

Prayer: *Dear God, I don't like to suffer. I don't like to see others suffer. So often pain seems undeserved and unjust. You have promised to sustain us. Help me to trust and feel the strength of your love. Amen.*

---

†Pastor, Seymour United Methodist Church, Seymour, Missouri.

Tuesday, May 19   Read 1 Peter 3:13-17.

You have worked long, hard hours on a controversial project. You have done a good job and look forward to positive reactions from others. Instead, you receive criticism and ridicule. Your Christian faith demands that you stand up for the results of your work, even though the results go against popular opinion. Your friends do not understand your faith decision. They urge you to change. Perhaps they laugh at you, become angry with you, or attack your character.

In such a circumstance you may feel alone and hurt. Your self-confidence and your faith in your God-given abilities begin to wilt like cut flowers. The sacrifices required by your faith seem so great. You anticipated the respect and admiration of others, and yet you seem to be the object of criticism, ridicule, misunderstanding, anger, and attack. How do you handle these feelings?

First Peter is a letter of encouragement to the Christian communities in Asia Minor that were experiencing persecution. They were bewildered by the cruel treatment and the suffering. Our everyday sacrifices may not be as painful or as life-threatening, but they are no less real. Like the early Christians, we are called to move beyond passive acceptance of our faith into an active witness of our faith. The directions in First Peter are specific: do not fear, reverence Christ as Lord, defend your faith with gentleness and reverence, and keep your conscience clear. Why? God is with us. The witness of our lives in times of tribulation can help someone else discover God's strength and love.

Prayer: *Caring and strengthening God, it is not easy to care for those who cause me to suffer. Help me. I want others to know you. Amen.*

Wednesday, May 20   Read 1 Peter 3:18-22.

How can we make ourselves trust God when floods of suffering overwhelm us? How do we overcome our fear? How can we save ourselves? This letter to the early Christians reminds us that we do not save ourselves. God saves us from the floods. Through Christ, God saved us once and for all. The hope that strengthens us resides in the example and the companionship of Jesus Christ.

Jesus Christ suffered for us so that we might be brought to God. Out of death, he gave life. As innocent sufferers we have the opportunity to share in the redemptive power of Christ's suffering. As we defend our Christian hope through our suffering, others may be brought to life with God in Christ. We can discover strength as we remember the example of Christ.

Through the mystery of resurrection, Christ is alive in the spirit. We are not alone. A living, creative power in our universe cares enough to suffer with us and give us life. The living companionship of Christ comforts us, sustains us, and empowers us.

In times of suffering and tribulation, you and I have a choice. We can give the whole of our hearts and minds to fear or we can trust in a loving and saving God. When faith and reverence reside in our hearts, no amount of pain and suffering can affect our integrity or our confidence. Suffering can be accepted, and through our suffering we can experience God's grace.

Prayer: *Loving and saving God, when I remember that Jesus Christ suffered for me, my own suffering seems easier to bear. If I follow his example, I know your saving love will shine through me. Help me to feel his strength and share his love. Amen.*

Thursday, May 21   Read Acts 17:22-25.

You are in the kitchen of an old house, and the paint is peeling off the window ledge above the sink. You open a cabinet door and take out a plate. It must be washed clean of roach leavings before you can use it. You open a lower cabinet door beneath the sink to get some soap, and you smell the rotten odor of something dead. You discover a mouse, stiff in its trap, and take it outside to throw it in the large metal drum that serves as your trash can.

As you walk onto the sagging porch, spring sunlight breaks into a thousand colors through a dew-spangled spiderweb in the tangled rose vines. The morning light hums with heavy, yellow bees hovering over sweet alyssum. The odor of honey fills the garden. You walk slowly along a crumbling stone path. Your mind makes no words. In child-silence you open your heart, your mind, your senses, your whole being to the neglected beds of red roses, blue columbines, yellow coreopsis, and white Shasta daisies. In the kaleidoscopic color and spring light of the ancient garden you sense something, a larger Reality for which you have no name. Something unknown is in this old place, and it shines in sudden beauty. From the decay and ugliness of poverty, you have walked to the edges of worship. You have discovered an altar to the unknown God.

Paul reminds us that the God who made the world does not live in shrines made by our human hands. This God lives in our darkness and in our light, in our ugliness and in our beauty, and gives life and breath to all.

Prayer: *Almighty God, if I live in ugliness and poverty, you are there. If I live in splendor and luxury, you are there. I want to see your beauty in darkness and in light. Help me. Amen.*

Friday, May 22   Read Acts 17:26-31.

In a time of pestilence in Athens, the Cretan poet Epimenides suggested that in order to appease the gods, they should release a flock of black and white sheep and watch where each one lay down. Each sheep should then be sacrificed at the nearest altar. If a sheep lay down where there was no known altar, it should be sacrificed to the unknown god. This ancient story offers one explanation for the altar to the unknown god noticed by Paul (see Acts 17:23) and used as a point of contact with the Athenians. Paul proposed to make this God known to them.

It may be difficult for you and me to find points of contact between our own scientific and technological age and the God revealed in the Bible. We suffer the pestilence of spiritual dryness and yet, in this darkness, we somehow grope after God. In our own way we "feel after" a palpable God with shape, color, and a voice. Paul reminds us that God created us to "feel after" God. Our cravings originate from the very God we seek.

Paul strains language and thought to make God's living nearness real for the Athenians. He quotes well-known lines from the poets Epimenides and Aratus and uses them to share his understanding of God. We live and move and have our being in God. We are God's offspring. In some inexplicable sense, we are the "stuff" of God. For Paul, God is not fixed in the static representations of art and imagination. God moves and breathes and feels in the active processes of life. God is not far from each one of us.

Prayer: *Living God, I know you are not far from me. I feel after you with hope. I want to find you. Take my hand and open my eyes. Amen.*

Saturday, May 23   Read John 14:15-18.

Jesus speaks of his imminent death and bodily departure in words of farewell to the disciples. He tells the disciples that love for him must issue in obedience. The strength, companionship, and comfort needed to live in love and obedience will be provided by the eternal presence of the Holy Spirit.

What does the presence of the Holy Spirit mean? The many words used in the ancient texts help us to have a fuller understanding of the functions of the Holy Spirit. The Greek word *parakletos* literally means "one called along beside another." The word *counselor* is closely related to this conception and compares the work of the Spirit to that of a legal counselor or advocate and to that of a teacher or adviser. The notions of being with, advising, and speaking for are included here. The word *comforter* has often been used to speak of the Holy Spirit. The root words of comfort are the Latin words *con* which means "with" and *fortis* which means "strength." Thus the word carries a history of strength as well as tenderness. Jesus also refers to the Holy Spirit as the "Spirit of truth." Like Jesus, the Holy Spirit knows and shares the true nature of God.

Jesus promises that this eternal, guiding, strengthening, comforting, Spirit of truth will dwell with and be in the disciples. They will know the presence of the Holy Spirit. Jesus will not leave them desolate.

Prayer: *Loving Christ, help me to know that the suggestions and promises to the disciples are for me as well. If I love you, I will obey your commandment to love. The Holy Spirit dwells with me and is in me. You will not leave me desolate. Help me to know your strengthening, guiding, comforting presence. Amen.*

Sunday, May 24   Read John 14:18-21.

Teilhard de Chardin reminded us that if we harnessed the energies of love we would discover fire for the second time in history. The analogy is a good one. Fire controlled and directed to constructive purposes has changed the shape of human existence. Such is the power of love.

The God-life of obedience to love, with its promise of life and oneness with God, was the vision of Jesus of Nazareth. In his vision, the constructive and creative force of love transcends the emotions associated with childlike and narcissistic human need. We often say "I love you" when we mean "I need you." The Greek word for divine love is *agape*, and such love is necessarily something greater than our human emotions. It is the selfless and self-giving love of God. Such love is a constructive, creative, active force that wills good for all creation.

In our simplest impulse to give or to will good for others, regardless of the feelings we might have for them, a tiny flame of divine love glows like a lit match in the dark. We instinctively recognize its beauty and power. We see light, and we feel the force that has the power to warm and transform all human experience. Understood this way, it is easy to see that love for Jesus demands obedience to his commandment to love.

Prayer: *Active and giving God, not only are you near me, you dwell within me and you act through me. I am living, breathing, and acting in your life and love. Thank you. I want to do your will. Amen.*

In God's Mighty Presence

May 25-31, 1987 **Robert D. Ingram†**
Monday, May 25 Read John 17:1-5.

There is an instinctive desire within humans to live and to keep on living. When our prehistoric ancestors first began wondering about the possibility of a greater being, their musings must have inevitably been fused with thoughts of how a relationship with this greater being could help them live longer and more abundantly. In his crucifixion and resurrection, Jesus reveals the Being who has the power to extend life eternally. He shows us the object of our deepest desire.

On the night of his betrayal, Jesus is praying with his disciples in the upper room. "This is eternal life: to know thee who alone art truly God" (NEB).

Our human task is clear. Our quest for life will find its goal in knowing God. This is not a knowing that can be acquired from textbooks or from scientific research. Nor can it be won by human achievements or by measuring up to a certain set of ethical standards. This knowing is given. It is given in God's coming and being present among us. As husbands and wives over the years come to understand and know what kind of person their spouse is, so do we come to know God through years of living together. In this knowing there is life. If our lives are to be preserved, it will be by receiving and living continually in the presence of the God who comes to each of us.

Suggestion for prayer: *Pray that you might be aware of and receptive to the presence of God in your life today.*

---

†Pastor, Grace United Methodist Church, Hicksville, Ohio.

Tuesday, May 26   Read Acts 1:6-14.

When I was a boy there was a 100-yard section of sidewalk that I often had to walk alone after dark. There were no street lights or houses, but there were numerous bushes where some thing or some evil person could have been hiding. With my imagination, the night sounds and shadows became very frightening. But that sidewalk was the only path into the world where I lived much of my life. Walking fast, whistling loudly, looking over my shoulder every few steps, and being scared to death was the best I could do.

Somehow I became aware that I really was not walking alone. God was with me wherever I went, even on dark sidewalks. God was a protector and would protect me. With my new awareness of God's spiritual presence, I gave up whistling loudly. I strolled boldly and slowly down that sidewalk, almost daring some horrible night creature to try to attack me. The fear was gone.

When Jesus was about to leave his disciples to enter into heaven, he made sure that they knew that they would not be left alone, saying, "You will receive power when the Holy Spirit comes upon you" (NEB). Fear would have been visible in the disciples. It would have made a mockery of the faith to which they were to witness. They needed the comfort and assurance of the Holy Spirit. Such an assurance would put power in their words and belief in the hearts of those who heard them.

There are many dark places where we must walk. The danger is often real, not just imagined. Yet, we can go into these places unafraid and full of power, and we can witness to the God whose mighty presence is with us.

Suggestion for prayer: *Where are the dark places to which you are sent? Thank God that you need not go alone.*

Wednesday, May 27   Read Psalm 68:1-6.

Every person has the potential to do good or to do bad. When we do the good, it is an offering to God; it pleases God. But, when we do the bad, it is a rebuke of God; we are an offense to the One who has given us the very freedom that we abuse. All humans share this predicament. Sometimes we act like servants; sometimes like enemies.

God is not so inconsistent. God's love is steady and constant over the ages. No matter how offensive and hostile we become to God, God never thinks of us as enemies. We are always children, and our Creator loves us with a long-suffering love that outlasts even decades of our tantrum-throwing.

The psalmist tells us that God's "enemies are scattered; those who hate him flee before him" (NEB). That which is evil cannot stand fast in God's presence. It is like smoke in the wind or wax in a fire. This is good news. As God's children, hostile though we may be, we are always welcomed into God's presence. Since evil cannot stand fast before God, it is driven out of our lives. We are purified in God's presence. So, instead of vainly trying to hide from God when we have done wrong, we need to run like injured children to our Creator, who can heal us and make us wholly good. Instead of rebelling and fighting against God, we need to carry our anger and resentment to the only One who can deal with it without becoming defensive and angry in return. God's love is constant and long-suffering. It can cope patiently even with the anger of our adolescent faith.

Suggestion for prayer: *Is there unconfessed wrongdoing in your life? Is there unexpressed anger or resentment? Take it to God in prayer, and be made whole.*

Thursday, May 28   Read Psalm 68:7-10.

The Hebrews traveled with God out of Egypt and in the wilderness for 40 years. Then they traveled with God, conquering the land they had been given. Jesus never left this land, but he traveled constantly within it. His disciples were practically driven out of the land to avoid persecution and death, yet they were not so much running away as they were being led to other places where they were to witness to their experience in Christ.

Of course, Christians travel in ways other than across the geography of our planet. Some travel with their minds, developing their intellects and the world's knowledge of God and creation. Some travel with their creative talents, finding new ways to express their experiences of being human and being with God. Others travel with their hearts, performing humble tasks of kindness. There are many ways to travel as Christians. We are not meant to settle down and be content with our present relationship with God. Nor are we to lock ourselves in some supposedly secure fortress of belongings and opinions. Our minds and hearts are to be open always to the new thing that God is doing. The journey is not only to God but with God.

All journeys present obstacles, hazards, and even times of great danger. All journeys cause weariness of spirit and body and expose us to temptation, doubt, and conflict. What is unique to the Christian journey is that we are never alone. As the psalmist says, we have a giant of a God going before us. Following behind such a God refreshes and renews us. Because of such a God, we can keep going.

Suggestion for prayer: *Pray that you may be faithful in following God on your life's journeys.*

Friday, May 29   Read 1 Peter 4:12-14.

Peter warned fellow Christians that they should not be surprised to be persecuted because of their faith. Yet, because the
complexity of all issues in our contemporary world casts doubt
upon any action, there is always room to question any individual's motivation. Family members may think we are crazy because
of stands we have taken. Jesus' family thought he was crazy (see
John 7:5). We may even doubt ourselves.

What Peter did not warn about was the uncertainty and doubt.
If our stand is going to anger people, we want to be sure that it is
really the stand Jesus wants of us. If our family is going to suffer
ostracism because of our actions, we want to be certain that we
are right. Peter did not warn about the doubt, yet it is just as much
a part of the fiery ordeal as is the anger of those who come
against us.

The problem is that the faith that guides our words and actions
is based on trust, not on proven fact. So, when we are persecuted
because of our faith, deep questions arise that cause doubts. We
feel that we might possibly be wrong. And yet, the persecution
has come, not because we have doubted but because we have
trusted enough to do something that has upset the world's status
quo. We are persecuted because we have had faith.

Here is a cause for joy. Not only have we suffered like Christ,
but we have also had faith like Christ. His Spirit has been in us
and has given us the faith to do what we have done. We have been
literally one with Christ, and it is the persecution that reveals this
blessing.

Suggestion for prayer: *Pray for those who suffer for their faith, that
they may endure with strength.*

Saturday, May 30   Read John 17:6-10.

Today's scripture is part of a prayer in which Jesus is preparing his disciples for his impending absence. Jesus speaks to God about his disciples as the ones that God had given him. Jesus would also speak of contemporary believers as those whom God has given him. He speaks of them, and us, as "mine," as though we belong to him. What does this belonging mean?

I have three children, and when I introduce them to someone, I say, "These are my children." Of course, I do not own them. I did not buy them as I did my car. They are "mine" only because God has given them to me, and I feel responsible for them. I love them. I provide for them and teach them how to behave. I share time with them and do all the other things that fathers do with children who are theirs. These are also the same things that Jesus did for his disciples because God had given them to him.

When my work takes me away from home, I do not stop caring about my children. They are still mine, and I still love them. In the same way, Jesus may be absent from those who are his, but he still loves each of us. He prays for us, and he provides for us by pouring out his Spirit upon each of us. Jesus does these things so that even in his absence we sense his continued presence. We are secure in his love and are aware of his influence in shaping and directing our lives. We imitate him and consciously model our lives after his example. We try to please him in everything we do and say. We do for others as a way to do for him. All these things make us realize that we really do belong to him.

Suggestion for prayer: *Take time now to consider how Jesus is present in your life, and thank God for this presence.*

Sunday, May 31   Read John 17:11, 20-23.

It is fitting that on Sunday, when most Christians are gathering to worship, we remember Jesus' prayer that we be one with one another just as Jesus is one with his Father. He prays, asking God to protect our unity and make us perfectly one. In such a unity we experience the presence of God perfectly.

However, a perfect, loving unity is not what will be experienced by most of us as we gather. Grudge-bearing and old wounds will bring division among us. Doctrines and denominations composed by human minds will impose artificial barriers. Jealous egos and self-imposing manners will add more division. Add to this worldly concerns such as economic status, racial prejudice, and social position that further disintegrate the unity, and one can quickly see why Christ prayed for God to protect our unity.

Whether there is any unity left in the church to be saved could be questioned, yet the fact that there is still a Christian church is a testimony that there is some unity among us. We still worship the same God and cling to the sacred writings of the early church. At times of famine, flood, earthquake, and other disasters, we quickly cooperate to bring relief to the victims. We work and pray for world peace and human justice. We count on the salvation offered us through Jesus' crucifixion and resurrection to provide us with eternal life. We call on the same Holy Spirit for comfort, strength, and direction in our daily lives. We are even trying to serve the same God when differing opinions throw us into conflict. Although it is not perfected, God is preserving a unity for us.

Suggestion for prayer: *Pray that God might both perfect and protect our unity.*

PENTECOST: THE BELIEVER'S BIRTHRIGHT

June 1-7, 1987   **Ruth Heaney†**
Monday, June 1   Read John 7:37-39.

It is autumn, and in Jerusalem the Feast of Tabernacles is being observed by devout Hebrew pilgrims. Jesus and his disciples are among them.

Included in the commemoration of the forty years of wandering is a gold pitcher filled with water. For seven days the pitcher is carried in the procession that winds into the Temple, its contents symbolizing the water God provided from the rock.

But now it is the eighth and final feast day, and the gold pitcher is missing. The Jews are celebrating their ancestors' arrival at the promised land, a land with thirst-quenching rivers and lakes.

It is during this last feast day that Jesus stands up and announces that he is the source of an even better water, a living water. Unaided by the Gospel writer's explanation that the living water is actually the Holy Spirit yet to be poured out (v. 39), those who hear Jesus are understandably confused and uncomfortable. Surely the enigmatic teacher approves to some degree of the traditions that link Israelites to their God or else he would not participate.

What point is he trying to make?

Prayer: *Lord, even though I have your written word to guide me, I— like your earthly contemporaries—am prone to cling to the fixed and the comfortable. Keep me, O Lord, from the danger of preferring the gold cup of staid tradition to your everchanging living water. Amen.*

---

†Christian writer, Wenonah, New Jersey.

Tuesday, June 2   Read Isaiah 44:1-8.

Why doesn't Jesus choose, instead, to stand up during the Feast of Tabernacles and declare that he is the source from which the Holy Spirit will flow? Those within earshot might be no less confounded. They know that God's Holy Spirit is already in existence (Gen. 1:1). Even the prophets have mentioned God's Spirit on occasion (see Isa. 63:10; Zech. 4:6).

On this final feast day, not even Jesus' own disciples realize that the Old Testament concept of God working through his Spirit is soon to pivot dramatically. The living water of Pentecost has yet to wash the spiritual scales from their eyes. When it does, Peter will proclaim the fulfillment of Joel's prophecy (Joel 2:28-32) in his Pentecostal sermon.

Isaiah's prophecy (today's Bible reading), however, is of interest because it foretells who will receive the outpouring of the Holy Spirit. Verse 5 explains that the recipients will be an expanded covenant people and will include all those who choose to call themselves by the name of Jacob and surname themselves by the name of Israel.

Jesus, too, has already said that many will come from the east and west and sit down with Abraham, Isaac, and Jacob in the kingdom of heaven while the children of the kingdom are cast out (Matt. 8:11-12).

Nobody understands yet.

Prayer: *Lord, there are times when I also don't understand what you are trying to tell me. Is it because I've been too fearful to wade deep enough into your living water? Please take my hand, Lord, and lead me to greater depths. Let me ultimately experience the joy of sitting with Abraham, Isaac, and Jacob in the kingdom of heaven. Amen.*

Wednesday, June 3   Read John 20:19-23.

It is now Easter evening in Jerusalem. Jesus' disciples huddle behind locked doors. After watching their leader die in disgrace, they wonder if they are next. Equally chilling is the fact that the mysterious heavenly kingdom Jesus attempted to establish has been aborted.

Mary Magdalene has already delivered Jesus' resurrection message (John 20:18), but it has been met with disbelief. The disciples remain convinced that they have failed Jesus—and he has failed them.

Into this fear-ridden scene, Jesus appears after his resurrection. Among the few remarks recorded of the reunion is that of Jesus when he breathes on those present and says, "Receive the Holy Spirit" (v. 22).

This is not the first time Jesus has spoken to them of the Holy Spirit. A few days earlier, at the Passover supper, Jesus explained both the conditions that will precede the Holy Spirit's arrival and the role the Holy Spirit will play: (1) Jesus will return to the Father and be seen by them no more; (2) Jesus will send the Holy Spirit after he leaves; (3) the Holy Spirit will act on Jesus' authority (see John 16:7-15).

On this first Easter evening, the disciples realize their Lord's embryonic kingdom is still intact. For the next forty days Jesus will instruct them before handing over its keys (see Matt. 16:19).

Until then, a breath of the Holy Spirit will suffice.

Prayer: *Lord, sometimes I'm frightened and sure you've forsaken me. Please come to me at those times through doors I've locked against the world. Remind me that I—even I—am needed for the work of your kingdom. Amen.*

Thursday, June 4   Read Acts 2:1-13.

Jesus' followers remain in Jerusalem—waiting. It has been ten days since he left to be with the Father. The risen Lord has charged them not to leave the city until they are baptized with the Holy Spirit (see Acts 1:4-5). Once they are baptized, he has explained, they will have the power they need to be his witnesses throughout the world (Acts 1:8).

Suddenly, with a rush of wind and tongues of fire, the Christian church is born. The Holy Spirit descends on the 120 gathered there (see Acts 1:15), and they are filled with living water. The simple become profound; the weak are made strong; the cowardly are now bold. Each is given the specific spiritual gifts he or she will need to be an effective witness (see 1 Cor. 12:11).

The disciples are not the only ones affected by the outpouring of the Holy Spirit. Pilgrims who have filed into Jerusalem to celebrate the Hebrew fruit harvest festival of Pentecost are caught up in an experience that isn't bounded by nationality or language. The fruit harvest pales beside the harvest of 3000 souls (see Acts 2:41).

Unfortunately, as in all times and places, there are those present who choose to mock what they cannot understand. "They are filled with new wine" (v. 13).

Twentieth-century mockers shrug off today's manifestations of the Holy Spirit with twentieth-century explanations: "Emotionalism." "Exhibitionism." "Psychological crutch."

Prayer: *Lord, let me not be numbered among those who fail to grasp the significance of Pentecost and what the Holy Spirit can do for me and through me. Amen.*

Friday, June 5   Read Acts 2:14-21.

In the wake of the baptism of the Holy Spirit, Peter has to raise his voice to be heard above the confusion. Thus, the keynote speech at the birthday celebration of the Christian church begins with a roar. The introduction, however, is deceptively simple. Peter begins by tackling the accusation that the disciples are drunk.

It is not a difficult task, even for a burly fisherman noted for his impetuosity, not for his eloquence. Peter merely points out that it is only nine o'clock in the morning. His audience knows that on the Sabbath, or a feast day such as Pentecost, Jews do not eat or drink before nine, the hour of morning prayer. Once the time of day has been noted, Peter's explanation is accepted without controversy.

This acceptance frees Peter to move into the remainder of the first of the three parts of his speech. Instead of drunkenness, he informs them, what bystanders have just witnessed is the out-pouring of the Holy Spirit as spoken by the prophet Joel. Peter quotes the prophecy for them.

To those present who know him, the difference between the pre-Pentecost Peter and the Pentecost Peter is astounding. Surely the Holy Spirit Jesus promised to send has arrived and has just finished witnessing through Peter.

Then, as now, actions speak louder than words.

Prayer: *Lord, we know that with you no limitations are ever involved. Yet many today who claim they are yours fail to receive the tremendous power of your Holy Spirit. What is blocking it? Who is blocking it? Lord, is it I? Amen.*

Saturday, June 6   Read 1 Corinthians 12:3*b*-11.

Empowered by the Holy Spirit at Pentecost, the disciples set forth from Jerusalem to carry out their Lord's parting instructions (see Matt. 28:19-20). They soon discover that the living water flows from them onto all who accept the good news (see Acts 10:44-47; 19:1-6).

As the Holy Spirit begins to seal and indwell believers everywhere, the converted Gentiles run into difficulty. How do they distinguish between gifts from the Holy Spirit and practices from their idol-worshiping past? Many of the emotional experiences are similar.

The church at Corinth writes to Paul for advice on this and other matters. His reply contains a lengthy section on spiritual gifts (see 1 Cor. 12:1–14:40).

For Paul, the acid test is that only the Holy Spirit will try to convict one of the divinity of Jesus (v. 3). Yet, for the benefit of his Corinthian readers, Paul goes on to recognize nine valid gifts of the Holy Spirit.

At the same time, he points out these facts: the gifts are from God (v. 6), the gifts are intended to benefit not only the recipient but also the body of believers to which that person belongs (v. 7), the gifts are distributed by the Holy Spirit as the Spirit sees fit (v. 11).

Despite initial confusion, it is obvious the living water Jesus promised is stimulating the growth of ability, power, and zeal in the early Christian church.

Suggestion for meditation: *The church of Jesus Christ still needs ability, power, and zeal to carry out its mission today. Are those vital ingredients present in my church? Are they present in me?*

Sunday, June 7 (Pentecost)

Read 1 Corinthians 12:12-13.

For all of us who are born of water and of the Spirit (see John 3:3-8), Pentecost is our birthright. It is a birthright that gives us spiritual freedom while binding us irrevocably to others baptized by the Holy Spirit.

Rather than a dichotomy, this is God's way of equipping the baptized individual (see Rom. 8:26-27) and the body of believers (see Acts 9:31). If there is any flaw in this plan, it is the human tendency to allow spiritual gifts to become a joyous end in themselves.

If we do fall into this error, we overlook the most important word of Pentecost—"Why?" The answer is the same in 1987 as it was when Jesus charged his original disciples. "Ye shall receive power when the Holy Spirit has come upon you; and you shall be my witnesses in Jerusalem and in all Judea and Samaria and to the end of the earth" (Acts 1:8).

The baptism of the Holy Spirit—foretold by John the Baptist (see Mark 1:8) and fulfilled by Jesus—has crossed centuries and miles to reach us (see Acts 2:38-39). It is our turn to use our spiritual gifts to point others to their source.

Living water, bottled within us, stagnates.

Prayer: *Lord, why have you given all to someone who deserves nothing? It is beyond my comprehension that you would allow your Holy Spirit to dwell in one as unfit as I. Thank you for the gifts you have entrusted to me, and forbid that I should ever take them for granted. Instead, show me each day a way to use them to witness effectively for you. Amen.*

POWER, PRESENCE, AND THE CHOSEN

June 8-14, 1987   **Leonard Thompson Wolcott†**
Monday, June 8   Read Deuteronomy 4:32-40.

An astrophysicist, explaining the development of the universe, said, "We now know the 'how' of the universe, but not the 'why'." Do you know why you are here, a finite jot in this vast space?

Moses, amazed at the wonder of the voice of God "speaking out of the midst of the fire," put off his shoes in worship, listened, and was sent to deliver a people God had chosen.

Deuteronomy recounts the power of God, who created humanity, chose a nation of people, spoke to them, delivered them from bondage, gave them an inheritance.

Why? "That you might know that the Lord is God"; that you might hear God's voice; that God might bridge the gulf between infinite holiness and human sinfulness (see John 1:14).

We understand the wonder of God's love and choice of us only in the context of God's immeasurable power. In spite of this ominous power, God lets us live, loves us, chooses us, speaks to us.

It is awesome. We don't deserve it. "Therefore . . . lay it to your heart. . . . Therefore you shall keep . . . his commandments . . . that it may go well with you."

Prayer: *We stand in awe before your unfathomable infinity, O God, in wonder that you should love us and have chosen us as your people. May we accept your choice by willing your will and doing your commandments. Amen.*

---

†Author, lecturer, former missionary to India, Ecuador, and Zaire, and teacher of missionaries, Scarritt College; Nashville, Tennessee.

Tuesday, June 9   Read Psalm 33:1-5.

Praise befits the righteous.

Much happiness depends on events. It comes and goes. Joy is "in the Lord," who comes and never goes. Joy is born in our awe at God's greatness. Joy grows in attention to God's goodness. The Lord acts with caring; we react with praise. There is much we do not understand. Yet, confident in God, we see the beauty of the universe and the wonder of life.

"Righteous" is the psalmist's designation of the chosen people. We are righteous through no personal achievement but through the Lord's choice of us and only in our relationship with and toward God. The righteous live a Godward life, receptive of the Spirit, in tune with God's purpose.

Because God is right, we join in righteousness. In the company of God's righteousness, we rejoice, we praise. Praise is the natural response of the upright to the uprightness of God. We play our instruments, we use our abilities, our disciplined talents, our lives, to praise the Lord. We sing a new song, new every morning, ever renewed by his ever-refreshing Spirit. We "shout in triumph" because we are God's chosen people.

Uprightness is cohesion with God's word—action that is upright. An upright people live in conformity with God's will that they might live by God's will.

Prayer: *Let us be aware of you, God, and of your word and action among us that we may take joy in them. Then we can do nothing but break out in praise. May our lives sing to you, reverberate with your righteousness. Amen.*

Wednesday, June 10   Read Psalm 33:4-7.

"The word of the Lord is upright" to an upright people.

These verses of the psalm sing of creation by the righteous, faithful, caring God. God's love defines righteousness: God's consistent intent is for just relationships. Such is right for us. God's love explains God's faithfulness: It never lets us down. If we kneel in awe before the overwhelming might of our Creator, we can also stand firm on the reliability of God's word.

Unless we are sensitive to God's benevolence, we can have no clear perception of the 'why' of creation; of life, the amazing product of creation; or of humankind, the ultimate in creation. When we grasp the theme of love in all God's work, we recognize that the magnificent creation "is full of the steadfast love of the Lord," which, with affection and kindness, incorporates God's people into God's purpose of community.

This love is never sentimental, never indulgent. We dare not take it lightly nor for granted. As it defines righteousness, so it is defined by righteousness. We receive it with trembling gratitude.

God loves to do righteousness toward the chosen people. God loves justice done by those people. God does goodness and expects and delights in goodness.

Never separate consciousness of God's love from the wonder and thunder of creation—massive and minute—which came into being by "the word of the Lord," the "breath of his mouth."

Prayer: *Almighty God, as we consider the mystery of your being, let us receive with gratitude your loving-kindness for us. Help us build the hours of this day and this life on the firm foundation of your righteousness. Amen.*

Thursday, June 11   Read Psalm 33:8-11.

Faith can have vitality. The practice of it can have vigor in a vivid awareness of God's power.

The psalmist has sung of the awesomeness of creation. The song reinforces our recognition of creative power. "For he spoke, and it came to be; he commanded, and it stood forth."

The creative word is a controlling word. God has the last, and lasting, word. The counsels, schemes, plans of nations are ephemeral. The Eternal frustrates their intent, makes them without effect. Human counsels, ideas, thoughts are superseded by those of God, which underlie and are the 'why' of the universe. Look at history; the rise and fall of nations; the Napoleons who sweep across the land causing the deaths of tens of thousands, the dislocation and suffering of millions. Such empires have fallen, their schemes in shreds. We are all subject to God's overruling.

The Lord examines all human endeavors (see Ps. 33:13-15). At God's mighty works, all the earth dare not but tremble. All are summoned to acknowledge the divine activity. Faith includes awe.

Because of God's power, the chosen people are assured, confident that the word spoken to them endures. God's designs for them cannot be frustrated. In weakness, we may change; in strength, God does not. In the light of God's power, the chosen people must place their counsels and intentions. We need to reframe our wills in the context of God's will.

Suggestion for meditation: *Contemplate the power of the Infinite. Face its reality. Look at your life, your plans, your hopes in the light of the Eternal will.*

Friday, June 12   Read Psalm 33:12.

We belong to the Almighty.

Conscious of this, we hear God and know God's love. We remember the Lord is God, and we keep the Lord's commandments (see Deut. 4:35-40). We rejoice in the Lord in praise and singing (see Ps. 33:1-3).

This is the happy experience of those who are chosen. And it is a group experience. "The nation" is a *people* who have in common their relationship to God. We are God's people by God's choice of us, not ours of God. We are a people who, in harmony with God, are in harmony with one another. Our happiness together is our journeying together in God's way. We, the finite, are enveloped by and move with the Infinite. Because the aim of God's plan is wholeness, God's people belong as a group to this wholeness, this salvation, this *shalom*.

We belong to God. We have surrendered ourselves to be God's possession, God's special property (see Exod. 19:5-6; 1 Pet. 2:9-10). Our identity is with the One who creates and controls our universe. Here we are at home with God, having responded to God's invitation. We enter into participation with the joy and beauty of God's creation. As instruments of God's upright, faithful, loving purpose, we have as our goal God's will, that our actions may be in unison with the Lord's action.

God, who gives us an inheritance, has given us a divine heritage. Here is enduring happiness.

Prayer: *We thank you, Lord, that you have made us your heritage. May we, together with all those who love you, enter the joy of your presence to be with you, to go with you, to do your will with you. Amen.*

Saturday, June 13   Read 2 Corinthians 13:5-14.

We have heard the ancient saying, "Know thyself." Today, there is emphasis on knowing "who you are." The ideal placed before us is to "feel good about ourselves," to "be comfortable with ourselves," to gain "self-realization."

Paul's challenge to the Corinthian Christians was not likely to make them comfortable with themselves. "Examine yourselves," "Scrutinize yourselves!" They were to realize not themselves but Jesus Christ, to recognize Christ in their lives.

Test yourself, as you would test a metal to verify its quality. Many Christians have the habit of self-examination, asking themselves, "Have I grown in Christ today?" In the light of the divine presence, "How are you doing?" Remember, it is just as wrong not to do right as it is to do wrong. Are you doing right? Are you holding on to the faith, living faithfully as God is faithful, uprightly as God's word is upright?

But what if we fail the test? What if we, God's people, live not as God's people; what if we forget God's power and neglect God's presence; what if we have no peace?

"Mend your ways" requires genuine repentance. Live in peace and "the God of love and peace will be with you." Here again is the promise of God's presence if we do not shut it out in our daily business!

The promise is granted in the experience of chosenness: the grace of Christ to live by, the love of God to live in, the fellowship united by the Holy Spirit.

Prayer: *O God, help us acknowledge our sins and mend our ways. Let your grace adorn us, your love fill us, your Spirit bind us with your people. Amen.*

Sunday, June 14   Read Matthew 28:16-20.

We are chosen and authorized to great work with our Lord.
Jesus had chosen his disciples. They had been with him in his
ministry. Now he commissions them to ministry, and he will be
with them.

There was a new dimension now, after the Resurrection. Like
Moses awed into worship by the voice that commissioned him at
the burning bush, the disciples worshiped their risen Lord.
Worship is a time to listen to God, to receive God's orders.

Jesus said, "All authority . . . has been given to me. Go,
therefore." "Authority" can translate as "power," "possibility."
Jesus gave his disciples authority, power, and the daring possibility to change the world. Note the limitless "all."

The mission was clear, direct, definite, and in the continuous
tense: "Keep at it."

1. Go, don't hesitate, and keep going.

2. Make disciples. Extend God's choosing to others who also,
by God's strength, can do God's bidding.

3. Baptize. Initiate new disciples into the total human experience of God as Creator, Son, Holy Spirit—Lord, Presence,
Power.

4. Teach all I have commanded. We share what we live by.

5. The commission is to be a carried out to all nations, all
peoples, all cultures, every time and space. None is left out of the
encompassing love of God.

And with the commission, again the promise: "I am with you
always." As you do God's bidding today, no task is beyond you.
God is with you.

Prayer: *Dear God, we accept your commission. We go in your authority. We claim your ever-staying presence. Amen.*

NEW BEGINNINGS!

June 15-21, 1987 **Ruth Hurtt†**
Monday, June 15 Read Genesis 28:10-11.

TOUCH ME! The moment I stepped inside the store, these two words labeled on a lampshade totally mystified me. Noticing my pensive stare, the clerk instructed, "Go ahead, touch it!" The chandelier bulbs visible through the crystal shade added a fragile beauty to the lamp, and I was fearful I would break it. But the clerk repeated, "Touch it!" As I touched it ever so lightly, I was amazed. There was instant light!

Something new had happened to me during my introduction to the "Touch Me Lamp." I had experienced a quiet receiving—a recognition of one of God's coincidences. Just recently I had been looking for ways to increase my awareness of the presence of God. But I had concentrated on sights and sounds. Now I sensed a need to retrain my heart and mind to listen for the quietness of God's touch. I shall never forget this place of new beginnings in my quest.

This week we will journey toward new beginnings. Today we meet Jacob who also came to a place he would never forget. Described as the original con man, he has ample time on his journey to reflect upon the deceiving person he has been. He arrives at a rock-sheltered place at sunset, ideal for camping. His tired body is ready for rest, but his loneliness and homesickness keep gnawing at his heart. Using a stone for a pillow, he lies down to sleep. And he dreams! We must rest, too, for a long journey awaits us.

Prayer: *O God, help us know your presence as we journey. Amen.*

---

†Free-lance writer, Harrisonburg, Virginia.

Tuesday, June 16   Read Genesis 28:12-15.

God's gift of each fresh day is a new beginning. Believe that! Yesterday may have found us struggling with overwhelming adversities. No matter. With a night's rest we can see things more clearly. "Weeping may tarry for the night, but joy comes with the morning" (Ps. 30:5). And we know that God has brought us through the pain or has strengthened us to endure it. Now we are ready to resume our journey.

When we met our first traveler, Jacob, he wondered if even a night's rest could help his weariness. Memories were too fresh of his cruel treatment of his father and brother. How like us when we limit our concept of God! Indeed, he fell asleep. And then came the dream. And the dream created a sprouting of the seeds for his "new beginning." What a sight for guilty eyes and heart to see—angels going up and down the stairway reaching from earth to heaven. Sleep researchers claim that if you are an average sleeper, you start a dream about every 90 minutes. In eight hours' sleep a single dream may last 45 minutes. This scientific information leads us to ponder Jacob's dream. We wonder about the possibilities of God's communication to us through our dreams today as God did in times long ago.

Imagine how deeply Jacob sensed God's presence when he heard God declare, "I am the Lord, the God of Abraham your father and the God of Isaac; the land on which you lie I will give to you and to your descendants." And the dream is not over yet!

Prayer: *Lord, your tender mercies are mystifying to us. We feel unworthy but are grateful for your love. Amen.*

Wednesday, June 17   Read Genesis 28:16-22.

We resume our journey as Jacob's dream is ending. Why have we lingered so long at this special place? The reason is now clear. It is the benchmark for the entire week's journey! The profound awareness of God's presence is the assurance we need for new beginnings. Jacob is so surprised at God's promises that he exclaims upon awakening, "The Lord is here! He is in this place, and I didn't know it!" (AP) His emotions are so awakened that he dedicates that special place as the house of God. Excitement builds as he realizes that God has not rejected him after all but has restored him. Could this be Jacob's Damascus Road experience?

How different are Jacob's thoughts as he prepares to leave that place he named Bethel. Even if he goes astray from God's guidance in future days, Bethel will remain as the memory jogger that will determine his destination, for he will remember where his new beginnings originated.

We bid farewell to Jacob and prepare for tomorrow's journey. But let us never forget that Jacob surely stands out as a work of God's grace. God comes to us even when we feel least worthy of God's presence.

Prayer: *Dear God, your grace is amazing! Help us remember that you make your presence known to us often in mysterious ways. Please give us listening hearts so that we will not miss your call or touch. Amen.*

Thursday, June 18   Read Psalm 91:1-4.

In our journeys of life the people we meet make the difference. How often we find ourselves at a place where we did not plan to go and meet someone who influences us greatly. As a result, our faith is strengthened and we learn anew about totally trusting God when we are faced with detours in our journeys.

Today the psalmist gives us a song of trust. And the traveler we meet projects the trust we need to learn for the balance of our seven-day journey. Meet Marie Coffman. She began her "journey of trust" on May 7, 1985, the day her illness was diagnosed as leukemia. Since that day, Marie has traveled through many deep valleys, and the journey continues with medical treatment and more waiting. Responding to my request for a sharing of her trust in God as she endures her illness, she said: "How wonderful to know that I have a God and Savior who is my refuge. I need not fear. I am trusting in his faithfulness completely and standing firmly on his promises."

Marie confesses that she cannot endure on her own strength but leans on God's strength, peace, love, and presence—and on God's promise never to leave or forsake us. Marie imparts the special peace of Christ to everyone who talks to her. And its strengthening effect lingers long after.

We have no guarantees that life's tragedies will not touch us. Yet when we discover that resting place of trust in our great and loving God, we experience a calm in the midst of life's storms. Knowing God's everlasting love is the antidote for our fears.

Prayer: *Forgive us, O God, when we fail to totally trust you. Thank you for giving those special people who teach us anew of your strength and ever-present love. Amen.*

Friday, June 19   Read Psalm 91:5-10.

"Our faith in tomorrow gives us strength to endure the pains of today." I wrote this to a friend in 1982 who was suffering from ALS, and it seems appropriate to share here as a help for the balance of our journey. Today's psalm passage tells us that we need not fear "the terror of the night, nor the arrow that flies by day." But we will experience a faith struggle before we find that confidence and peace which enable us to trust God totally when unexpected crises come upon us. A serious illness or a significant material loss can teach us that we cannot survive on our own strength. It is then we receive a quiet knowledge that God is our strength and refuge.

As is all scripture, today's psalm is relevant for today. We can face all dangers by trusting in our God of all tomorrows. What happened on the first Easter teaches us the real meaning of life—life for which there is always a future. Christ was resurrected! Christ lives! And our belief in Christ as Savior assures us of eternal life. We then no longer need to fear what may happen to our earthly bodies, and we have the confidence that Paul had: "Neither death, nor life, nor angels, nor principalities, nor things present, nor things to come, nor powers, nor height, nor depth, nor anything else in all creation, will be able to separate us from the love of God in Christ Jesus our Lord" (Rom. 8:38).

Prayer: *Dear Lord, thank you for your everlasting arms of love that comfort us in our pain and sorrows. We lean on your strength for tomorrow's journey. Amen.*

Saturday, June 20   Read Romans 5:12-19.

Let's go to prison today. I share an experience from my prison visitation ministry which fits perfectly into today's scripture written by the traveler who knew all about prisons: Paul.

The prisoner we will visit today is serving a sentence for the crime she committed. Yet she is enjoying true freedom! How? Since she entered prison, she has accepted Jesus Christ as her Savior. And that has made all the difference! She had known about Christ before but had always rejected him. But now she knows the true meaning of forgiveness and true freedom. She expressed it poignantly in a letter to me:

> I am ashamed to say a tragedy had to take place in my life for me to find our Lord. On the other hand I am grateful to God for his forgiveness. . . . The girls in here just don't understand how I can be so happy and content after what I've done. Of course they don't know the mental anguish I've been through, but they just shake their heads no when I tell them, "God has forgiven me and it's in his hands now."

All of us inherited the guilty sentence of sin as the result of Adam's disobedience, but Christ's death and resurrection resulted in God's pardon. With repentent and desirous hearts we ask for forgiveness of our sins, and God freely gives it with great love. Then sin is no longer able to crush our hopes for reconciliation of all relationships, for we are now unified with Christ and are truly free! And because of God's great love for us, we have new beginnings and new life in Christ.

Prayer: *We are overwhelmed, dear Lord, by your gift of grace through Jesus, your Son. Help us to accept your great love and to share that good news with others. Amen.*

Sunday, June 21   Read Matthew 10:24-33.

Our journey has ended. But we have not arrived—we have a long way to go! Even though we have experienced new beginnings each new day, life's journeys never end.

The wonderful gift of God's grace has become more precious to me, especially when we remember Jacob, our first fellow traveler, and others. And we have been reassured of the quieting touch of God's presence. When we reflect upon courageous Marie's trust in the faithfulness of God, we learn that in the quietness of trust we find strength. Sometimes our faith will falter and our adversities plague us, making it harder to hang on. But then we meet other travelers, and God's love is revealed anew as we are reminded that our hope is in Christ. We have learned that there is no journey in which Christ does not accompany us; no suffering that he has not endured; no sin that he will not forgive; no life that is not eternal by belief in him and his resurrection.

Today's scripture reading reminds us of the sparrows and, in turn, reassures us of how much God cares for us. What a privilege to witness for God to those who reject God or may not know of God's love! What a joy to reach out with encouragement to become what God intends us to be!

I have enjoyed our journey together and shall miss all of you. We could not have made it without constant prayers for God's guidance. Keep expecting to see rainbows (new hope) and butterflies (new beginnings). May God's love be the strengthener for your difficult days and for your new beginnings.

Prayer: *Dear God, thank you for being so patient with us during our journey. Guide us in our new beginnings. We love you. Help us to spread love and joy for you. Amen.*

STRENGTH THROUGH TESTING

June 22-28, 1987   **James L. Merrell†**
Monday, June 22   Read Genesis 32:22-32.

Wrestling with God

A key incident in the early history of Israel is the encounter between Jacob and a stranger who represents God. The two do not simply settle down by campfire to discuss theology or the market value of sheep. They tussle in a fierce wrestling match. Jacob persists until he gains a victory and receives the divine blessing.

As we mature in faith, we gain a greater appreciation for the underlying truth of this story. Our faith grows through *struggle*. Think of some profoundly confident and joyous Christians. Their spiritual achievements have not come easily. Their radiant faith is the outcome of a fierce, ongoing battle between human and divine concepts, values, and will.

God may have one direction for our lives while we choose another. So our purposes clash. And we often find, gratefully, that God's strength prevails. But the struggle is fierce—as rough-and-tumble as that between Jacob and the angel. It can be painful. We have other points of competition with the Almighty. Sometimes we will not believe God, and we must know bitter defeat in order to learn the deeper lesson. Sometimes we want to pin God so that we may hold this elusive deity in our firm grasp.

Our wrestling with God enlivens our spirits and reminds us that we have a living, relevant faith.

Prayer: *Eternal God, we thank you that you have given us a challenge so that we may struggle—and grow. Amen.*

---

†Ordained minister, Christian Church (Disciples of Christ); editor, *The Disciple*; St. Louis, Missouri.

Tuesday, June 23   Read Psalm 17:1-7.

Ready for the exam

The psalmist appears to be overly exuberant and boastful in saying to God, "Look, I've led an exemplary life—and now you may come and put me to the test and I will be ready and will prove it to you!" (AP) But there is something to admire here as we ponder the bold sense of assurance that is reflected in these words. The writer does not doubt for a moment that the spiritual test would be passed with an A plus!

When Jesus told the parable of the wise and foolish maidens, he added a note of commendation to the kind of thinking we find in Psalm 17. Jesus urged his listeners to be prepared—to live such a faithful life that they will be ready no matter when the test comes.

There is sound spiritual advice here for all of us. We should live each day with such faithfulness that we will have no fear of the ultimate judgment—or of any lesser daily testing that comes our way. We will know that we are prepared. It is not to say that we will pass with a 100% grade—for there is imperfection in all of us. But we will be able to live in confidence, knowing we have done our best and are ready to give an account to God as stewards of the gospel.

Our boastfulness, however, must never become arrogance. There is a fine line here, and we must watch that we do not move away from the spirit of Psalm 17 and become so overly confident of our worth that we think more highly of ourselves than we should. Our assurance must always be tempered with humility. We know we are prepared for the test, but it is God who sets the standards and finally determines our grade.

Prayer: *O God, help us to live such a life of obedience that we will have no fear of the day of accounting. Amen.*

Wednesday, June 24   Read Psalm 17:15.

Face to face

Some American corporations have been debating the legality and ethical implications of using lie detection equipment in screening potential employees. Business has claimed that it is necessary to find ways of testing individuals in regard to their moral values because of the high rate of white collar crime.

Electronic devices are only the most recent tools in the age-old effort to get into a person's heart and test for goodness and evil. Humanity has created all sorts of sinister and brutal methods, as well as subtle and sophisticated ones, to ferret out the truth. Still, the true person remains an enigma, always hidden from full view, always safe from total exposure.

One of the striking concepts of our biblical heritage is that the true test of our character comes as we stand face to face with God. Before the Almighty One, we are naked, unmasked, vulnerable. There is no hiding, no room for pretense. The Bible speaks of God as the one who knows the inmost secrets of our hearts. This is a sobering concept, because we like to keep our souls hidden from scrutiny; but it is also a joyous thought because it means that the God we serve is concerned with all persons as they are—and not swayed by our pretense or blocked by our protective walls.

The psalmist was glad to be able to "behold thy face in righteousness." Here is the supreme confidence of one who has struggled against temptation and has won enough battles to have no fear about meeting God face to face. Will we also live such transparently faithful lives that we will have no fear of such a "lie detector" test?

Prayer: *Thank you, O God, for the joy that comes as we put our spirits in tune with yours. Amen.*

Thursday, June 25   Read Romans 6:1-4.

Faithful to the death

When we think of Christian martyrs—those who have given up life rather than surrender to evil—we usually dwell on those faithful men and women of the first few years of the Christian era. But the surprising truth is that there have been more martyrs in the past two or three decades than at any other time in the past twenty centuries. Each day, more and more believers give up their lives for the sake of the gospel.

Martyrs today are those who have resisted political or religious tyranny. They do not willingly seek out death but simply carry out their faithful witness, thus antagonizing the powers and principalities. In the end, the presence of such truth and goodness can no longer be tolerated. With Jesus, the forces of evil used the cross as the instrument to silence the truth. In our times the weapons are many.

The Letter to the Romans is a reminder that martyrdom is one of the risks one gladly accepts in becoming a follower of Jesus Christ. Our baptism—this act by which we are joined to Christ and his community of faith—is a graphic symbol of death. It is a burial with Christ—so that we might experience the power and joy of the resurrection that follows.

Are we prepared for this supreme test? Most of us live relatively safe and secure, but we must always keep in mind the possibility that at some point our testing may be a matter of life and death. We can only live faithfully from day to day, abiding in the strength of the living Christ, so that we will remain steadfast if and when we are called to put our lives on the line.

Prayer: *In life and death, O Lord, we are yours. Amen.*

Friday, June 26   Read Romans 6:5-11.

Freed for joyous living

Daily crucifixion is an experience that all of us will know again and again in life if we are faithful to our commitment to the Savior. We may not face the ultimate test of martyrdom, but all of us are called by Christ to help bear and share his cross.

A Jamaican pastor once preached on this theme to a small, isolated congregation. He asked them to bring forward symbols of oppressive elements in life which Christ called them to reject or resist. So they brought an array of weapons, rum bottles, lottery tickets, and even marijuana. These were among the many temptations they faced every day. To disclaim them publicly within the community of faith was to experience a measure of crucifixion—to bear deep hurt for the sake of greater good. The simple service was a moving experience for everyone—a time of honesty and growth.

Jesus' call to his disciples was that they should take up the cross and follow him. Our passage today from Romans goes further in that it speaks not only of carrying the cross but also about going on to the ultimate end—so that our "old self" is "crucified with him." This is the testing Jesus puts before us every day. We are called upon to die to the old life of sin so that we might experience the joyous resurrected life.

We know how hard it is to give up our old ways and follow Christ. Death is the correct way to speak of this experience, for it is often traumatic and painful to change our patterns of living. But the happy reality is that we thus become free, through this crucifixion experience, to know life as it was meant to be.

Prayer: *Help us to crucify the old self, O God, so that we may find new life in and through the living Christ. Amen.*

Saturday, June 27 Read Matthew 10:34-38.

The family struggle

The question on a church's outdoor signboard was provocative: "Is Your Religion in Your Wife's Name?" Often spouses do not share the same religious values, and at times there may be a clash. Sometimes a person's commitment to the truth will mean that others within the same family will become hostile.

This is a difficult challenge. We all want to enjoy a happy family experience, and the thought of division within the household over religious matters is unpleasant to contemplate. Often the spiritually minded in the family will yield to the opposition in order to keep peace and to prevent conflict. But at what cost do we avoid conflict?

Jesus surely wants the home to be a place of joy for every person. But he would have us realize that there may be times when our commitment to the gospel will create painful conflict within the family circle. We may have to choose whether to follow Christ or to yield to human desire.

We often think of young people who reject church-going. Yet often it is parents who are the problem. Some youth are drawn toward faith but find no support from father or mother.

We must always look for ways to help those of all ages and circumstances who are reaching out for help beyond their families, who sincerely love those within their household but realize there is a call beyond the human family toward the community of faith.

Prayer: *We are grateful for the larger household of faith, O God. We pray that we may be faithful to our participation in it even as we love our human kin. Amen.*

Sunday, June 28   Read Matthew 10:39-42.

Passing the hardest test

Some observers charge that ours is perhaps the most selfish, self-centered era of recent history. There are bright spots, such as the massive responses to natural disasters. But for the most part, people tend to place a heavy priority on personal gain. In his teaching, Jesus recognized and dealt with this common response. "Don't seek so hard to hold on to life," Jesus intimates. "Let go. Lose your life in servanthood. Then you will really have something enduring."

Such a teaching is hard for us to understand and to follow. Yet those who have lost their lives in loving service tell us that they really found their lives for the first time. The tragic thing is that so many people are like the rich young aristocrat who heard such a message from Jesus and then went away with sorrow without even trying to put this concept into practice. We are afraid of giving up what we prize so highly, of surrendering what we have worked so hard to attain.

This may well be the key test of the Christian life—choosing between loyalties. We face this test whenever we write a check or set our activities calendar. We face it in daily conversations. Do our own interests come first? Or do we let go of our own wants long enough to consider the question of what Christ would have us do?

We never know the full joy of life if we spend every waking hour trying to hold tightly to it. Incredible peace and purpose can be ours when we seek to follow Jesus above everything else.

Prayer: *Servant Savior, help us to find true life through you. Amen.*

GOD DELIVERS

June 29–July 5, 1987   **Thomas R. Logsdon†**
Monday, June 29   Read Psalm 123.

A restaurant in our town takes your order by phone, prepares it, and brings it to your front door. Their motto is, "We Deliver."

So does God. God, the Great Deliverer, delivers us in all kinds of ways from all kinds of problems. God is never too busy to listen and always willing to help—though often in God's own way and time.

God delivers us from pride. Whenever we are tempted to look down on someone, God says, "Look up at me!" The only way we can do this is through the eyes of a servant. Thinking about God's greatness cures us of our pride.

God doesn't leave us humbled, however. When other people look down on us, God lifts us up. God reminds us that, even though we are servants, we are servants of an almighty God. And by grace God calls us "friends" (see John 15:15). God bought us at great price, and we are among God's most treasured possessions.

Prayer: *Lord, let me see through the eyes of a servant. Deliver me from pride. Thank you, God, for calling me "friend." In Jesus' name. Amen.*

---

†Pastor, Lewistown United Methodist Church, Lewistown, Illinois.

Tuesday, June 30   Read Matthew 11:28-30.

God delivers us by helping carry our burdens.

A yoke is a piece of wood carved to fit the neck and shoulders of two draft animals so they can pull together and share a common load. An easy way to teach a young animal what is expected is to yoke it with a larger, more experienced one. The larger animal carries most of the weight, but the younger one carries enough to get a feel for the yoke. As the young one grows and matures, it carries more and more weight until, eventually, it carries half the load.

While God takes away many of our burdens, some we have to carry. Even then God tells us, "Take my yoke upon you, and learn from me."

To wear a yoke means to stick out your neck and share another person's burdens—after all, your yokefellow isn't going to drop his or her burdens just to help you carry yours. A lot of people don't want to do this. They fear the other person's burdens might be heavier than their own.

Jesus makes a perfect yokefellow. He says, "My yoke is easy, and my burden is light." Besides, he has even been known to carry more than his share of the load.

Prayer: *God, teach me to stick my neck out and share your burden as you share mine. Let me grow more like Jesus as I share his yoke. In Jesus' name. Amen.*

Wednesday, July 1   Read Exodus 1:6-14.

God delivers us in spite of our suffering.

Poor Hebrews! Joseph saved the Egyptians from starvation, and they rewarded him by making his family slaves. Yet Abraham's children were not forgotten. God told Moses, "I have heard the groaning of the people of Israel whom the Egyptians hold in bondage and I have remembered my covenant" (Exod. 6:5).

Why did God let the people fall so far, and why did God wait so long before bringing them out? Similar things happen to us. There are times we suffer in spite of, or even because of, our faith. Like Joseph, we often help others, only to have them turn on us.

Yet, even in the Hebrews' suffering, God's covenant was slowly unfolding. God had promised Abraham the land of Canaan, but Abraham was also promised that his descendants would be as many as the dust of the earth (see Gen. 13:14-17). Even when the promised land seemed a million miles away, God was still bringing the covenant made with the Hebrews to pass, for the more the Egyptians oppressed the Hebrews, "the more they multiplied and the more they spread abroad" (Exod. 1:12).

Maybe God is delivering us, even in the midst of our suffering.

Prayer: *God, I know there are times I have to suffer. I ask only that you strengthen me to endure it, as you keep your covenant alive in my life. In Jesus' name. Amen.*

Thursday, July 2   Read Exodus 1:15-21.

God delivers us from doing wrong.

Three cheers for Shiphrah and Puah, the Jewish midwives. They knew Pharaoh. They knew that anyone who would order them to kill babies would have no qualms about killing midwives for refusing to do his will. Besides, their refusal did not change anything—Pharaoh just found another way to kill the babies, as they must have known he would. Yet they still refused to do his dirty work. Even though they feared Pharaoh, they feared God more.

Whom do you fear most, God or the agents of evil? God does not always bail his servants out. As the three young men told King Nebuchadnezzar before he threw them into the furnace, "If it be so, our God whom we serve is able to deliver us from the burning fiery furnace; and he will deliver us out of your hand, O king. But if not, be it known to you, O king, that we will not serve your gods or worship the golden image which you have set up" (Dan. 3:17-18).

The midwives feared God, and their respect for God helped them face the fire of Pharaoh's wrath. The three young men feared God, and their respect for God helped them face the fire of the furnace. How about you?

We discover that the young men were delivered from the furnace, and that they also obtained jobs in the Babylonian government. The midwives were delivered from Pharaoh's anger, and they also bore children of their own.

Prayer: *God, strengthen me to face the fires of life, and let me always choose your path. In Jesus' name. Amen.*

Friday, July 3   Read Exodus 1:22–2:10.

God delivers us by changing our plans into better ones.

Moses' mother knew her son had to die. She kept him hidden as long as she could, but eventually she knew she would have to throw him into the river. If she didn't do it, someone less gentle would.

If he had to die, at least he would not die in vain. I don't think Moses' mother expected Pharaoh's daughter to adopt the boy, but I do think she meant him to be found. "Maybe," she must have thought, "if Pharaoh's daughter finds my son floating in the Nile, she might have pity on my people and convince her father to change his mind."

By her father's law, Pharaoh's daughter should have thrown the baby in the river herself. Instead, she called for a Hebrew woman to nurse the child, and the woman who was brought turned out to be Moses' mother. God had taken her plan and made it better.

Sometimes God does the same for us. If we offer our plans to God for approval, God might take them and make them even better.

Prayer: *O God, teach me to submit my plans to you, that you might make them better. In Jesus' name. Amen.*

Saturday, July 4   Read Matthew 11:25-27.

God delivers us from ignorance.

It would be very difficult, almost impossible, to learn to drive a car or play a musical instrument by reading a book. Some understandings can be learned only through experience.

We can learn a lot about God by looking at creation—just as we can learn about an artist by looking at her work. But knowing God and knowing about God are two different things. The only way to know God is through experiencing God. The only complete way to experience God is through Jesus Christ. As Jesus said, "I am the way, and the truth, and the life; no one comes to the Father, but by me. If you had known me, you would have known my Father also; henceforth you know him and have seen him" (John 14:6-7).

We need to know God because God is the source of all light and life. God created us with certain basic needs: food, water, shelter, love—and the wisdom that comes from knowing our Creator. Without these things we can never reach our full potential.

We are delivered from ignorance by being in relationship with the source of all wisdom—God. God does this by first giving us a relationship with Jesus Christ. Because all things have been revealed to the Son, Jesus is able to reveal all things to us, including God. "For the Lord gives wisdom; from his mouth come knowledge and understanding" (Prov. 2:6).

Prayer: *Lord, deliver me from my ignorance, and make me wise by making me one with you. In Jesus' name. Amen.*

Sunday, July 5   Read Romans 7:14-25.

God delivers us from the power of sin.

A lot of people misunderstand sin. They think of sin as simply "doing something wrong." But sin is far more than that. Sin is a destructive force lurking inside each of us. Sin constantly pressures us to do wrong. Even when we succeed in doing good and avoiding evil, sin is still there making life difficult. Trying to live a Christian life without coping with the power of sin is like treating the symptoms of a disease without dealing with the disease itself.

Paul knew this firsthand. He tried being good, but it was hard. "I do not understand my own actions," he said. "For I do not do the good I want, but the evil I do not want is what I do. . . . So I find it to be a law that when I want to do right, evil lies close at hand" (Rom. 7:15, 19, 21).

Paul had discovered a basic truth. Even when he did right, it was hard; and when he quit working at doing right, he fell back into doing wrong. But Paul had also discovered how to overcome that problem. "Wretched man that I am!" he cried. "Who will deliver me from this body of death? Thanks be to God through Jesus Christ our Lord!" (Rom. 7:24-25)

Even though we have to take responsibility for our actions, God through Christ takes away the power of sin in our lives. Sin may pressure us to do wrong, but God strengthens us to do right. Why make doing good and avoiding evil any harder than it is? Why don't we open ourselves to God, the Great Deliverer, who delivers us from the power of sin!

Prayer: *Loving God, deliver me from sin and strengthen me that I may serve you. In Jesus' name. Amen.*

GROWING IN THE SPIRIT

July 6-12, 1987   **L. June Stevenson†**
Monday, July 6   Read Psalm 69:13-15.

I was in some of the most desperate areas of Ethiopia during a recent drought. Although rain had not fallen in months, people ploughed the dry land each day and planted what seeds they had. The hope of these people, many of them Christians, lay in the belief that God would ultimately provide for their needs.

Quoting from Habakkuk 3:17-18, one of the church leaders said that though "the fields yield no food . . . yet I will rejoice in the Lord, I will joy in the God of my salvation."

The psalmist displays the same faith and hope. Though desperate and despairing at the unfortunate circumstances of his life, his greatest desire is that his God, the God of his people Israel, will answer his prayer to deliver him not only from his enemies but from death's very door.

"At an acceptable time, O God," he says. Not immediately, perhaps not even tomorrow, but in God's own time. All this in the face of death, beyond which for the psalmist there was no hope of immortality.

What a great heritage we have been handed by the psalmists! How reassuring to see our own faith journeys in the light of a nation that trusted in God even as it yearned for fuller understanding. "Blessed are those who have not seen and yet believe" (John 20:29).

Suggestion for meditation: *Today I will rejoice in the roots of my faith.*

---

†Editor, *Glad Tidings*, Women's Missionary Society, The Presbyterian Church in Canada, Don Mills, Ontario, Canada.

Tuesday, July 7   Read Matthew 13:1-9.

I saw firsthand the problems that people in a drought-stricken country like Ethiopia have in growing food. My shoes were brown with dust at the end of the day, my nose filled with dust. Everything was dry. I began to understand the seeming futility of planting seeds. Sometimes when the rains come, they wash the seeds right out of the newly planted ground. Sometimes the rains do not come soon enough, and the sprouts wither and die in the parched ground. Sometimes the seeds are eaten before they can be planted. There are no guarantees for the sower.

In the parable of the sower, Jesus was preparing his faithful followers for the unavoidable truth that their words, however enthusiastically strewn, would not always produce the desired results.

With people, like the land, the conditions for growth must exist. If not, the seed will be destroyed or die before it can take root. Not everyone has the same sensitivity of hearing or the same ability to act upon what they hear.

Could it be that the psalmist we heard of yesterday was like fertile ground—that he had the "ears to hear"? I believe he did, that he had the right attitude for receiving the word. Not everyone has. Let us learn to be patient in our hope.

Suggestion for meditation: *Can I be patient today to allow the Spirit to work in God's own time?*

Wednesday, July 8   Read Matthew 13:8-9, 18-23.

What a joy it was for the disciples to sit beside the sea and listen to the Master. What puzzlement when his words sank in. What is it we are to hear? What can all this mean to us?

What the disciples would begin to realize was that in Christ, God was fulfilling the expectation of his people Israel. God had indeed come to answer the prayers of the faithful, like the psalmist in Monday's reading. In the parable, Jesus was confirming the kingdom of God as a presence already at work in God's people in the person and work of Christ Jesus.

One thing was clear. As Jesus' followers, the disciples were responsible for sowing the seed, the good news of the kingdom of God. Their work would not always be productive. In fact, often it might seem as if they had failed. Yet, Christ left no doubt in their minds that although part of the seed might never grow, their efforts would ultimately yield results.

Are we more concerned about results than actions? Are we impatient with the slow growth of the church? Do our efforts not bear fruit quickly enough?

Remember, we are assured that in good time, the Master Gardener will gather in the harvest, and it will be abundant!

Suggestion for meditation: *I will remember that the work of the Spirit will bear fruit in God's own time.*

Thursday, July 9   Read Exodus 2:11-22.

I was only in Ethiopia for two weeks, but I truly believe that it was in God's plan for me to be there at that time. Yet, I was anxious and uneasy at the unfamiliarity of the land and customs, and disturbed by the terrible suffering I saw.

Moses must have felt strange, too. Having grown up in Pharaoh's court and sensing a greater purpose to his life, he might have been unhappy and confused at suddenly finding himself an exile in a strange land. Apparently, however, he settled down and even had a family.

It is not easy to adjust to a foreign country or unusual circumstances in life. I have learned from experience that growing spiritually is growing wherever you are.

I recall once, as a young person in deep emotional distress, wishing I could begin my life all over somewhere else. My doctor said, "I can't pick you up by the roots and transplant you. I can only help you where you are planted now."

I couldn't understand that at the time, but now I can relate it to the old saying, "Bloom where you are planted." Make the most of life wherever God puts you—whether it be for a lifetime or for a short stay; whether it be in suffering or in joy. We are growing for God as we journey in life. Let us grow graciously.

Suggestion for meditation: *Am I blooming where God has planted me?*

Friday, July 10   Read Romans 8:9-11.

One Christmas a friend gave me an amaryllis bulb. It was the kind of gift you have to wait to enjoy—one that keeps you in a state of anticipation and curiosity. What a thrill I had watching the phenomenal growth of that plant.

As I planted it, I wondered how a magnificent red flower like the one on the box might grow from that ugly, rough brown bulb. But, before my eyes, the amaryllis grew almost daily to a height of over two feet. One February day there was a glorious burst of spring in my living room and a lot of joy in my heart.

Those who do not have the "ears to hear" see only the rough onion shape. Their hearts are closed to the potential of a spiritual growth that is almost beyond imagining. Yet, the kingdom of God is in our midst, silently, gloriously bringing those who hear with their hearts to full bloom.

The kingdom of God is a gift given freely and for our pleasure. It is a gift that grows from within—slowly and miraculously. Is the kingdom of God coming to full bloom within you?

Prayer: *Thank you, God, for the gift of the Holy Spirit. May I grow day by day toward the likeness of Christ, that I may truly live in your kingdom on earth. Amen.*

Saturday, July 11   Read Psalm 69:6-9.

Nature is full of wonders. Even if shielded from the right elements, a plant will stretch and reach out beyond itself in search of what it needs to grow. Long, sturdy potato tendrils grow right through the bag in a dark cupboard, and plants defy obstruction by cracking cement walls that hide the sun.

We are like plants. From the tiniest seeds, we have our beginnings. As we grow, we develop layers—like the amaryllis bulb—of understanding and wisdom. And, like the plant that grows in spite of obstacles, within each person there is a force that struggles and perseveres against odds toward full potential. One day, like that beautiful red blossom in my living room, a person will burst forth in the form and shape that God intended.

The psalmist sought to live the best way he could, to serve God and be a good example to others. For the psalmist, God was a powerful being—but a being definitely transcendent.

The new life that Paul speaks about in yesterday's reading is the Spirit of God dwelling in us—the kingdom of God which Jesus brought to earth which is given to those who have heard the Good News.

If the Spirit dwells in us, all those things which obstruct our growth will no longer have any power over us. We will develop as God intends. We will indeed bear fruit.

Prayer: *Holy Spirit, dwell in me, that I may become what you intend me to be. Amen.*

Sunday, July 12   Read Romans 8:12-17.

"I never promised you a rose garden," the psychiatrist in a popular book said to his patient. I can relate to those words. The same doctor who said he could not transplant me also told me life would never be a garden of roses. Even if it were, we all know that roses have thorns.

Living with the Spirit is not a promise of life without suffering. Greater than that, such living offers the promise of joy *in* suffering!

What privileges we inherit, Paul tells the Romans. We are now sons and daughters of God. No longer is God a distant eternal being to be feared but a loving parent who dwells within us.

As children of God, we also have an overwhelming sense of belonging to a great fellowship of believers. And this special relationship allows us the greatest of privileges—the inheritance of eternal life.

Paul takes us beyond the hope of the psalmist for release from death. In verse 17 he says, "We are children of God, and if children, then heirs . . . provided we suffer with him in order that we may also be glorified with him."

The crown of thorns foreshadowed Christ's death and resurrection. Our suffering will be our joy in him.

Suggestion for meditation: *Today I will bear the thorns as I delight in the roses.*

THE VISION OF GOD

July 13-19, 1987   **Bruce A. Mitchell**†
Monday, July 13   Read Exodus 3:1-6.

I remember how, when I was a boy, we took a family trip across the United States. Leaving the hills of New York and Pennsylvania, we saw the landscape change from hills to plains, and, moving into the Southwest, we saw mesas and desert land. Then came the day when my father announced, "Tomorrow we go to the Grand Canyon."

Driving out of Flagstaff, Arizona, after an hour or so on the road, we suddenly saw the canyon before us. Never had I seen anything so deep, so wide, so awesome. I could only marvel at the immensity of it.

Later in the same trip we visited Carlsbad Caverns in New Mexico. The same thoughts hit me: *How long has this been here? How did it come to be? How long will it remain?*

In a sense, both the Grand Canyon and Carlsbad Caverns are like the burning bush that mystified Moses—lasting examples of the never-consuming love of God.

I view things like the Grand Canyon and Carlsbad Caverns and see, in their magnificence, the very presence of God—not a transitory presence, but a reminder of God's eternal presence, power, and creative ability.

So it was for Moses as he saw a living, non-consuming presence of God in the bush. For us, the marvel is the living presence of God in all we see about us as we see a vision of God in everything that is.

Prayer: *O great Creator, help us focus on your living presence in all that is. Amen.*

---

†Associate Pastor, Aloma United Methodist Church, Winter Park, Florida.

Tuesday, July 14   Read Exodus 3:10-12.

I can hear the protest of Moses: "But I'm not the person for a job like that!"

Moses had stopped by the wayside and was mystified by a burning bush which was not consumed by the flames. Yet in this Moses realized that it was, in fact, God calling him, and the call went beyond a discussion of faith. The call really became a test of just how far Moses was willing to go in response to God.

The world hasn't really changed too much since the days of Moses. There continues to be reluctance on the part of humanity to accept God's call in terms of God's vision for humankind.

As we look about us, we may recognize the power of God in all we see. But then as we feel the call of God to do something or to play a certain role in making the world a better place, we back off. Perhaps we say things like, "I'm just not qualified for that. I'm sure someone else could do it better."

Maybe we say, "I'd like to help with that project, but I've got so many demands on my time." Our priority for the work of God often is low; we respond to God's call when it fits into the schedule of our other events.

Moses was one who didn't feel qualified. He may have truly wanted to respond to God, but he feared his own human limitations.

Reflecting on this, we must realize, just as Moses finally did, that our human ability may never be obvious until we trust God enough to say yes in faith.

Prayer: *Great God, forgive me when I respond more readily to my call than to your call. Amen.*

Wednesday, July 15   Read Psalm 103.

Some years ago, while working in the aerospace industry, I was asked (along with everyone else in my department) to complete what the company called a "personal profile form." I was to evaluate, as honestly as possible, the strengths, weaknesses, and potentials I had to offer the company.

I looked in a mirror and saw a short, slightly graying, fortyish individual complete with glasses and middle-age bulge. Looking more closely, I saw an individual who loves to write, paint landscapes, and take pictures. The longer I looked, the more detailed the picture became. In the process, I envisioned who I was and who I felt I might be in times ahead.

In some ways, this is what the psalmist has done in today's reading. Instead of looking at self, however, the psalmist paints a vivid vision of God.

The psalmist describes a God who is loving, forgiving, and just. We hear the psalmist describe God as a healer and as one who is kind and loving.

The further we read, the more detailed the picture becomes. Suddenly the reader realizes the awesome example God has set for all of us.

Going back to the mirror, I found myself asking how open I have been to becoming like God wants me to be. It did not take long for me to realize how far short of the example and goal God has set for all of us my own life falls.

The psalmist says, "I bless the holy name of God with all my heart." My "mirror" tells me how far I have fallen short of the mark and how much more I must try to pattern my life after God.

Prayer: *Loving God, forgive me when I do not measure up to what I should be, and strengthen my faith that I may grow in grace. Amen.*

Thursday, July 16 Read Matthew 13:24-30.

I wonder what heaven is really like.

We all have read stories, heard messages, seen paintings, watched motion pictures, which are intended to communicate a vision of heaven.

A book in my library may oversimplify heaven. It says, "Heaven is the place where God dwells." That being the case, we may see heaven here, in this spot, at this precise moment in time.

Sometimes you hear people talking about some very special spot—perhaps a hilltop, a lakeside, or a seashore—as their "special corner of heaven." An old love song sums up the joy of such a relationship by saying musically, "I'm in heaven."

Do we create a "heaven" in our lives by "sowing good seeds?" Do we, in some ways, create something of heaven when we unselfishly love another person? Do we help build a heaven on earth as we seek justice for the persecuted, food for the hungry, love for the abused? Do we sow seeds of heaven as we proclaim the power of Christ to all we meet and as we share our faith with people who may have lost hope themselves?

Perhaps heaven is beyond anything we can see. Yet we must believe that heaven is something eternal, gained through seeds of faith, trust, and love, sown in human lives. Perhaps because of the limitations of human vision we cannot see the real picture of heaven, yet in faith we know there is something beyond what we can understand. For this we can be glad.

Prayer: *Great Power above all powers, give us the power to sow seeds of faith, hope, and love that we may grow to know the fullness of heaven itself. Amen.*

Friday, July 17   Read Matthew 13:36-43.

Not long ago my wife and I watched a Broadway musical produced by our local civic theater players. Our seats were good ones—first row in the balcony.

During the intermission, we amused ourselves by looking over the edge of the balcony, seeking familiar faces among those who had orchestra seats. Once in a while we would see someone we knew, and occasionally they would look up, see us, and wave.

I wonder if God is "sitting in the balcony," looking out over all the world, evaluating what humankind is up to. God's vision of humanity is, in many ways, summed up in today's scripture passage. God can sit in the balcony, look out over all the people of the world, and see some who are good and faithful to the purposes of God. Others may be people who are passively involved with God, going through the motions of being Christian so long as the call of Christ does not interfere with so-called more important priorities.

Then there are those who want no part of the church, Christ, faith, or God. Their world revolves around making the most for themselves, having the best time they can in the time they have.

God, in the balcony, sees all. In today's scripture passage, Jesus reminds us that we are never apart from God.

With that in mind, we need to ask ourselves, "What is God's vision of me, you, and all humanity?"

Prayer: *Lord God, mold my life that I may grow to be completely responsive to your will. Amen.*

Saturday, July 18   Read Romans 8:18-25.

Rolling out of bed, I looked out the window to see a snow-covered yard. I was not eager to go outside in the sub-zero temperatures, much less struggle with balky cars. It was a morning that generated thoughts of warm weather, tropical breezes, and soft surf washing up on a snow-white beach.

Today's scripture passage is something like that. It looks beyond a cloudy, snowy, rainy day of human frustration to a vision of hope beyond comprehension.

All too often we look only at immediate situations, only at what is right at hand. Perhaps we are facing a situation involving adverse weather. Perhaps it's a financial or employment crisis. Maybe it's a concern about a health situation threatening our well-being or life itself.

However, Paul, in today's reading offers us hope that transcends even the direst of human situations. Paul reminds us that trials faced in day-to-day life are really insignificant when we consider the hope of the Resurrection.

It is then, says Paul, that fears, frustrations, and failures of the moment are blown away as lightly as a thistle seed in a summer breeze. It is then that all who believe will find the fulfillment of faith.

Paul wrote about this hope:

If we see what we hope for, then it is not really hope. . . . But if we hope for what we do not see, we wait for it with patience (TEV).

Prayer: *Great God of all, give us confidence enough to hope and faith enough to believe. Amen.*

Sunday, July 19   Read Matthew 13:43.

"Let those with ears, listen!"

Jesus admonishes not just the select few who surrounded him during his earthly ministry to be attentive to God; he tells all people from all times that there is a need to experience the presence of God in all there is.

The ultimate vision of God is wrapped up in the eternal sound of surf breaking on the beach. The ultimate vision of God is encompassed in the winds, clouds, and infinite distance of the sky.

The ultimate vision of God is contained in all of nature—in the wonders of the world—in God's handiwork in forming and reforming the universe. On the one hand, we can experience the massive power of God in the eruption of Mount St. Helen's, yet we also see the eternal God in the tiny seedlings sprouting on its devastated mountainsides. Life is destroyed, yet life springs anew.

The ultimate vision of God is measured in the infinite number of stars and planets. The ultimate vision of God is experienced in the joy of birth and the innocent smile of a child receiving love from a parent.

The ultimate vision of God is wrapped in something beyond the tangible and touchable. The ultimate vision of God is knowledge, for all who will listen, believe, and respond that God has a plan beyond what humans can imagine or manufacture, an assurance and promise too good to refuse.

Prayer: *Lord of all, place within me the willingness to seek the seemingly unattainable and to have the faith to believe it is within my reach through Christ. Amen.*

LOOKING FOR THE KINGDOM

July 20-26, 1987   **J. Stephen Lang**†
Monday, July 20   Read Psalm 105:1-11.

The much-used phrase "kingdom of God" has a rich history in scripture. While the phrase itself does not occur in the Old Testament, God's sovereignty over all creation is implied throughout the Bible. It is an eternal fact, manifested most clearly in God's dealings with the chosen people, the Hebrews. As the Israelites well knew, God was sovereign over all human activities, even those of the nations outside Israel.

While the Hebrews were aware that God was sovereign, they were also aware—painfully so—that God's rule was not universally recognized or obeyed, not even in Israel itself. They looked forward to a time when God's rule would be gratefully acknowledged. They yearned for a messianic age when God would rule in a fuller sense than before. We know that this became so with the work of Jesus, whose teachings and deeds showed that God's rule was not only a future ideal to hope for but also a present spiritual reality for those who would cling to God.

Today's scripture reading speaks of God's rule in the world, made known through the signs and wonders God had shown on behalf of believers. It also speaks of promise, the promise of a future inheritance for those who acknowledge and obey God's rule.

Prayer: *Sovereign God, remind us that you guide and direct the universe and that you delight when we acknowledge your benevolent rule. Keep us mindful of your kingdom, which is and which is to come. Amen.*

---

†Book editor, Tyndale House Publishers, Wheaton, Illinois.

Tuesday, July 21   Read Exodus 3:13-17.

Devout people of Israel expected the kingdom of God to be fully manifested by demonstrations of God's mighty power. Signs and wonders would occur, and there would be evidences of the breaking of the power of evil in the world. The Hebrews already had evidence that God could act in this dramatic fashion, for God showed this power in delivering the Hebrews from their misery in Egypt.

Today's reading shows God promising to lead the oppressed Hebrew people into a land flowing with milk and honey. Later, generations in Israel—including those alive in Jesus' time—did not forget that the Sovereign God would work wonders and would, in time, defeat all evil.

Those who worship the Sovereign God have continued to deliver the oppressed from misery. In Victorian London, William Booth and his tireless family devoted themselves to helping slum dwellers. East London in the 1860s was hardly an image of heaven, but Booth and his followers—later called the Salvation Army—provided food, shelter, clothing, and spiritual nurture as they witnessed to God's rule in their own lives.

Toyohiko Kagawa (1888-1960) labored for years to combat poverty, prostitution, and exploitation of workers in the Tokyo slums. Not without cause was his mission called the "Kingdom of God Movement." Those who benefited from Kagawa's efforts could see evidence that the coming kingdom was manifesting itself already in the work of those who love and serve the Sovereign God.

Prayer: *God of the present and future kingdom, empower us to do your work in breaking down the power of evil and in nurturing others. Help us witness to your rule, a rule rooted in your unfailing love. Amen.*

Wednesday, July 22   Read Exodus 3:18-20.

Moses has been instructed by God to approach mighty Pharaoh and announce that the elders of Israel wished to take a journey into the wilderness to offer a sacrifice to God. But God already knows that Pharaoh will not allow this gesture of worship, so God makes a dramatic promise: Stubborn Pharaoh will release Israel after God performs miracles on behalf of the Hebrews.

Evil never gives in easily. Pharaoh was powerful—and obstinate. But God, who rules even when human beings fail to acknowledge the divine rule, was more powerful. The whole Book of Exodus reminds us that even the most deeply rooted evil can be removed by God.

The New Testament, especially the Gospels, are full of evidences that God works to smash the power of evil. Yet the New Testament makes it clear that the final victory is not yet won. With Christ, God's power and rule were manifested dramatically, yet even Christ acknowledged that the kingdom, now present to some degree, is still to come. We must await God's good time in overthrowing evil forever.

In the meantime, knowing that we serve a loving and just God, we work for love and justice, as Jesus did. We try, as did the high-minded Puritans who sought to build the kingdom of God in Massachusetts, to create a just and caring society. The Puritans failed. So will we, for all our noble efforts will not fully bring the kingdom into being. But God blesses our efforts at making the divine rule and will known to a world riddled with evil.

Prayer: *Loving and compassionate God, instill in our hearts the burning desire to accomplish good in the world and to witness to your rule. Amen.*

Thursday, July 23   Read Matthew 13:44-46.

God is sovereign whether we admit it or not. Jesus proclaimed that God's rule—God's kingdom—was at hand and that men and women should accept that truth and act accordingly by repenting and dedicating themselves to God.

God's rule is an objective fact. For believers, it is also a present spiritual reality, felt in individuals and in the community of believers. We live in relation to the present kingdom (God's rule in our lives) and to the future kingdom (God's consummated rule, which we know will come).

For believers, the kingdom—both present and future—is a wonderful thing, as Jesus' two parables show. He was stating in no uncertain terms that those who want God's kingdom to come will desire it as they desire nothing else.

I am reminded of a song from my favorite movie, *Oliver!* The poor orphan, Oliver Twist, falls in with a gang of London pickpockets. The gang's hideout is hardly the loving home Oliver seeks so desperately, yet briefly he is stirred by the beauty and gentleness of Nancy, a cutthroat's mistress. Oliver and his companions serenade Nancy with the delightful "I'd Do Anything for You," expressing their desire to serve with devotion when they encounter kindness and beauty.

Like Oliver, we would all do well to devote ourselves to whatever beauty we find in a sin-ridden world. Like the merchant in Jesus' parable, we do well to make any sacrifice for God's kingdom.

Prayer: *Loving God, help us to hold nothing back as we seek your kingdom. Amen.*

Friday, July 24　　　　　　　Read Matthew 13:47-52.

One aspect of God's kingdom is judgment, much emphasized in the preaching of John the Baptist but, as today's reading shows, also a part of Jesus' teaching. It was the belief of Jesus—and many of his pious contemporaries who looked for the kingdom—that the Sovereign God would eventually judge all people, separating the useful from the useless, the good from the wicked. Only when the useless and rotten elements were discarded would God's rule be fully established. Earlier generations had assumed that God's wrath would fall upon the Gentiles, but John the Baptist, Jesus, and others knew that even the Jews had to prepare for God's coming with sincere repentance.

God as judge is not a popular theme today, but it is an integral part of any teaching about the kingdom. The theme of judgment need not threaten us. In fact, looked at positively, it is a stimulus to righteousness, for if we know that God looks with disfavor on human sin, we rightly try to avoid what displeases God. We act not out of fear, though the God of the universe is a fearsome force, but out of a positive devotion, a zeal for what pleases a just and loving God.

Jesus' parable of the net may make us uneasy. It need not. In fact it should provide us with solace, for it reminds us that whatever is opposed to God's love and justice will have no place in the coming kingdom. It also reminds us of how serious our witness in the world is, for many persons have not heard the good news of the kingdom.

Prayer: *Holy God, remind us that in your love you judge evil. Remove from us all that is not devoted to you. Make us holy, for you are holy. Amen.*

Saturday, July 25 Read Romans 8:26-30;
Genesis 45:4-8.

Paul told the Christians at Rome that even things that seem evil or unpleasant are, because God loves us, made to produce a good end.

This was not a radically new teaching, as the reading from Genesis shows. Joseph, viceroy of Egypt in spite of the fact that his brothers had sold him as a slave, observes that God took a horrible act and made it have a good result.

In the famous hymn, "O Love That Wilt Not Let Me Go," George Matheson recognized that the Sovereign God would prove this sovereignty by bringing joy out of tears:

> O Joy that seekest me through pain,
> I cannot close my heart to thee;
> I trace the rainbow through the rain,
> And feel the promise is not vain
> That morn shall tearless be.*

The ruling God is able to quiet evil and to work good for those who love God. Perhaps this power is nowhere displayed better than in cases like those of Joseph, where an apparent evil act led, in time, to a great work. We are nearsighted, often unaware that things will—in time, in God's time—work for the best for those devoted to God and God's kingdom.

Devotional exercise: *Think of examples from your own life and from the lives of people you know of how God worked to bring goodness out of what was evil or unpleasant. Give praise for God's power in extending the divine rule over all areas of our life.*

---

*The United Methodist *Book of Hymns*, no. 234.

Sunday, July 26   Read Romans 8:29-30;
                                              Psalm 105:3-5.

"Glory in his holy name; let the hearts of those who seek the Lord rejoice" (NIV). Perhaps Paul had this verse in mind when he wrote to the church at Rome, for in today's reading he speaks of the joyful destiny that awaits believers: They will be conformed to the likeness of Christ, and they will be both justified and glorified. These verses follow the statement that all things work for good for those who love God. Those who cling to God have a glorious destiny awaiting them: glory itself.

This glorification begins now, as we let ourselves be shaped by God into Christ's image. The kingdom of God is a present reality because we are already gathered to Christ and are already being made like him. When the world beholds us—individual Christians and the gathered church—they should have an idea of what the final kingdom will be like.

We need not be contemptuous of this world. It is God's good creation, needing our labors to transform and ennoble it. Yet the New Testament makes it clear that this world is not our final destiny. While we can delight in the here and now and be thankful that a gracious God uses our present circumstances for our good, we can look forward to the coming kingdom, glorious and triumphant.

Suggestion for prayer: *Meditate on these lines from Joseph Addison's hymn, "When All Thy Mercies, O My God":*

> Through every period of my life
> Thy goodness I'll pursue;
> And after death, in distant worlds,
> The glorious theme renew.* Amen.

---

*The United Methodist *Book of Hymns*, no. 70.

ON BEING CONNECTED

July 27–August 2, 1987   **Norene D. Martin**†
Monday, July 27   Read Exodus 12:1.

"The Lord spake unto Moses. . . ." How wonderful to be Moses and hear God so clearly; how comforting to be sure that it really is the Lord you hear.

I reflect often on Moses—his failures, his disappointments, his reluctance. I say to myself, *How easy it would be to respond obediently to God's will if I could actually hear a voice and see a burning bush that was not consumed. Maybe I could do as well as Moses if I were chosen.*

In the emptiness that I sometimes feel, am I failing to heed the small voice, the persistent nagging of my conscience, the perpetual nudging that comes from within my being and calls me to a better life? Does the story of Moses so mislead me about the experience of the presence of God that I subconsciously expect some dramatic revelation, leaving me unaware of the presence in all the small, good things in my life? Do I put aside what is immediately at hand waiting vainly for a bright vision?

I am surely a very fortunate and blessed woman. I have health, husband, children, grandchildren, friends, job. I live with a sense of connectedness to the universe. In all this the Lord is indeed speaking to me. If I don't feel that presence, it is I who am absent, not God.

Prayer: *Lord, give me moments of quiet in which I may listen for your word. Deliver me from the busyness which separates me from you. Amen.*

---

†Director, Cathedral College of the Laity, Washington, D.C.

Tuesday, July 28   Read Exodus 12:2-14

The story of the Passover, told and retold through the ages, is that of a family feast commemorating delivery from bondage. The observance bound families together, knit family to community, community to the nation of Israel, Israel to God. The faithful had no identity crisis: they were God's chosen.

Reflect on the similarity to American Thanksgiving. Family members gather. Because we are so scattered this gathering crowds airports, roads, train and bus terminals. We celebrate with a feast of commemoration. Television screens, in a way, bind us to the community as the ubiquitous football games relentlessly proceed. Occasional interruptions for news may present the poor and homeless in long lines awaiting their celebratory meal. Even in homes where grace is not normally said before meals, the youngest or oldest person present may well be asked to express thanksgiving for family, food, and friends. This may not be consciously religious, yet surely it suggests that the presence of the Divine is palpable and real enough to require some acknowledgement.

Such celebrations tell our hearts again that one blessing of life is a sense of connection, of being grounded in a tradition, rooted in a place. We create family myths as we go along, and they form part of the web in which we are happily and hopelessly entangled. In most families, religious tradition plays an important role, whether recognized as such or not. We have been set down in families, in places, and in time. Our strength comes from interdependence: we need one another.

Prayer: *Lord, help me to see that I am a small part of a great universe, that I have a role to play which is only mine. Amen.*

Wednesday, July 29   Read Psalm 93.

God is ruler over the earth and its people, the supreme being to whom we owe obedience. How we need this reassurance in a time of missiles, summits, and terrorism! Sometimes these are seemingly senseless, directionless, random developments of which we are incapable of making rational sense and over which we have apparently lost control. In days long gone, primitive people feared that the sun might not come up one day. This fear has returned: indeed, it might not. Our sanity requires an assurance of ultimate meaning and order.

We are sometimes disappointed when we seek this assurance in regular church services. Even here we have been invaded by excessive activity as the needs of the institution press in. Pledging canvasses, bazaars, meetings, programs are all distractions as we listen for the Good News. All these play a steady counterpoint to the majestic and inevitable march of the church seasons.

We can be delivered from panic by quiet observance of the great events that reflect our religious heritage and by assurance that "your laws are eternal, Lord, and your Temple is holy indeed, forever and ever" (TEV). What a comforting assurance in a time of planned obsolescence! If only we really believed it.

Prayer: *Help me to understand, Lord, the infinity, the everlastingness of your rule so that I may ground my life accordingly. Deliver me from petty, transitory concerns. Amen.*

Thursday, July 30   Read Psalm 143:1-10.

"The enemy hath persecuted my soul." I need to be delivered from my enemies. These are words to take to heart, on which to meditate long and hard. It is not an easy task to explore what about oneself invites persecution. There are layers of self-protection and self-justification to strip away. It has always seemed paradoxical to me that when I have reached rock bottom, and even in solitude am suffering from embarrassment as I take a good look at myself, suddenly there is a flash of joy! I am delivered from my silliness. I have reached out and been refreshed.

One of the times I need to carefully examine the kind of inner commitment I am making is when I feel most pleased with myself. I am reminded of a story of a friend of mine, a devoutly religious man. He learned that one of his ancestors had been a French Huguenot, burned at the stake for religious convictions. My friend then confessed with some chagrin that, as Lent began, he had vowed to eliminate some excesses—not necessities—from his life and now had grave questions about how this "sacrifice" might be received. Commitment and its consequences, when truly understood, never lead to a feeling of self-righteousness. I am doing only what I have to do.

In asking for deliverance from enemies it is possible that I am asking for deliverance from myself, that there are no enemies "out there" nearly so fearsome as those within.

Prayer: *Lord, help me to perceive the true nature of my enemies so that, with you, I may realistically deal with them. Amen.*

Friday, July 31   Read Matthew 14:13-23.

Surely the story of the feeding of the multitude is one of the more delightful narratives in the Bible. Close your eyes and picture the scene: Jesus was seeking a place apart, for he needed to be alone, needed to replenish his resources. He was followed by a crowd of people seeking deliverance from their many hurts and, perhaps, also longing simply to be with him. He is moved by them and goes among them healing and blessing. Meanwhile, the sun has gone down and evening has overtaken the crowd. The disciples would have sent the people off to nearby villages for food, but Jesus said, "No, we'll feed them." The disciples responded quite reasonably that there wasn't enough food to go around. And then the miracle. Not only was there enough—there was a lot left over.

One of the clearest conclusions to be drawn from this story is that our faith must have some concrete manifestations; our behavior must be different because it is grounded in faith. Sometimes our inner spiritual needs can wait until after our service to others: people do need to be fed. Another conclusion is that our resources for relating to other people and their needs are without limitations; they will expand with use. Compassion does not have to be meted out in measured doses; there is enough to go around. True faith has hands callused from work. When we feel at the end of our rope, then is the time to expect a miracle. And when we are quite finished with the task before us, then we may release ourselves from worldly demands, go apart, and refresh ourselves by prayer and meditation.

Prayer: *Lord, help me not to walk away from demands being made on me, no matter how ill-timed. I know I can return to you for rest and strengthening. Amen.*

Saturday, August 1   Read James 2:5-10.

We live in a day of instant communication, visual and oral. Satellites bring us live scenes of war, famine, disaster, and life from all around the world. We are in great peril of linking with global concerns to the extent of ignoring what is immediately at hand. "Global concerns" frequently seem like a scapegoat to me. Sometimes I feel there is very little that I alone can do to alleviate world hunger. But can I do something to alleviate hurt in my own neighborhood? The answer had to be affirmative if I am in any way sensitive to the life around me.

Something happened in my neighborhood that gave me real cause for reflection. I live in a "good" neighborhood: no visible poverty, adequate services. One day a fire broke out in the house immediately behind mine, caused by a can of Sterno. Investigation by health authorities showed that an elderly brother and sister had been living in the house with no heat, light, phone, or running water. All utility services had been cut off for lack of payment of bills. This kind of deprivation does not take place in a few days; it takes many weeks to reach this stage—weeks during which neighbors could have helped.

I made a lot of excuses for myself: I am at work all day so I do not see much of what goes on in the neighborhood; my own family makes demands on some of my spare time; I need leisure for exercise and recreation. Yet, none of this helped. I had simply been totally negligent in carrying out the mandate that I should love my neighbor. I had offended in one point; hence I am guilty of all.

Prayer: *Lord, keep my attention focused on those things I can do and keep me from being negligent of the needs of others, especially those close at hand. Amen.*

Sunday, August 2   Read Romans 8:31-39.

One of the most comforting elements in the Christian heritage is that we know the end of the story; we know we are saved. Nothing that we do or that is done to us can separate us from the love of Christ. This conviction anchors our lives. And it should make us fearless in living our lives as disciples.

As I grow older I become more and more convinced that faithfulness lies in small things, and that consistency is harder here than in grander gestures. To be thoughtful and considerate, caring and helpful to family, friends, and co-workers really puts me to the test. It is my behavior in these contexts by which I am known. It is my attitude to those around me that will color how I respond instinctively. When I fall from grace—and that's often—I have the assurance that I have God's forgiveness.

How can I hold in my consciousness at all times my union with Christ? I am fortunate to have spent some time with a Hindu monk from whom I learned ways to approach continuing awareness of the divine. A moment of silent withdrawal accompanied by controlled breathing can bring an amazing calm in the midst of a quarrel or a dispute. The repetition of a brief prayer that you can hold in your mind like a mantra helps keep priorities straight. I am always pleased and surprised at how often one can say a short prayer—while waiting for the telephone to be answered at the other end, waiting in line at the grocery store, riding bus or subway. All of us have many times like these which we could use to stay close to Christ.

Prayer: *Lord, help me to be more mindful of you and of others than of myself. Deliver me from preoccupation with concerns of no lasting importance so that I can be open to receive you. Amen.*

ACCEPTING GOD'S PRESENCE IN THE DARKNESS

August 3-9, 1987   **Lance Webb†**
Monday, August 3   Read Exodus 14:19-22.

God is always present in our darkness

Like the Israelites with the Egyptian army behind them and the Red Sea in front of them, we are in the terrifying darkness of human evil and unbelief. The darkness threatens the destruction of all we hold dear. But the mighty God is present as symbolized in this remarkable story.

Like the Israelites, we are terrified because we cannot see the presence of God moving even now as in all past history. The pillar of cloud by day and the pillar of fire by night symbolize God's presence—the God who goes before us to guide us as we travel. When we find the Egyptians behind us and the Red Sea in front and we see no way out, we are in despair. The supreme truth is that throughout the night, the pillar of cloud brings darkness to the one side and light to the other!

The resurrection of Jesus is the great fact of God's presence. God was on the cross with his Son! For those who cannot see what God is doing, there is only darkness; but for countless persons through the ages, the other side of the Cross is light.

Prayer: *Dear Lord, when we see no way out of the darkness of illness and death before us and the discouragement, frustration, and seeming defeat behind us, help us trust the light of your presence to open up the way and enable us to walk through the deep waters on dry land. In the name of the risen Christ. Amen.*

---

†Bishop (retired), The United Methodist Church; consultant for spiritual formation with The Upper Room; Dallas, Texas.

Tuesday, August 4 Read Psalm 106:7-15.

How hard to remember! How easy to forget!

When everything is going our way, we, like the people of Israel, find it easy to forget our past experiences of rebellion and resulting distress and the many kindnesses of God who saved us from our Red Sea disasters. The 106th psalm is a realistic portrayal of our human predicament. Why is it as hard for us to remember that life is beautiful and worth living only as we continually recognize and overcome our sin of self-sufficiency? One day we awaken to the truth that even our prayers are hurtful instead of helpful! The psalmist describes it in sad realism:

> They soon forgot what he had done and did not wait for his counsel. . . . So he gave them what they asked for, but sent a wasting disease upon them (NIV).

God sent "leanness into their soul" as the King James Version puts it. Our self-centered narcissism, the proud little self that wants our own way on our own terms—this is the "wasting disease" that besets us as persons, families, and as a people. There are always plenty of Egyptians ready to enslave us. Yes, God gives us what we ask, if we want it enough, but our souls are lean and hungry and soon life falls in on us.

So over and over the same human story of pride and folly is told. The amazing truth of God waiting to heal and forgive is the basis for the first lines of this great psalm, "Praise the Lord. Give thanks to the Lord, for he is good; his love endures forever" (NIV).

Prayer: *Dear Lord, deliver me from my self-centered pride that spoils even my prayers. Help me to remember whose I am and instead of forgetting your love, to praise you. Amen.*

Wednesday, August 5   Read Matthew 14:22-33.

Looking at the storm rather than at Jesus

Peter's response in the frightening storm on the lake to the invitation of Jesus—"Take Courage! It is I. Don't be afraid!" (NIV)—points to our very human temptation to put our attention on the perils and to forget the Presence. We, too, may have for the moment a genuine assent to the presence of the One who can enable us to walk on the heaving waves of our fears. With Simon Peter, we cry, "Lord if it is you, tell me to come to you in the stormy waters!" (AP) For a moment as we look to the Mighty Ruler of winds and waves, we are able to do what seems impossible. But then even as we walk, we forget and take our attention off of the Lord and put it on ourselves and the fearful waves that threaten us. "When [Peter] saw the wind, he was afraid and, beginning to sink, cried out, "Lord, save me!" (NIV)

There are those who say we are foolish to accept the invitation of one we call God who comes to us in Jesus inviting us to give our complete trust to him as we walk life's troubled seas. Peter, too, thought it was foolish when he saw his Master on trial for his life. Again Peter let his fears sink him in the roaring winds of human hate and evil. And Peter denied he knew Jesus! Only when Peter met the risen Christ by the lake did he remember that the love of Jesus was the almighty love that creates, sustains, and rules even the stormy seas of human evil and fear. Only then did he become Peter the Rock, able to obey Jesus' invitation, "Feed my sheep" (John 21:17).

Prayer: *Yes, Lord, I am frail and weak. But in thee I have resources infinitely greater than my weakness. "I am weak, but thou art mighty; Hold me with thy powerful hand."* * *Amen.*

---

*William Williams, "Guide Me, O Thou Great Jehovah," the United Methodist *Book of Hymns*, no. 271.

Thursday, August 6   Read Matthew 14:28-29;
                                             Philippians 4:4-9.

Looking to Jesus rather than at the storm

The power to put our attention where we choose is the greatest single gift of our human freedom. When Jesus' presence walking on the sea was known to Peter and Jesus invited him to come to him, Peter's attention was wholly on Jesus. But when Peter took his attention off Jesus and put it on himself and the storm, he sank. There are times when we find ourselves sinking in the confusions and evils of our own lives and times. Consciously putting our attention on God as revealed in Jesus and near to us in the Holy Spirit, we find the hand of God reaching out to us as Jesus did to Peter, "and the peace of God, which passes all understanding, will keep your hearts and your minds in Christ Jesus."

"What gets your attention gets you." Therefore, cries Paul, writing from prison in Rome and soon to be executed by Nero, "Delight yourselves in the Lord, yes, find your joy in him at all times . . . and never forget the nearness of your Lord" (Phillips).

From Paul to the most confused and uncertain person of us all, the great hope of our deliverance from the evils within and without is a disciplined, regular, consciously practiced putting of our attention on the living Christ.

Suggestion for prayer: *Take a few minutes of complete silence as you pray the "Jesus Prayer": "Lord Jesus Christ, Son of God, have mercy on me!" Over and over, slowly, think of the reality and nature of the One-who-is-present. When you awaken in the night with anxious fears, pray this prayer again and again, and the peace of God, the courage and strength to sleep and work, to fulfill your mission, will be yours.*

Friday, August 7   Read Psalm 106:1-9; 42:1-8.

Remembering with thanksgiving God's past action

Another of God's priceless gifts in our darkness is the power of memory, what the saints have termed "recollection." In both Psalm 106 and 42, as well as in many other places in the biblical account of God's ministry to his rebellious children, the writer is calling people to remember.

"Give thanks to the Lord, for he is good; his love endures forever. Who can proclaim the mighty acts of the Lord or fully declare his praise?" (NIV) The psalmist's answer is: Only those who remember his loving "kindnesses" in the past. It is no wonder that the most joyful celebration for the Jews is the Passover as they remember their deliverance from slavery in Egypt; and the most powerful sacrament for Christians is rightfully called the Eucharist, which means "the great thanksgiving," as we celebrate the wondrous love of God in the life, suffering, death, and resurrection of Jesus.

"Do this in remembrance of me" (Luke 22:19). Remembering is a central part of Communion, but this *anamnesis* ("to remember") is more than just memory—it is a *re-presenting* of God's presence with Jesus in Gethsemane and on the cross of pain. So with the writer of Psalm 42, we cry, "My soul is downcast within me; therefore I will remember you. . . . By day the Lord directs his love, at night his song is with me."

We are what we remember! Hence the daily, regular recollection of who we are in the love of God as we accept God's presence in forgiveness, guidance, and deliverance, becomes the doorway by which God's light of wholeness and healing enters into our present darkness with hope for the future.

Prayer: *O mighty God of love and compassion, I give thanks for your wondrous acts in the past and trust your loving-kindness to lead me all my journey through. Amen.*

Saturday, August 8

Read Exodus 14:13-15;
Matthew 14:28-31.

God's presence accepted by trust

We can sympathize with the Israelites as they grumbled over the impossible situation at the Red Sea. It took a supreme act of trust in God for Moses to answer them, "Do not be afraid. Stand firm and you will see the deliverance the Lord will bring you today" (NIV). It took even more faith for him to stretch out his hands over the waters and believe they would part! It also took an act of trust, inspired by Moses, for the Israelites to step out on the ground once covered by the sea "with a wall of water on their right and on their left" (NIV).

Whatever took place that day, we may be sure of one thing: They would never have crossed the Red Sea and continued on to the promised land except by an act of trust in God inspired by Moses. Prayer at its best may begin with grumbling complaint, but it always ends in an act of ultimate trust.

If we are to be freed of enslavement to our self, with its fears, its hurts, and failures preventing us from being God's instruments of peace and healing, it will be by our response to the glory of God as seen in the face of Jesus Christ and in the lives of those who, like Moses, reveal God's Spirit. As Peter said on that stormy night, "Lord, if it's you, tell me to come to you on the water" (AP). When we recognize God in the face of Christ and in the faces of others who act on their faith, we, too, can step out with the wall of water on the right and on the left.

This is not just poetry; this is a fact of human experience: an affirmation and an act make the truth of God's loving presence a fact. God is greater than our fears.

Prayer: *Lord, it is you who bids me come to you across the seas of evil and finitude. Help me now to serve you in trust. Amen.*

Sunday, August 9   Read John 15:9-17; Rom. 9:1-5.

God's presence accepted in acts of caring love

Of this I am sure: We will know the presence of God as long as we keep God's supreme command to love even as we are loved.

One of the best illustrations of this fact is in the life of Paul, the apostle of love. In the Letter to the Romans, Paul speaks frankly of the "great sorrow and unceasing anguish in my heart . . . for the sake of my brothers, those of my own race, the people of Israel" because they have forgotten their heritage. "Theirs is the adoption as sons; theirs the divine glory, the covenants, the receiving of the law, the temple worship and the promises." Paul is echoing the sad words of Psalm 106, "They forgot the God who saved them" (v. 21, NIV), and, therefore, could not accept the Christ who fulfilled these promises. Paul foresaw the suffering that comes to all, even the chosen people of God, when they forget and deny the saving, life-giving presence of God. Paul cried out in the agony of one who cares deeply for those he loves: "I could wish that I myself were cursed and cut off from Christ for the sake of my brothers" (NIV).

We are saved when we stay near to our Lord, who "loved us and gave himself up for us" (Eph. 5:2, NIV).

The heart of the Good News is in the First Epistle of John:

> This is love: not that we loved God, but that he loved us and sent his Son as an atoning sacrifice for our sins. Dear friends, since God so loved us, we also ought to love one another. . . . If we love each other, God lives in us (4:10-12, NIV).

The darkness in our world will be extinguished only by the light of loving acts in which God's love is made known.

Prayer: *Dear Lord, nothing can separate us from your love, so teach us to know your presence in our acts of love today. Amen.*

OUR RESPONSIBILITY IN THE COVENANT

August 10-16, 1987   **Homer Noley†**
Monday, August 10   Read Exodus 16:9-12.

The people of Israel had seen the power of God in the rod held by Moses. They had seen the plagues which devastated the Egyptians. They had experienced the miraculous crossing of the sea.

Then why were the people huddled in the Wilderness of Sin complaining of deprivation? It seemed to the people of Israel that even the condition of slavery was better as long as they had enough food and water.

They were not simply rescued from Egypt; they were *called* out of Egypt for reasons they did not yet comprehend. Since they did not comprehend God's purpose for them, they were a people without a mission. It was only when they were able to perceive that God had a plan for them that they were able to move forcefully as God's people. Survival was no longer the end they sought, but survival was necessary for the nation to achieve God's purpose.

So it is with us. We were not simply called out of our old lives; we were called into our new lives with a mission. Unless that mission is recognized by the church and by individuals, our spiritual community will disintegrate. Unlike Israel huddled in the wilderness, we know our mission. Will we accept it?

Prayer: *Our God of covenant, help us accept ourselves as people in mission. Forgive our reluctance to be in mission. Strengthen our resolve to persevere in the work to which you have called us. Amen.*

---

†Pastor, Grace Memorial–Sycamore United Methodist Church, Independence, Kansas.

Tuesday, August 11   Read Exodus 16:6-8.

"What are we?" Moses spoke in a moment of frustration as he tried to show the people that they were quarreling not with himself and Aaron but with God. "What are we?" was meant to subordinate his role to God's plan. However, if understood another way, the remark could strip us of whatever notions we may have of ourselves. The people of Israel were seeing themselves simply as mortal creatures needing only those things required for mortal sustenance. Moses spoke to the people and said, "When the Lord gives you in the evening flesh to eat and in the morning bread to the full, because the Lord has heard your murmurings which you murmur against him—what are we?"

What indeed! When our bellies are full and we live in relative comfort, what are we—other than mortal creatures with our bellies full?

We need a better concept of ourselves to get us off ground zero. God created us in his image. Have we tarnished that image?

Prayer: *Dear Lord, open our eyes so that we may see ourselves as you intend. Amen.*

Questions for reflection: *Who do I really think I am in relation to other people? in relation to God? Do I tend to think too highly of myself or not highly enough? Read Romans 12:1-3 and Psalm 8.*

Wednesday, August 12   Read Exodus 16:13-15.

In 1934, over two thousand Native American people of almost thirty tribes gathered in Middle San Bois Methodist Church near Quinton, Oklahoma. This was an annual meeting of the Indian Mission Conference of Oklahoma. That year the conference would report a total membership of 2,767, seventy-nine local churches, and 104 local preachers.

These were the depression years, and the entire country was experiencing intense hardship. The native people of the Indian Mission of Oklahoma had their own way of confronting those hardships. The church was a spiritual haven for many as the people shared both spiritual and material gifts. The church building was the central building, and located in a semi-circle around the church were several camphouses. The camphouses were used for preparing and serving meals to all of the participants whether Methodist or not, delegate or not. Never were people charged for their meals. The people camped for a week.

The Sabbath day began with an early morning worship service, breakfast, Sunday school and the preaching service. After the noon meal there would be a "singing" and an afternoon preaching service. Then there was more singing, the evening meal, and the evening preaching service. So the people did more than survive. They transformed hardship into a spiritual experience that sustains them to this day.

Prayer: *O Lord, open our eyes to your providence and make us thankful. Amen.*

Questions for reflection: *Is my faith active and joyful—a source of strength—in times of crisis? Or do I panic and withdraw from others and from God when struggle and pain come? Read and meditate on Philippians 4:10-13.*

Thursday, August 13   Read Romans 11:13-16, 29-32.

Once we have received the gospel, it is incumbent upon us to be willing to share it with others. The apostle Paul was undaunted by his rejection by the Jewish community. Rather, he saw it as an opportunity to focus attention on the matter of taking the gospel to the gentile world. Through his work he led the early Christian church to a more profound expression of God's mission on earth. How strange it must have seemed to the Jewish community for one of their kinsmen to be preaching a gospel of love to their oppressors.

It is no different than when we in the contemporary church struggle against reluctance to carry the gospel to the far corners of the earth to a people we don't even know.

The mission of the gospel is universal in scope and requires the boldness and persistance of Paul-like witnesses.

Prayer: *O Lord, instill within us the kind of boldness and perseverance that opens the door to the gospel for people everywhere. Amen.*

Questions for reflection: *In what ways have I worked to carry the gospel message of God's love to those in my neighborhood? to those in the place I work or with whom I spend much of my time each day? How have I helped send the gospel message to those in other countries?*

Friday, August 14   Read Matthew 15:21-28.

"Send her away, for she is crying after us" complained the disciples of Jesus. While the disciples were complaining that the woman was whining after them, they were doing a little whining themselves. The grieving woman was perhaps grasping desperately for every straw, no matter how faint the hope. But in Jesus she saw more than just a faint hope. She sensed certain help for her suffering daughter. It did not occur to the disciples that they might help her. After all, she was a Canaanite woman. And Jesus' words to her seemed unduly harsh. But the instant Jesus saw the strength of her appeal and her faith couched in humility, he responded to her pleas. It should have been a lesson to the disciples that God's mercy extends beyond cultural and political considerations.

Do we still harbor our own private criteria by which we judge whether another has the right to seek God's mercy?

Prayer: *Dear God, help us to open doors, not close them, for others seeking your mercy. Amen.*

Questions for reflection: *When have I been guilty of judging someone's worth? Have I set my own standards that all others must meet in order to be worthy of God's love and care? Who, specifically, do I feel God would really help "if they would just realize how sinful they are"?*

Saturday, August 15   Read Psalm 78:1-3, 13-20.

What sort of people would we be if we used God the way a genie was used in the *Arabian Nights* fantasies? Instead of seeking God's guidance in our quest for salvation, we would develop our own prescription for salvation and give God instructions on how to deal with us. While the notion may sound silly, it may illustrate how we relate ourselves to God and God's providence. We certainly have our own ideas about what we would like God to do for us. Fortunately, for us, God has his own perception of our needs and responds to our prayers accordingly.

It is not good for us to develop the attitude that God owes us something so that we approach God simply to demand payment—our just due. The children of Israel had magnified their place in the covenant relationship to the extent that they were putting God to the test and making demands on the Almighty.

Let us remember our place in the covenant relationship and put in perspective our concept of God's providence and our own responsibilities in that covenant relationship.

Prayer: *O Lord, forgive our impatience and accept our gratitude for your providence. Amen.*

Questions for reflection: *Does my praying become an exercise of telling God how God should respond? How can I work to strengthen my covenant with God so that in my praying I remember my responsibilities and God's promises to hear and be faithful to me?*

Sunday, August 16   Read Exodus 16:4-5.

People need security. It would be a good thing if we could be free from worry for the rest of our lives—at least we think so. The miracle of manna from heaven provided a sense of security for the people of Israel only if they had faith that the miracle would be repeated the next day and the day after and so on. But the Lord said, "The people shall go out and gather a day's portion every day, that I may prove them, whether they will walk in my law or not." Some of the people were still fearful and attempted to store some of the manna for the next day, but it spoiled.

Jesus said, "Pray then like this: Give us this day our daily bread" (Matt. 6:9,11), perhaps prompting the same kind of faith. He encouraged people not to worry about what they should eat or what they should wear because God will provide those things. The point is that mere existence is not the whole purpose of life. While we need certain provisions for living, we live for a purpose that exceeds bare existence.

Prayer: *O Lord, still our fearful hearts and lead us to do your will. Amen.*

Questions for reflection: *What, specifically, have I worried about that has consumed too much of my time and energy? In what ways have I tried to live too far beyond "this day"? Have I asked God for too much at one time?*

BEYOND DOUBT AND FEAR

August 17-23, 1987   **Donald E. Kohlstaedt†**
Monday, August 17   Read Exodus 17:1-7.

Countless people in today's world face problems as severe as
the congregation of Israel met with in the wilderness. Famine in
Africa makes no distinction between Christians there and people
of other faiths. Much more than in past eras, wars affect God's
people wherever they are as much as they affect worshipers of
gods other than the God of Bible revelation.

Likewise, economic conditions make little distinction, especially among the poor of all nations. No different from Old
and New Testament times, "You always have the poor with you"
(Matt. 26:11). Just as the people of God in the wilderness began
to berate their leader, Moses, so, when things go wrong now
people complain about their government officials. Complaints
may be well grounded when people under oppressive regimes
protest, but the Israelites in the wilderness acknowledged Moses
as their God-appointed leader. So Moses had to point out to the
people that their chidings really were a charge that God was
letting them down. How easily that syndrome can undermine the
peace even of people who affirm their belief in God.

This week we want to see how gracious are God's promises
and discover anew the wideness of God's mercy and compassion.

Prayer: *God of grace and glory, grant us to see with eyes of faith your
moving in history. May we rest in your saving intention as you call us to
your eternal kingdom. Amen.*

---

†United Methodist lay speaker, conference lay delegate, and adult church
school teacher, Spokane, Washington.

Tuesday, August 18   Read Psalm 95:7*b*-11.

Immediately after songs and words of thanksgiving to God, the psalmist remembers the trials of his forbears in their wilderness wanderings. There is almost a sob of heartbreak when he breaks off from praise with the words, "O that today you would hearken to his voice!" The allusion is unmistakable. The Exodus reading yesterday is the psalmist's reference. Massah (testing) and Meribah (contention) convey the doubt—even skepticism—the people of Israel expressed concerning God's providence. No wonder God responded with grief to their rebelliousness.

What shall we do then when famine conditions in today's world are placed before our very eyes? Heartbreaking adversities face multitudes in greater numbers by far than the children of Israel in the wilderness. Shall we ask, Does not God care that millions live in utter impoverishment, countless families languish in refugee camps, children starve or die for lack of clean water while a privileged minority have more than enough of everything? At least, we must recognize that vast disparities in living conditions are caused by human sin, not ordained by God. No more than slavery was God-ordained are economic ways and means that fail to provide just distribution of a nation's resources.

Prayer: *Forgive us, O God, when we "pass by on the other side" in the face of human need. Our sympathies go out to our brothers and sisters who are denied even the basics of decent living. We pray for them and for ourselves, that we never become hardened and uncaring. Amen.*

Wednesday, August 19   Read Matthew 16:13-20.

From the rock Moses struck to bring forth water, to Peter the "rock" on which Christ builds his church, we see God bringing to fruition the divine plan of human redemption. The prophetic message all through the Old Testament was in the final analysis forward-looking and hopeful. Many more times than in Psalm 95 God had to express his displeasure with a "stiff-necked," often disobedient people, and this displeasure led to the most severe penalties. But in their own land or in exile under the conquering heel of an adversary, Israel was always given assurance that God had never forgotten them nor given up on them.

Could we ever imagine God is about to give up on one final generation? If we really think that human fallibility—with great potential for self-destruction—will end this planet's livability, shouldn't we have second thoughts? Jesus looked beyond the human potential for destroying what God had created and promised that the "powers of death" could not prevail against his church. If the church were to be preserved through ages to come, surely human existence is also to be preserved. After the Flood, God promised Noah, "While the earth remains, seedtime and harvest, cold and heat, summer and winter, day and night, shall not cease" (Gen. 8:22). So it has been all these millenia, while the door to our redemption remains open. But is there a deep disappointment in God's heart that many will not accept the invitation to life?

Prayer: *For all who accept your invitation to life, O God, there is joy and eager anticipation. With utmost confidence we pray, "Thy kingdom come." Through Christ our Lord. Amen.*

Thursday, August 20   Read Psalm 95:1-7*a*.

With what exuberant joy the psalmist begins Psalm 95! The word *rock*, used many times in the Psalms, speaks to us of the steadfastness, the faithfulness, and unchangeableness of God. Always there when we call, God is the king of all creation. All human conceptions of God never come close to the reality of God's splendor and glory. Nature as seen in the terrestrial world attests to God's power; elsewhere the psalmist tells us the heavens declare God's glory. The psalmist knows that God is infinitely worthy to receive the worship, praise, and adoration of all sentient creatures, including every human being ever born. So he rightly calls on God's people to worship and bow down before their Maker! As sheep are to the shepherd, so are we before God. We need only reflect on the "sheepishness" of sheep to see the analogy. Our wisdom compared with the wisdom of God is as the wisdom of sheep compared with the wisdom of the shepherd.

In the light of the sovereign power and authority of God, dare we carp when we take into account the state of our world? Our Lord Jesus Christ also lived in a world of ostentatious wealth and human pride alongside wretched poverty, miscarriages of justice, violence, and cruelty. That God came to the world as one of us in Jesus Christ declares God's loving concern and depth of longing for us to be saved from sin.

Prayer: *Great is thy faithfulness, O God. Our heart's desire is to be on your side and to see our world through the eyes of Jesus, our Lord. Awaken us and give us vision. Amen.*

Friday, August 21   Read Hebrews 12:12-14.

Exhortations to encourage the faint-hearted abound in scripture. Moses cried to the people as they faced the Red Sea with Pharaoh's army behind, "Fear not, stand firm, and see the salvation of the Lord, which he will work for you today" (Exod. 14:13). Jesus enjoined the disciples through a parable that they "ought always to pray and not lose heart" (Luke 18:1).

At the same time, the scripture writers make it clear that fallen humanity lives in a world of human alienation from God which inevitably leads to strife and enmity—unless the grace of God intervenes. From beginning to end sin building a barrier between the soul and God takes away peace and opens the door to everything opposed to God. And without holiness, no one will see the Lord, says the writer to the Hebrews. The other side is the beatitude of Jesus, "Blessed are the pure in heart, for they shall see God" (Matt. 5:8).

Has modern society ceased to distinguish between the rightness of right and the wrongness of wrong? In his book *Whatever Became of Sin?* Karl Menninger asked some important questions about sin, some of which seem to have been ignored to the present time. Whether we name it sin or simply attribute certain behaviors to our "human condition," evil is all around us. And the faithful need to look continually to the Bible—the Judeo-Christian revelation—for the answer.

Prayer: *O God, give us a sensitive conscience and quickness to perceive anything in ourselves that dulls our responsiveness to your Spirit. Through Christ our Lord. Amen.*

Saturday, August 22   Read Hebrews 12:15-17.

It can be said that the kind of persons we are determines the choices we make. In this passage, Esau is identified as "immoral or irreligious" because he did not sufficiently value his birthright. His wily brother, Jacob, caught him at an unguarded moment, but Esau is blamed because he "sold his birthright for a single meal." When Esau realized what he had done, he was remorseful, but it was too late. His loss was final when the patriarchal blessing was given to his brother through dissimulation and trickery.

How seriously we must take the warning not to fail to obtain the grace of God! We have been looking at some of the seeming contradictions to the sovereign power of God—a suffering, endangered humanity looking toward a future with more hazards than past generations ever faced. If ever people of faith needed to affirm their allegiance to the God who is the author of that faith it is now! How greatly the civilized world, long exposed to Christian witness, needs to be reminded that persons are here who take their Christian commitment so seriously and intensely that nothing can turn them aside as Esau was turned aside! For us Christians this means self-denial, the bearing of our crosses— whatever God lays upon us. It means disciplined living. When we consider the alternatives with Esau as an example, are not the issues quite clear?

Prayer: *God of creation, help us to feel to the depths of our being the compulsion of your Spirit. May we rise in wholehearted obedience so that we will not later feel your hand in judgment on our half-commitments and trifling. In Jesus Christ's holy name. Amen.*

Sunday, August 23 Read Romans 11:33-36.

After agonizing appraisals of the state of our world, we can with relief take our stand on the truth of God! Like Paul, who was disheartened by those who rejected the good news of salvation through Christ, we, too, can still give God the glory, though frustrated by our generation's wanton ignorance of God's saving intention.

Is it not amazing that after a laborious intellectual pursuit through labyrinths of argument, Paul could suddenly break off with a paean of praise to God—a joyously exultant song of worship, thanksgiving, and triumph! This was the way of psalmists; it has been the way of God's saints through the ages. The writings of Augustine, Francis, Teresa, Jeremy Taylor, Richard Baxter, John Milton, John Wesley and a great host of other past-generation saints bear this out. We can never doubt that countless obscure saints alive today along with famous spiritual leaders offer their heartfelt praises to God. Probably every devout Christian has a list of great Christians of this century.

If we are on God's side, how could we ever give way to panic? "Perfect love casts out fear" (1 John 4:18). The love of God in Paul's heart made him express his tribute to the goodness of God. It could only be expressed in exclamations of joy or in rational questions of how life could not be fashioned any other way. Christians in today's world have the same grounds for believing in God's triumph at last. To God be the glory, now and forevermore!

Suggestion for meditation: *Examine your faith to see if it gives you utmost confidence in the triumph of righteousness and a victorious outcome for God's people.*

BEING TRUE TO THE CHRIST WITHIN

August 24-30, 1987   **Sr. Mary Michael, SSM†**
Monday, August 24   Read Exodus 19:1-9.

Jesus taught by his own example that a life directed to following God's will is the richest, simplest, best life anyone can ever have on this earth. Our Mother Superior once told me that the Creator didn't make any mistakes in designing any of us, that God gave us all we shall ever need to do whatever is asked of us. She said that if we do what God asks of us, we will be supremely happy.

I know in my own depths that God does dwell within us at the innermost core of our being. The most important discovery, therefore, that we can ever make in life is the searching out of what this innermost core of our own being tells us is right for us to be doing. Once we make this discovery, we can then give ourselves wholeheartedly to the purpose for which God created us. If we are doing what the innermost core of our own being tells us to do, we are then living in harmony with God, with others "so far as it lies with [us]," (Rom. 12:18, NEB) and with ourselves. We shall be doing God's will, and we shall have found highest earthly fulfillment and joy.

It is during our times of prayer that we learn ever more and more surely that we are loved, forgiven, accepted, and trusted by God. And it is from experiencing God's great love for us from prayer that we find that will to respond with all the love of our being to God and God's truth deep within.

Prayer: *O Christ, grant us the grace to do whatever you ask. Amen.*

---

†Sister of St. Margaret; Associate Chaplain, Germantown Hospital; Vice-president of Prayer and Worship, Episcopal Church Women of the Diocese of Pennsylvania; Philadelphia, Pennsylvania.

Tuesday, August 25   Read Romans 12:1-13.

One of the most trenchant collects in Episcopalians' *Book of Common Prayer* beseeches God to give us "the grace to hear, read, mark, learn, and inwardly digest the scriptures." If we were to do what Paul tells us to do in today's reading from the Letter to the Romans, we would find the one sure way to begin to grow in what scripture often speaks of as wisdom.

The wisdom of the Bible is God-given and really means knowledge *of* God—experiencing God's love and presence in our lives—not just knowing *about* God. If we are to let our minds be remade and our whole nature be transformed, prayerful study and pondering of scripture is a necessity.

If we hear, read, mark, learn, and inwardly digest scripture, we shall find that the theme that runs through the Bible from the Book of Genesis to the Book of Revelation is God's self-giving love, no matter what the cost. God-given wisdom requires us to pay attention to the word of God even though at times it "cuts more keenly than any two-edged sword" (Heb. 4:12, NEB), as it does here in the concept of self-giving. Many of us today don't like the idea of self-offering, believing that it means self-destruction rather than self-fulfillment.

But the Christian way of sacrificial love is the way of self-transcendence, the way to go beyond our infinitely little selves, the way to be true to the Christ dwelling within. If we really mean it when we call Jesus our Lord, he becomes our model. We seek to love as he loves, to be generous as he is generous; to be concerned for all people as he is.

Prayer: *Dear Christ, let us not call you "Lord, Lord" while failing to do what you tell us. Amen.*

Wednesday, August 26   Read Matthew 16:21-23.

In today's reading we find Jesus telling the disciples God's plan for the salvation—the healing, the wholeness—of the human race. The plan involves Christ's free-will acceptance of suffering and death at the hands of the so-called religious leaders of the day. Peter, quite understandably, was so horrified by the thought of such an inglorious end for his beloved Messiah—whom he had doubtless always believed would some day free his people from Roman domination—that he remonstrated vehemently with Jesus.

To what must have been Peter's great surprise, Jesus said that Peter was at the moment playing the devil's role. Peter was doing this by trying to deflect Jesus from the course of utter trust in and devotion to God's will. "You think as men think, not as God thinks," Jesus declared (NEB).

What Peter didn't know then—and what it may take the rest of us almost a lifetime to realize—is that God's wisdom is not the same as our human wisdom. Christ's suffering and death for love of us broke our hard hearts and led us into a deep and abiding relationship, a relationship where love becomes our treasure and our joy. God's wisdom is, indeed, not our wisdom; nor are God's ways our ways.

Prayer: *Teach us, Lord Christ, to respond with love to your great love for us. Amen.*

Thursday, August 27   Read Matthew 16:24-28.

For more than a year before I entered the convent over thirty years ago, I was torn between a great desire to do so and resistance to doing it. I thought going into the convent would mean giving up my family, my friends, my job, my apartment, my freedom to go and come as I pleased and to do or refrain from doing whatever I wished. I feared that I could never bear to live faithfully according to the customary three vows of poverty, chastity, and obedience.

I spent much time in prayerful thought about whether or not it was true that God was calling me to such a life. In these times, however, the verse from scripture that came often to my mind was, "I have loved thee with an everlasting love: therefore with loving-kindness have I drawn thee" (Jer. 31:3, KJV).

I became gradually more and more convinced deep in my heart that the convent was the way I was being asked to follow God—a way which is not the least bit superior to any other. But I believed that if it was truly the way to which I was being guided by God, it would be the best possible way for me to draw closer to God and to strive to become all God asked. I knew that if I didn't answer what my deepest self told me was God's call to me, I would be letting the pearl of great price slip through my fingers.

Suggestion for meditation: *What will we gain by winning the whole world, if we do so at the cost of our true self? Or what could we give that would buy our self back?*

Friday, August 28   Read 1 Corinthians 2:6-13.

We considered the other day God's hidden wisdom not being the same as ours. Today we want to consider God's hidden wisdom, God's secret purpose framed from the very beginning to bring us to our full glory. We are not writing about worldly wisdom, exhibited by those who live as if God didn't exist at all. We are writing about the God-given wisdom which we receive from the Holy Spirit, who comes to dwell within us at our baptism and who becomes ever more real to us as we find God in others, in prayer, and in sacrament.

When Jesus lived here on earth among us, he told us to ask, seek, and knock in prayer (see Luke 11:9-10). He also told us we would be given the gift of the Holy Spirit (see Luke 11:13). God's hidden wisdom, God's secret purpose, is that Christ will dwell within each one of us always to empower, transform, and guide us. Whether we know it or not, a battle between light and darkness has been going on here for thousands of years. Christ came to earth to fight and win the battle for us.

What gives Christians unshakeable joy is the fact that Christ does live within us—loving us, accepting us, forgiving us— enabling us to strive to become like Christ and to do whatever God asks. In this way we are growing ever more true to the Christ within.

Suggestion for meditation: *Everyone who asks receives, the one who seeks finds, and to the one who knocks, the door will be opened.*

Saturday, August 29 Read Matthew 16:25-26.

Last summer I stood for a long time in St. Paul's Cathedral in London, contemplating Holman Hunt's magnificent painting of Christ, *The Light of the World*. In the light of such love for us all as the painting reveals, we cannot help seeing with searing clarity our own sin. But we also see Christ's great love, compassion, and healing freely offered to each one of us.

A few days later I stood before one of the great glories of Coventry Cathedral—the Baptistry Window designed by John Piper. The window represented for me that Christ's light, truth, and love are far greater than all of our darkness, confusion, and sin. These negatives were represented by the darker colors— reds, greens, and blues—surrounding the glowing circle of light in the center of the window.

Both the painting and the window spoke far more loudly than any words could of the living Christ within me and within every baptized Christian. We are not fully alive, I think—not our truest, deepest selves—until we know the joy of Christ's love and presence within us.

Prayer: *O Christ, you are the source, guide, and goal of all that is. To you be glory forever! Amen.*

Sunday, August 30   Read Matthew 16:21-28.

The doctrine of the Cross is "sheer folly" (1 Cor. 1:18, NEB) to those who live as if God doesn't exist at all. But to those of us who believe that we are in Christ Jesus by God's act (our baptism), the cross—the way of willingly losing everything, even life itself, to remain loyal to the Lord Christ—is the one and only way to gain true life, real life, eternal life (see 1 Cor. 1:24-31).

Two of the noblest people on earth today—both winners of Nobel Peace Prizes—are Bishop Desmond Tutu of Johannesburg and Mother Teresa of Calcutta. Bishop Tutu has for years been fearlessly contending for righteousness and justice for his people in Africa, in spite of the persecution or suffering that others have inflicted upon him. Mother Teresa has been giving food and shelter to "the poorest of the poor" in India for many years, no matter how great the cost to her in energy, labor, and hardship.

Bishop Tutu and Mother Teresa are doing what they believe to be God's will. They are, therefore, in all the great good that they are doing, being utterly true to their Christ self. I believe that both of them (if they took time to think about it!) would consider themselves richly blessed and completely fulfilled. They have found their greatest joy, as their Lord Christ did, in doing God's will.

Suggestion for meditation: *What self am I trying to fulfill—my Christ self or my me-first self?*

A POWERFUL AND LOVING GOD

August 31–September 6, 1987   **Harvey and Gayla Estes†**
Monday, August 31   Read Exodus 19:16-20.

This scripture deals with a theophany—the appearance of God on Mount Sinai. Like many Old Testament passages, it does not rest easily on modern-day ears. We admit to an uncomfortableness with the awful display of the power and authority of God as we read of thunders and lightnings, thick clouds, smoke, fire, and the quaking mountain. Little wonder that the Hebrew people trembled. We prefer to see God present in the beauty of nature—in sunsets and rainbows—more than in thunderclouds and earthquakes.

This preference often extends to our theology. We pick and choose a theology to match our own desires. We select a church on the basis of how well it suits our lifestyle. Perhaps we are more closely akin to the Hebrew children than we realize. They, too, chose to create their own theology. They fashioned their own god—a golden calf—to match their own desires and concepts of what God should be like.

We sometimes sentimentalize God as a God of love to the point that we no longer allow divine authority to hold us accountable. Like the ancient Hebrews, we, too, need those moments when we stand trembling, awestruck by the God of majesty and power.

Prayer: *Almighty God, help us to accept your power and authority in our lives as well as your gracious love. Amen.*

---

†Harvey Estes is pastor of Cokesbury United Methodist Church, Stedman, North Carolina. Gayla Estes is an ordained United Methodist minister, a member of the North Carolina Annual Conference.

Tuesday, September 1   Read Exodus 19:21-25.

We often sing "Just a Closer Walk with Thee," and we do well to have such a desire. But sometimes we need the God who is far away. Like the Israelites, who were told not to break through to Mount Sinai, at times we need to see God at a distance lest we become presumptuous.

No matter how much we may hunger for divine intimacy, familiarity can also breed contempt. A religion teacher once told his class, "Some people talk as if they have sat down to eat breakfast with Almighty God." Certainly at communion we are invited to God's table, but not as equals! To have Jesus in your heart is not the same as having God in your hip pocket!

I became painfully aware of this my first semester in seminary. After preaching all summer on a field education assignment, my first Old Testament course hit me like a ton of Bibles! It drove home to me the presumptuousness of preaching. Who am I to stand in the sanctuary and dare to interpret God's word? I became so intimidated that if someone had asked me, "Does the Bible say that God loves us?" I would have replied with fear and trembling, "Let me check a commentary and get back to you."

It was almost a year before I tried to preach again, and even today I still feel scared whenever I go into the pulpit. But it's a good "scared"; it has grown into a sense of awe through which the Spirit says, "I am with you, but do not forget that I am God."

Prayer: *We thank you, most holy God, for being both near and far away. Help us to walk close to you as children walk with a loving parent; but help us also to see you atop a mountain of fire, challenging our presumptuousness with your authority. Amen.*

Wednesday, September 2   Read Matthew 18:15-17.

How does the church deal with an erring member? This is a tough question on a delicate subject. In all Christian fellowship from time to time there may be a member who not only sins but continues unrepentant. That person's actions may not only hurt another member but may also hurt the entire church. How does the individual Christian and the church community deal with such a person?

Most of the time the response of the church is either to ignore such behavior and hope that the unrepentant one has a change of heart, or to gossip about it. We are reluctant to come right out and confront such persons because we are reminded of another passage in Matthew: "Judge not, that you be not judged" (7:1).

In dealing with this situation we should remember that our aim is not to judge or condemn. In our personal relationships with fellow Christians it is possible to discipline in love without being self-righteous about it. Our first concern should be for the person and not the fear that the person may make the church look bad. Our purpose should be one of reconciliation: to reconcile the offender with the offended, with the community of faith, and with God.

Spiritual growth and Christian unity within the church have too often been hampered by hurt feelings among members. Dealing with discord in the church uses up a great deal of energy that we could spend on sharing Christ with others. Think of the ministry we could accomplish if we could only put our grievances behind us and get on with God's work!

Prayer: *O God, help us to hold each other accountable in Christian love so that we may resolve our conflicts, live in peace, and minister to others. Amen.*

Thursday, September 3   Read Matthew 18:18-20.

"Call out the names of some of the saints that have meant a lot to you." At an All Saint's Day celebration in Duke Chapel, the liturgist invited us to offer up this unusual prayer. After a moment of silence, a few people began to speak up: St. Paul, St. Francis, Susanna Wesley, Martin Luther, Mother Teresa, Martin Luther King, Jr. Something about calling out their names seemed to evoke their presence.

Unlike Shakespeare's Juliet, who questioned, "What's in a name?" Matthew wrote for a culture that linked people's names very closely to their character. In writing "Where two or three are gathered in my name," Matthew emphasizes the name of Jesus in a way that evokes his presence. Rather than making an apology for poor church attendance, the Evangelist affirms the power of Christ's presence whether the number gathered is great or small.

If the church is ever to claim the high authority and power that Jesus offers (v. 18), we can only do it when we act in his name, in his character. But what would the church look like if the name of Christ characterized all our gatherings, right down to the smallest prayer groups of two or three? John Wesley traveled all over England preaching and organizing class meetings, society meetings, building what would later become the Methodist Church from the building blocks of small groups committed to scriptural holiness. And some say he prevented a bloody revolution like the one in France simply by offering Christ to rich and poor alike.

Prayer: *Jesus, help us to cultivate your character in our hearts that we may proclaim your name in power. Amen.*

Friday, September 4   Read Psalm 115:1-11.

The psalmist was lucky. The idols of his day had blind eyes, dumb lips, immobile hands and feet. Today we confront idols far livelier; we have only to turn on our television sets to watch them glide into our homes. Soap opera idols tempt us to place lust ahead of love; commercial idols lure us to put things above people; entertainment idols entice us to value amusement more than fulfillment. Sometimes I think I would rather argue against the stone totems of ancient Palestine than confront the electronic images of a consumer society.

Perhaps we today need even more to give glory to God who is in the heavens (v. 3) rather than to a god trapped in things. Only the unseen Power that rules our hearts, our minds, our relationships, can deliver us from idolatry. We may think ourselves far removed from primitive cultures that worship images, yet does not an affluent society often run the risk of putting things first, of lifting up our own material idols?

Like the ancient Hebrews, who found no real power in "the work of men's hands" made of silver and gold, we, too, may discover our salvation elsewhere. A CROP Walk (to raise money for world hunger) underlined this for my wife and me. It blessed us to see youth, often preoccupied with clothes, cars, and cruising, suddenly discover a greater fulfillment in ministering to hungry people in the name of Jesus. As they finished the ten-mile course, they *looked* materially impoverished—hot and sweaty in their jogging rags. But a Spirit walked with them that made them richer than kings.

Prayer: *Fill us with your Spirit, O God, that we may lay aside our idols. Amen.*

Saturday, September 5   Read Romans 13:1-7.

"There is no authority except from God." What a comfort to know that all real authority is morally grounded! The world tempts us to believe that authority and power (the same word in New Testament Greek) come from money, arms, politics, influence. But Paul reminds us that first of all authority must be credible before God.

Paul was blessed with the opportunity to live under good rulers. They punished those who did wrong (v. 4), gave approval to those who did good (v. 3), and were for this reason worthy to be supported by taxes paid by the citizens (v. 6). Needless to say, not all governments fit this description. In occupied France during World War II, one would hardly have said to the French Resistance, "Be subject to the governing authorities. . . those that exist have been instituted by God." The Nazi regime bore little resemblance to the Roman government of Paul's day.

This scripture does not negate the occasional necessity of civil disobedience against governing structures that do not function as "God's servant" (v. 4). But in a time when defying authority has become all too popular, a liberal dose of Paul's conservatism can be sobering.

I spoke recently with someone who had traveled to Washington, D.C. Upon returning he was asked, "What were they demonstrating against *this* week?" It saddens me to see the prophetic voice drowned out by every political bandwagon that comes down the pike. In light of this scripture, we need to remember that we must respect authority before we can call it to account.

Prayer: *Almighty God, strengthen our government when it acts as your servant; call it to account when it does not. Amen.*

Sunday, September 6   Read Romans 13:8-10.

Think about a time when you felt the overwhelming presence of God's love for you. For me that time comes during worship. We all feel a special joy and closeness when we take Holy Communion with other members of the Body of Christ. I remember particular Communion services: beneath the Chrismon tree on Christmas Eve, with my confirmation class at Pentecost, at an Easter sunrise service with the youth choir.

As we remember times such as these, Paul's words to us have a particular meaning. Paul talks about a debt of love. We may keep all of the law. We may be up-to-date on all our financial responsibilities. But we will always have that debt of love. When we think of all that God has done for us through Jesus Christ—the love shown to us through Christ's birth, death, and resurrection—none of us could ever claim to have paid back what God has given so generously. All we can hope to do is to accept this gracious love for us and then love our neighbor in response.

Paul also talks about love as the fulfillment of the law. He quotes several of the commandments which are stated in the negative—the thou-shalt-nots. But he then quotes another Old Testament commandment, one that Jesus held up as similar to the great commandment: You shall love your neighbor as yourself.

Love is the spirit behind the law. Love is the complete fulfillment of the law. If we truly love our neighbor, then keeping the commandments comes more naturally and easily. God's abundant love enables us to live according to his law.

Prayer: *O gracious God, thank you for the abundant love you have shown us. May we acknowledge the debt of love we have by sharing that love with all people. Amen.*

PARADOX OF LAW, FEAR, AND LOVE

September 7-13, 1987
Monday, September 7

Robert L. King†
Read Exodus 20:1-20;
Romans 14:7-9;
Matthew 18:31-33;
Psalm 19:7-14.

If the four scriptures are read in the order suggested, it is plain we are going to move through a lot of territory this week, and there are some apparent paradoxes to be reconciled.

The Exodus passage deals primarily with law and fear; the Romans passage with ownership; Matthew with a demand to forgive others; and the psalm with love of the law. So we progress from law and fear, through a definition of ownership, to a demand for forgiveness, to a statement of love of the law.

To integrate the ideas in these scriptures, we must consider the paradox of fear and love; of God owning us, which challenges our love of freedom, and of the threat in Matthew of forgiving others or else!

This week, we will examine each of the five ideas (law, fear of the Lord, ownership, forgiveness, and love of the law) separately, then try to tie them together. Our primary effort will be to find a way to truly agree with the psalmist as he declares so eloquently his love of the Lord and his desire to be purified by the law.

In your meditation for today, consider the nature of the Ten Commandments: their aim, the possibilities for compliance, and the dilemma they present.

Prayer: *Lord, we know we cannot please you on our own power. Lead us in your way. Amen.*

---

†Member, lay reader, and chalice bearer, Grace Episcopal Church, Middleway, West Virginia.

Tuesday, September 8   Read Exodus 20:1-17;
                                            Romans 7:15-24.

"I am the Lord your God, who brought you out of the land of Egypt, out of the house of bondage."

With these words, God claims a people and reminds them that God has freed them from bondage; yet there is a price for that freedom: obeying the Lord's commandments. But wait; look at the nature of these commandments. Four are aimed at how those people are to interact with God, while the remainder deal with proper interaction among God's people. Our New Owner seems to be as much or more concerned with how we treat each other. As we review these laws, who would not want to be treated this well!

Given the very positive nature of these commandments and the source from which we received them, it is strange that we often treat them so lightly. We worry about the bad effects of pollution, drugs, and other negative aspects of modern living, yet we seem to ignore the terrible prices we pay when we disobey the commandments. Could it be that, deep down, we realize that we simply cannot live up to these commandments, and we cannot face the thought of failure? As a result we act as if we are being casual about all this. But we know we are failing God, and we are paralyzed by our fear.

In your meditation for today, continue to consider the nature of the Ten Commandments: their aim, the possibilities for compliance, and the dilemma they present. Then ask yourself whether your guilt at lack of compliance is paralyzing you from trying.

Prayer: *Lord, show us how we are failing you in living up to your law. Amen.*

Wednesday, September 9   Read Exodus 20:18-21.

"Be not afraid! God has come to test you, so you may revere Him enough not to sin."*

This particular verse has been translated a number of ways, but I find the above version easiest to understand and to deal with. To be afraid is to be paralyzed in panic; it is a passive emotion which implies the inability to deal rationally with a fearsome issue. On the other hand, "to revere" implies the ability to show reverence for; to take a positive move toward the thing revered, or at least to deal with in a rational, positive way; in other words, to be in awe of but not paralyzed by.

As I was struggling with understanding this paradox, a major hurricane moved up the Atlantic coast, threatening the northern Virginia-Maryland-West Virginia area. This was my first experience with a threatening hurricane, and, as a midwesterner, I found it particularly frightening. My first reaction was to freeze in panic. But then I saw that the better solution was to follow the guidance given by experts and take the necessary precautions out of respect for the storm and its power. Unquestionably, I was in awe of the power of the storm, but I could take appropriate action.

When I am faced with God's awesome power and my weakness, the best course may be to take the necessary precautions by obeying God's commandments as best I can out of awe, respect, and reverence for God's desires and power.

Prayer: *Lord, teach us to actively revere you by doing our best to obey your commandments. Amen.*

---

*Exodus 20:20, *The Holy Bible, The Berkeley Version in Modern English* (Grand Rapids, Michigan: Zondervan Publishing House, 1960).

Thursday, September 10   Read Romans 14:7-9.

"So then, whether we live or whether we die, we are the Lord's."

This passage continues the idea of the first commandment. In Exodus, God pronounced, "I am the Lord your God, who brought you out . . . of bondage." Paul simply says that God owns us, dead or alive!

Consider how we act toward something we own. Normally we are concerned about our property. We guard it very carefully; we tend it with care; we maintain it; we want only the best for it. Certainly, if we are very possessive, we would do nothing to harm it.

If that is true of human beings, think how a loving God must consider us. And if God treats those valued things in a way that humans do (only, of course, infinitely better) then we must look again at the Lord's laws and commandments. They are the wise and loving judgments and concerns of an Owner who loves us so much that only the best is willed for us. An Owner who asks that we do our very best. In spite of our nature, God knows we can and should aspire to the highest level of excellence. Thus, God sets ideals of behavior for us to follow with respect to our relations with our Lord and with others. Even though we cannot completely meet those ideals, we must aspire to them if we are to experience the full joy of living as God's children.

Today, consider the good fortune of being owned by a beneficial, loving, and infinitely wise God. Consider the idea that all human beings are the property of that Owner. At the same time, consider the consequences of abusing the property of such an Owner.

Prayer: *Thank you, Lord, for showing your love for me by expecting the very best from me. Amen.*

Friday, September 11
Read Matthew 18:21-35;
1 Corinthians 13:4-7.

"Lord, how often shall my brother sin against me, and I forgive him?"

At times, the phrasing of some of Christ's words bothers me; the words sound so harsh. It helps me to remember that some of that is the prophetic style of the time. It is consistent with the style of the earlier Old Testament prophets. If we get past the harshness, we see that Jesus is simply helping us to see that our own failures are forgiven by God and that we must pass on that forgiveness to others.

In the trauma of living up to the ideal we are called to emulate, we simply must realize that others are also struggling—and often failing—just as we are. Our Christian walk asks more of us than just tolerance; it asks that we try to love our fellow pilgrims on this planet in the same way that God loves us—endlessly and fully.

As we consider this passage, we may realize that forgiveness is the healing salve that makes it possible to survive in a frantic, bruising world. As you go through your day, try to really forgive those around you for the small slights you suffer, and see if your day isn't better. Start with the "idiot" who cuts you off in traffic this morning, and then the "loudmouth" in the office who spends all his time talking right at your desk, and then your "inconsiderate" boss.

Prayer: *Lord, help me to realize that your kingdom is made up of some really messed-up folks, just like me. And Lord, help me to see in them the same diamond in the rough that you see! Amen.*

Saturday, September 12   Read Psalm 19:7-11.

"The law of the Lord is perfect, reviving the soul; the testimony of the Lord is sure, making wise the simple."

God's laws are perfect. Having thought of everything, God describes the ideal relationship with our Lord and with other human beings. God's laws protect us from ourselves and from harming each other; they provide a wise way of life and we can know joy and freedom from fear. They cannot spoil; they are timeless.

If we love God, honor our parents, avoid harming our fellows, deal honestly with our spouses, do not steal or lie, and maintain gratitude for what we have rather than coveting what others have, we will be less likely to harm others.

If humanity could do all these things to the fullest, we could live a life free of fear and guilt—a life in full communion with our God and with others. So, whose fault is it that we are not living in this utopia, God's or ours? We truly must cease being afraid of God and begin to revere God and God's ways by following these commandments.

Prayer: *Lord, I love you and need your guidance. Help me to want to truly walk in your ways. Amen.*

Sunday, September 13   Read Psalm 19:12-14.

"No one can see his own errors; deliver me, Lord, from hidden faults" (TEV).

I hope we come to the end of this week with an enhanced understanding of the apparent paradoxes we struggled with earlier this week. We have seen that God jealously protects us, even from ourselves. Because of God's love and protection, God demands of us the very best that is in us. Unfortunately, we cannot always live up to that ideal. As we see the beauty of those commandments, we also become aware that we cannot always obey them and we become afraid. But the Bible shows us that God forgives us and commands us to do the same to others, since we all share a common Lord who is jealous of our well-being. Understanding that, we can see the perfect nature of God's law, and we can rejoice in God's grace and love.

Even so, we know we fail, and we do need God's help to see our shortcomings. We can ask for help in being aware, since we know that we are pardoned even before we ask. With God's help, we can be safe from doing deliberate wrongs and, thus, free of guilt. In this state we can come and, with our whole heart, claim God as our rock and redeemer and ask that our words and innermost thoughts be acceptable. Amen and God bless!

Prayer: *Lord, truly let the words of my mouth and the meditations of my heart be acceptable in thy sight because you really are my rock and redeemer! Amen.*

WAITING FOR GOD

September 14-20, 1987
Monday, September 14

David F. Ensminger†
Read Exodus 32:1-14.

Waiting is a part of life.

We cannot go through a day of any week in which we do not spend some time in waiting. We wait for change at the market. We wait at a traffic light. We wait for other people.

In the scripture for today the Israelites are waiting for Moses. When he was so long in coming down from Mount Sinai, they were upset by the delay.

On a deeper level, they were waiting for God. The Hebrews had waited 600 years for freedom and now they were on hold again. They grew tired of waiting and decided to be passive no longer.

The Hebrews, with the help of Aaron, made themselves a god. They could serve (wait on) this god while they waited for the promises to be fulfilled. They made an idol and called it "lord" and "sat down to eat and drink and to indulge in revelry" (NIV).

Waiting is a part of life. Waiting for God is part of our Judeo-Christian history. Our ancestors waited for the Messiah, and we now wait for the Second Advent. Yet, we, like the ancient Hebrews, need to learn the secret of waiting for the Lord and the dangers inherent in waiting: idol worship, frustration, and separation from God.

Today, let us affirm waiting as a part of life and pray we can wait in faith, not in faithlessness.

Prayer: *Come, Holy Ghost, and touch me as I wait. Amen.*

---

†Pastor, Wesley Memorial United Methodist Church, Johnson City, Tennessee.

Tuesday, September 15   Read Psalm 106:7-8,
                                                 19-23.

Waiting is a part of life.

There is really nothing we do in our lives that does not require some form of waiting. Television commercials remind us to "please allow 6-8 weeks for delivery." Sometimes we wait months or years for legal matters to be corrected.

The key to waiting is in the attitude we have while we wait, and in what we do while we wait.

The psalmist reminds us that one danger is forgetting why we wait or for whom we are waiting. He reminds us that the Israelites "gave no thought" (NIV) to God's miracles; and "they forgot the God who saved them" (NIV).

As we wait for healing, guidance, or divine light in our life, we often fail to recall the mighty acts of God, and, therefore, forget God. This can lead us to forget *why* we wait: salvation.

The way to wait for the goodness of God is in anticipation. And the way to remain excited is to recall the "miracles . . . and awesome deeds" (NIV) of our God.

Waiting is a part of life, and it involves our faithfulness to remember the one for whom we wait, lest we forget God.

Prayer: *Thank you, God, for your deeds and wonders in my life. Amen.*

Friday, September 18   Read Psalm 46.

Waiting is a part of life.

Perhaps the most difficult part of waiting is knowing what to do while we wait. We have already seen the problem that befell the Israelites as they waited. Their experience can remind us that idle hands are the devil's workshop. We must be about God's work if our waiting is to be worthwhile.

Scripture gives another way to wait for God. Not only does it recount the power of God, "an ever present help in trouble" (NIV), it tells us to wait for God by *putting away* our business and frantic activity—even our warfare!

"Be still, and know that I am God" (NIV).

It is not impossible to be totally still, and there are times when it seems that being quiet and still would be wrong. However, we all understand and feel the power that comes in silence and waiting.

The psalm gives us a promise that the way to wait for God is by being still. To do nothing is something we must learn or we run the risk of missing God because we are leaning on our own understanding.

Waiting is a part of life. Waiting for God is part of the Christian experience. Waiting in stillness is part of coming into the knowledge of God.

"Be still and know."

Devotional exercise: *Sit quietly. Open your mind to God's presence and direction that can come in stillness.*

Saturday, September 19   Read Isaiah 40:29-31.

Waiting is a part of life.

Often life is unfair. Energy gets expended but nothing is accomplished. Many times we become frustrated because waiting is a part of our lives.

However, many people are learning that waiting itself is not bad. It is our attitude while we wait that wears us out. Grumbling and complaining weaken us and make us less likely to enjoy what we have waited for even when it comes.

Waiting for God may be like that. The people of Israel grumbled, the laborers in the vineyard grumbled, and often we complain because we have to wait to get an insight or some knowledge for our life.

However, waiting for God is scriptural and encouraged in our tradition. We are told by Isaiah that it is in waiting that we find strength, power, and the ability to "soar" and "walk and not be faint" (NIV).

God expects us to wait; when we are true followers, we will wait. Add to that the promises of strength for those who wait and we would be foolish not to wait . . . for God.

Prayer: *Come, Lord, while I wait, so I can live for you. Amen.*

Sunday, September 20   Read Psalm 23.

Waiting is a part of life.

Life has a common nature no matter where we live or how long we live. Part of that nature includes waiting.

We are always waiting. We wait for the mail, a meal, news, or a new day. And in our Christian faith, we wait for God.

We wait for God to be born in us or reborn. We wait for a new burst of awe and wonder. We wait for the Second Advent and a final infilling of the Holy Spirit, but we wait.

The fact that we wait is not bad. The scripture reminds us that part of having faith and being faithful is waiting. The important part of waiting is attitude and action.

When we wait for God, we recall God's goodness (through the valley of the shadow, anointing our heads with oil); we become renewed (by the still waters); we are promised life abundant (goodness and mercy all the days of life).

Waiting is a part of life. Waiting for God is a part of faith. We need not be afraid to wait, for we can be sure that as we wait, God will come.

Prayer: *Come, Lord; I wait for you. Amen.*

A PECULIAR PEOPLE

September 21-27, 1987
Monday, September 21

John M. Gessell†
Read Exodus 33:12-17.

"I know you by name," God told Moses.

Moses, weighed down by the heavy burdens of leading God's own people, appealed to God for support in uncertainty.

Then God answered, "I will go with you in person and set your mind at rest. . . . I will do this thing that you have asked, because you have found favour with me, and I know you by name" (NEB).

Knowing by name is an intimate declaration of grace and favor. It comforted Moses. It declares a companionship—"I, John, take thee, Mary." "You have found favor with me; I will go with you." Naming and knowing by name is power. Adam named the creatures and so declared their being. God names those appointed for great purposes, who belong to God in a peculiar way. Abram becomes Abraham the father of nations; Jacob becomes Israel by whom a chosen people are known; Saul becomes Paul the apostle of Christ; and Jesus is named before Mary by Gabriel, the archangel of light, for he shall be the Savior of his people.

The holy name of God reveals God's inmost nature—"Those who acknowledge thy name may trust in thee" (Ps. 9:10, NEB). And so we who call Jesus Lord are baptized into his name and no other (see 1 Cor. 1:13-15)—into the name above all other names—and we become one with Christ and Christ with us.

Prayer: *O God, give us grace that we may know thee as we are known by thee. Amen.*

---

†Priest of the Episcopal Church; Professor of Christian Ethics, Emeritus, The University of the South, Sewanee, Tennessee.

Tuesday, September 22   Read Exodus 33:17-23.

Moses stepped aside, took off his shoes, and met Yahweh at the fiery bush. There he and Yahweh became friends, called each other by name. There God first pledged to go with Moses. This God who dwelt on high, who manifested himself in the burning bush, in lightnings which played fitfully around Sinai, and in the fiery pillar leading Israel on by night, now renews the covenant.

God responds to Moses' perplexity by promising to go with him and seals the promise in a theophany which reveals the character of the Eternal. "I know you by name," God says. "You have found favor in my sight. . . . I will make all my goodness pass before you, and will proclaim before you my name."

Yahweh, the friend on the journey, attended Moses, the aging leader who did not spare himself in caring for the people who blamed him for everything. Moses, driven to distraction by the quarrelsome and rebellious flock he had been given, was reassured by Yahweh's revelation of friendship. The divine name conveys at once a power, a presence, a gracious will of the One who can be trusted to do what is promised. There is this certainty and stability at the heart of the universe.

Later on, Yahweh reassured the descendants of the people whom Moses had led. "But you, Israel my servant, you, Jacob whom I have chosen, race of Abraham my friend, I have taken you up . . . have chosen you and not cast you off" (Isa. 41:8-9, NEB). In the words of Jesus, "You did not choose me, but I chose you" (John 15:16). Here lies the mystery of "chosenness," Yahweh and God's "peculiar people."

Prayer: *Loving God, you have given yourself to me; may I give myself to you. Amen.*

Wednesday, September 23   Read Psalm 99.

This psalm is a hymn of praise to the glory of God's holy name, the God who had made a self-revelation to Moses as a pledge of faithfulness.

God's character, glory, and goodness were made known to Moses as gracious and reconciling mercy. Although no human can plumb the mystery of God, we can know the Holy One as "the Lord, a god compassionate and gracious, long-suffering, ever constant and true" (Exod. 34:6-7, NEB).

The psalmist weaves these qualities of God's character into this rhapsody of ecstatic joy that Israel should have the Lord as their God. The holy God loves justice and establishes equity and deals righteously with the people. The Lord is the God who forgives and declares the people's innocence.

The psalm invites us to worship the Holy One of Israel in trembling awe. For the Lord has chosen people and has entered into covenant with them. With this covenant has come the holy law, the keeping of which is an act of joy and praise, the highest form of worship and service.

This consciousness of the intimate relation between God and God's people is expressed in Deuteronomy 14:2 in terms of chosenness: The Lord has chosen you out of all the peoples on earth to be his special possession" (NEB). This sense of being God's own people is universalized in First Peter 2:9: "You are a chosen race, a royal priesthood, a dedicated nation, and a people claimed by God for his own" (NEB).

This is the destiny which God has prepared for all humanity, for God has elected all to salvation.

Prayer: *Thou art compassionate and gracious, O Lord God, slow to anger and of great mercy. Blessed art thou forever and ever. Amen.*

Thursday, September 24   Read Phil. 2:1, 5-11.

God's own people, God's peculiar people, are those chosen, elected, to new life in Jesus Christ. God's universal purpose from the beginning of creation is to bring all creatures to himself, to fulfill creative love, the perfection of all creation. Jesus as the Christ came to call all of us as elected, chosen people, God's new creation.

We have this life with God whose name we know and who knows us by name. We share this life in common in the Body of Christ. God is with us, and that presence is experienced "in the Spirit." God's peculiar people know and experience God's presence by the encouragement and support of the Holy Spirit in the church. This is the Spirit who is *for* us, *with* us, who actively supports us, the One who is with us and stands by our side and offers us God's strengthening aid. This is the Spirit Jesus promised to send to us, the Spirit who is both the giver of life and in whom we love one another.

Thus comes the joyful outburst of Paul's hymn to the name of Jesus in whom we have, as God's peculiar people, this amazing new life. This is one of the most beautiful hymns in scripture and shows signs of being composed with great care.

Though of the nature of God, Jesus voluntarily "emptied" himself and "came down from heaven" (see also 2 Cor. 8:9). Jesus became the servant whose suffering and death brought about our salvation. At the name by which he is known, "every knee shall bow . . . and every tongue confess" that this Jesus "God has made . . . both Lord and Christ" (Acts 2:36).

Prayer: *O holy Jesus, at your name may we bow the knee and with our tongues confess your Lordship. Amen.*

Friday, September 25   Read Phil. 2:2-4, 12-13.

"Have this mind in you which is in Christ Jesus" reads also, "Let your bearing towards one another arise out of your life in Christ Jesus" (NEB). The force of the reading is "be of the same mind."

Being of the same mind with Christ Jesus involves two things which are peculiar to Christians: love of neighbor and loyalty (or obedience) to God.

Life in Christ, "our common life in Christ" (NEB), yields stirring of the heart, sharing of the spirit, warmth of affection and compassion—that same love Christ has for us directed toward one another. So, Paul writes to the Christians in Philippi, "Let your bearing towards one another arise out of your life in Christ Jesus." This is obedience.

We are not called to love the neighbor for the neighbor's sake alone, or because he or she deserves it. If God loved us because we deserved it, most of us would be unloved. God's love is unmerited—it is grace. This is the overwhelming mystery of God's gracious love. We are, then, to love the neighbor because God loves him and her, and because Christ died for him and her also. This is the peculiar motive of God's peculiar people.

And who is that neighbor, the one with whom we are to be reconciled in love and in God's love? He or she is the companion whom I am commanded to love as myself and also my most loyal neighbor. He or she is also my enemy, the one who fights against me. My neighbor is the one, near or far, in need. In anyone's hunger, nakedness, imprisonment and illness, I see the neighbor whom I am to love in obedience to God.

Prayer: *We confess to you, O gracious God, that we have not loved you with our whole heart nor our neighbors as ourselves. Amen.*

Saturday, September 26   Read Matthew 21:28-32.

Obedience is hard, sometimes. Obedience to God is demanded of Christians. "I am the Lord, your God. . . . You shall have no other gods before me" is a claim to our exclusive loyalty. This claim takes priority above all lesser claims. Loyalty to God gives all lesser loyalties their meaning. Neither power, nor money, nor nuclear deterrence, nor human loves can claim our absolute loyalty lest they become idolatrous.

This obedience to God is not to be qualified; it qualifies the Christian believers in their faithfulness to God. The way to illustrate this is by pointing to the virtue of obedience in Jesus whose loyalty to God was absolute, leading him to death on the cross. We are to be faithful as Jesus was faithful.

Jesus illustrated this requirement in the parable in today's reading. "Which of these two did as his father wished?" (NEB) Why, the first son, of course, Jesus' listeners replied. He did the bidding of his father even though he said he would not. Even the sinners and the rebellious may enter the kingdom of God in that love which is loyalty, the commitment of the self to God and to God's cause.

Most of us do not recognize the extent to which we are endemically polytheists. We know that power, and money, and nuclear deterrence, and human love are not God. But we are deluded when we give them our ultimate loyalty and obedience. Then they go by the name of God and proclaim the extent of our idolatry. That obedience which is peculiar to the faithful believer is that he or she loves the Lord with all heart and mind and strength.

Prayer: *Strengthen us in obedience, Lord, that we may show forth thy praise with our tongues and in our lives. Amen.*

Sunday, September 27   Read Exodus 33:17;
                                               Philippians 2:9-11;
                                               Matthew 21:30-31.

The worship and service of God is the Christian's vocation. We are to live each day as God's own peculiar people, as if nothing else were important. Then all things are given their own appropriate importance.

A Hasid story nicely illustrates this primacy of praise as the beginning and ending of the life of love and obedience:

Reb Yitzchak Luria prayed with extraordinary devoutness during the Days of Awe, the High Holy Days. Then he was told from heaven that there was one man in a certain town who prayed better than he did. The celebrated sage traveled there, called for the man, and asked him, "Are you a Torah scholar?" "No," said the man. "Do you know how to pray?" "No," said the man. "Then what did you do during the Days of Awe?" Answered the man, "Rabbi, I don't even know the alphabet—only from A to J. So when I came to the synagogue, and I saw all the congregation praying so devotedly, all aloud, while I can't pray at all, my heart broke inside of me. And this is what I said: 'A B C D E F G H I J. Master of the Universe, put together all these letters into words the way you understand, and I hope you'll find them acceptable.' That's what I said with a broken heart, but with all my strength. Then I started over again from the beginning: 'A B C . . . .' "

And these were the words that made more impact on the Holy One, Blessed Be He, than all the learned prayers of the saintly Reb Yitzchak Luria.

Prayer: *Sovereignty and glory and kingly power are yours everlastingly, O God. You did create all things, and by your will they were created and have their being. To you be praise and honor for ever and ever. Amen.*

THE MEANS JUSTIFIES THE END

September 28–October 4, 1987   **Jerry Litherland†**
Monday, September 28   Read Philippians 3:12-14.

To get there you must run

Paul speaks of the prize, God's call through Christ Jesus to the "life above"—a prize promised to be freely given, but hard won.

A poor young man was heard expounding on the evils of modern society and the rights he deserved because he felt cheated. A more experienced soul stepped out of the audience pushing a wheelbarrow with a pick and shovel. With solemn expression shaped by years of struggle, he assured the youth, "Indeed, the world does owe you a living. It's yours for the taking. Here are your tools. Go and take it."

The mystery of free grace is elusive until God reveals it in the fullness of each individual's time. That gift cannot be earned, yet it must be worked for. It requires no great wisdom to know we must keep running, but why fight it day after day? Grace is sufficient to each day's needs, but the promise of eternal grace makes it possible to run the whole race.

Some translations of this passage in Philippians liken the pressing on to spiritual maturity to a runner who runs a race. The prize awaiting the runner must be worth the price paid, or the race will be lost. Paul's run, straight toward the goal, sustained him from the Damascus road to Rome and beyond.

Prayer: *O God, renew the vision of my high calling that today's race may be run at my best. Amen.*

---

†Director of Human Resources, Archbold Memorial Hospital, Thomasville, Georgia.

Tuesday, September 29   Read Philippians 3:15-16.

The mature runner will run the best race

Pacing oneself, reading the course, and knowing one's capacity are important to an experienced runner. The knowledge of the "how to's" belongs to someone else until it has become yours as the experience of having been there. Hours of well-planned practice, while working to understand the meaning of each new milepost, are required to develop a mature runner. Some progress more rapidly than others, but with determination each pushes on until becoming the best runner he or she can be.

Paul leaves little room for discussion when he tells those hearing that they must have the same attitude as he if they are to be spiritually mature. He says confidently that if we don't have the proper attitude now, God will make it clear to us in the future. We must run, but we must run toward the mark. In verse 15 he adds another condition—you must run according to the rules.

Paul made the rules plain to all at Philippi, and only by committing themselves to the rules could the Philippians enter the race. Through the running of the race toward the mark—and according to the rules—God would make things clear.

The spiritually mature runner absorbs the rules through study of the word. He or she learns through daily experience to pace the steps to the long run, to know when to sprint and when to hold back. The harder the run, the better the runner understands his or her capacity.

Prayer: *O Lord, help me run a good race today that tomorrow's race may be better. Amen.*

Wednesday, September 30   Read Philippians 3:17-21.

Follow my example

"Don't do as I do; do as I say" is a common expression that many of us wish to avoid. Many are the times we have known what we wanted to achieve; yet when the smoke cleared, we found less than we had hoped. To say, "Nobody's perfect" is but small consolation when our idealistic hopes have been rudely handled by harsh reality.

Paul exhorts those who hear to follow his example. He tells us to run straight to the goal, which is eternal life, and to run as a mature runner according to the rules. Paul wishes his hearers to imitate him in the manner in which he is still running—not looking to the past but running hard in the present with an eye on the future.

Paul warns of those with different attitudes, who will end up in hell because they don't follow the rules. Most important, Paul says that with tears. Compassion for the lost is a characteristic of the mature spiritual runner. Having been there, the experienced runner knows the shortcomings of the lost.

Paul ends this passage by saying that we are citizens of heaven. He exhorts us to be like him—mature runners with eyes on the goal, running according to the rules. Because we are citizens of heaven, running the race in the grace of God, we will be with God for all eternity.

Prayer: *O God, let me truly see the person I am becoming and not dwell on the person I have been. Let me glimpse the future in my experience of today. Amen.*

Thursday, October 1   Read Numbers 27:12-14.

Run because you must

The Lord commands Moses to go up Mount Abarim and look out over the promised land. Then the Lord tells Moses that he will die without entering the promised land because he sinned in days past.

Moses, already aged, had left an adopted land and suffered the abuses of the pharaoh. He had born the fickleness of his people in forty years of wandering in the wilderness. Now, with the promised land in sight, he is told he will never live there because of one sin. That would be enough to anger anyone, but Moses' concern is not for himself but for his people. He prays that God will provide a leader to care for them. The years of struggle in a race he never wished to run had caused him to run the perfect race. The abuse of his people could not put out the fire of care and concern he bore them to the end of his days.

Many people have found themselves in a position not of their own choosing, with challenges to meet and jobs they would rather not do. An unusual courage is required at a time like this—a courage born of care and concern, a courage that will keep the runner running. As the mature runners run the race according to the rules, God replaces the "ought to" with a "want to" for those he has struggled with and loved.

Prayer: *O Lord, grant me a vision of the future, that I might see those I love into the promised land. Amen.*

Friday, October 2   Read Numbers 27:18-23.

Enable others as you go

Moses saw his people in danger of losing God's gift. The promised land was only a short distance away, but his people were as sheep without a shepherd. He knew that without a leader the prize would be lost.

Through years of leadership Moses had come to a knowledge and understanding of his people that only living, loving, and caring can give. This gave him a vision of their needs, and he prayed for a leader to continue the work to which he had given his life.

Immortality is an eternal quest; however, Moses' concern was born not of his own desire for fame and fortune but rather for caring that his children would share the promised land.

God points to Joshua as the new leader and tells Moses to give Joshua some of his, Moses', own authority. Joshua will be given advice to lead, by Eleazar the priest, but it is through the authority Moses gives him that the community of Israel will obey him. Moses had earned his position of leadership, and the authority granted him by his people was that which he passed on to Joshua.

Happy is the person who can pass on a torch earned through running the good race so that others, too, might run the race to which he or she has given or will give a lifetime.

Prayer: *O God, grant me the vision that will lead me in a life of service. Let my life so shine that others might follow my example and continue in service through your grace. Amen.*

Saturday, October 3   Read Psalm 81:1-10.

You must know the Power Source

"Because my daddy said so" was the response given by a small boy when a neighbor asked why he was going home. Unquestioned authority is an institution fast dying in an enlightened world and properly so. But what kind of a world might it be if there were a leader who could be trusted to use such authority justly and wisely? We might find that utopian state sought after in the minds of political theorists of all ages. The small boy mentioned above held his father in awe, but in later years the picture will change, not because the father changes but because the boy changes. As time passes, the boy may again hold his father in awe, when his own identity is secure and he and his father can be individuals.

How often we have read about the awesome picture of God portrayed in Old Testament literature and attributed it to childlike understandings. In our enlightened state we often speak the definitive word about who and what is real. In doing so, we allow succeeding generations to nod in understanding at our childlike portraits of God.

When we have grown sufficiently to understanding that God will be our God and we will be God's people (see Rev. 21:1-4), we will have matured. Until then we must keep an open mind to a voice sometimes heard from strange corners.

Who knows but from the mouths of babes (childlike understanding) will come real pearls.

Prayer: *O Lord, open our ears to hear your voice in the past, present, and future. Amen.*

Sunday, October 4 Read Matthew 21:33-43.

A race that is run well justifies the reward

Growing the best grapes for the production of good wine is as much an art as it is a science. The right soil, the right environment, the years of tending plants to the fruit-bearing stage, and the care of the young crop must be measured with care.

The owner of Matthew's vineyard must have planned and developed his vineyard carefully. Surely he chose his tenants with care. With this good business judgment he had every right to expect a reasonable profit. But he lost his profit, his servants, and a son as well. Plans had been made and implemented to ensure a successful venture for all. But everyone lost, because the rules of the contract were violated by greedy tenants.

Paul tells us in Philippians that a race well run by mature runners according to the rules is the key to citizenship in heaven. Because the greedy tenants failed to follow through with their agreement, they lost their lives. Others were given a chance at the reward if they would follow the rules and give the owner his proper share.

Success is no guarantee of the "life above." The right product attained by the wrong means will end badly. The eternal reward comes when the mature runner has run a good race straight toward the goal and according to the rules.

Prayer: *O Lord, let today's race be one acceptable in your eyes as a step toward eternal life. Amen.*

To Be God's People

October 5-11, 1987   **David Randell Boone†**
Monday, October 5   Read Deuteronomy 14:1-8.

In a few weeks, on November 1, we will celebrate All Saints Day. Celebrating All Saints Day affirms the mystical fellowship in Christ that all God's covenant people enjoy. And the special point of the festival is that this fellowship includes all our spiritual forbears in Israel and all those of the church who have passed on into eternity. On this occasion we often sing William How's great lines:

> O blest communion, fellowship divine!
> We feebly struggle, they in glory shine;
> Yet all are one in thee, for all are thine.
> Alleluia, Alleluia!*

In the Bible, to be a saint means to be holy, consecrated, and set apart for God. Christians are part of a people God has chosen to be special or *peculiar* (see 1 Peter 2:9, kJv). Christian life reflects values and practices that are visibly distinctive.

Even Israel's grieving and dietary customs were distinctive, so that God's covenant community could be distinguished from non-covenanted neighbors. Not eating pork reminds Hebrews of the blessings of Jewishness. What practices in our lives remind *us* that we are saints of God?

Prayer: *God of Abraham and Sarah, I am grateful for the joys and responsibilities of being called apart for you. Amen.*

---

†Pastor, Harpeth Presbyterian Church, Brentwood, Tennessee.
*"For All the Saints," the United Methodist *Book of Hymns,* no. 536.

Tuesday, October 6   Read Psalm 135:1-4.

Like other psalms, Psalm 135 was used in the worship of the Jerusalem Temple. It was to be sung by "you that stand in the house of the LORD." When the Revised Standard Version prints LORD in all capitals, we are to understand that the Hebrew text has God's distinctive, proper name: Yahweh. Actually, Yahweh is only an educated guess about how the name would have been pronounced, since 1) ancient Hebrew had no written vowels, and 2) it was taboo for anyone, even a priest or scribe, to speak this proper name of the God of Israel. Hebrew faith took its responsibility to hallow God's name very seriously indeed.

Not only is Yahweh's name special. For our psalm contrasts Yahweh's power and goodness with the impotent, lifeless gods of neighboring nations. And the later verses (15-18) confirm the impression of the author as a proud national poet thumbing his nose at foreigners with the taunt, "Our God is better than your god" (AP). The writer believed this, not because Yahweh was some sort of mascot for Israel but because of his people's experience of God's saving actions in nature and in human history.

Hebrew faith rather turned the mascot image on its head: Israel belonged to God. God chose Abraham's and Sarah's descendants to be his own special possession. This notion was heady stuff, and therefore it was sometimes hard for Hebrews to stay humble. It took the prophets to remind their fellow Jews that being God's chosen people was not an inexhaustible bowl of cherries (see Amos 3:1-2).

Prayer: *Mysterious One, whether we are yours by birth or adoption, we can never deserve such steadfast love. Keep us humble and ready to extend the love we have learned from you to every person we meet today. Amen.*

Wednesday, October 7   Read Psalm 135:5-7.

This section of Psalm 135 celebrates Yahweh's lordship over nature. Note in verse 5 of the Revised Standard Version text the two forms LORD and Lord, reflecting God's proper name and, in the second instance, the Hebrew word for one who has mastery and control and therefore deserves respect.

God does what he pleases meteorologically. I once heard a Protestant theologian say that by asking one simple question he could learn a lot about one's personal theology. The question was: "Do you pray for changes in the weather?"

I asked this of a farmer in my congregation. His answer: Absolutely not. "Even when you are needing rain badly?" I pressed. "No, not even then," he responded, "because what is good weather for one person's pleasure or prosperity can be disaster for someone else. Best to leave it with God." Together we agreed that the Book of Common Prayer petition for "seasonal weather" is a good compromise!

Whether the weather is seasonal or extreme, the psalmist's faith is that God is immanently involved in it in a causal way. Our modern passive constructions—"clouds are forming" or "it is raining"—are foreign to Hebrew thought on the weather, which boldly claims that "God makes the clouds rise," and "God makes lightnings for the rain."

The Creator of the natural world is still involved in it. When we witness a variety of climates and seasons, the rich hues and teeming fertility of land, water, forest, mountain, and sky, the lyric beauty of a sunrise or the awesome power of a volcano, we are moved to adore and also respect this God!

Prayer: *Author of all life, open my senses to feel you moving within nature. Amen.*

Thursday, October 8   Read Psalm 135:8-14.

We move now from considering the greatness of Yahweh, Lord of nature to Yahweh, Lord of history. Reflection on God's purposeful directing of human history begins with the exodus experience, conceived here as *the* redeeming event whereby God chose Israel. The exodus informed Israel's collective consciousness of God's identity and that of the nation of Israel. Yahweh heard the cries of an oppressed slave people and brought them out of slavery to freedom in a new land. A compassionate God, Yahweh gets his hands dirty to help human beings in pain. That God is gracious and compassionate has always been the fundamental thing for Jews and Christians to confess when asked to articulate their faith.

This liberating God still "vindicate(s) his people." We perceive God's work of deliverance today in places where people live in exceptional bondage. In South Africa and in other places humans cry out to God for help in becoming free. And faith discerns God's Spirit creatively stirring upon the face of the chaotic waters of political oppression.

What about violence? The repeated verbs "smote" and "slew" provoke the sad thought that liberation movements, whether of the past or the present, are seldom without physical conflict. God smote the firstborn of Egypt, both human and animal. Americans recall that we have taken up arms in the cause of freedom many times. Yet the terrible reality of bloodshed, now made unavoidable by television news, leads us to hope with Martin Luther King, Jr., that freedom for oppressed people may be achieved through nonviolent means.

Prayer: *God, our champion, in choosing us to be your people you made us free. Show us how we can cooperate with your purpose of freedom for all people. Amen.*

Friday, October 9   Read Philippians 4:1-3.

When Paul pleaded with Euodia and Syntyche to agree in the Lord, he probably did not think they were going to achieve an identical understanding on whatever it was that had caused their argument. What he meant was: "For God's sake, put your differences in perspective and stop allowing them to disrupt the church's corporate life. Agree to disagree. Don't let your conflicting pride destroy the community of God's people you have both worked so hard to plant."

All congregations have a Euodia and Syntyche problem from time to time. And it is not just the women's problem! It is human, and many Christians get caught up in it. What is important is how we handle it.

Those of us who live in cities often choose simply to leave one congregation for another, seeking to avoid unpleasantness or seeking a group where our will can dominate more easily. Sometimes that works. More often, we find that we are faced with new conflicts in the new situation. Chronic church-hoppers seem to have little capacity for real community life.

Euodia and Syntyche were without such options. For it is almost certain that they belonged to the only Christian group in Philippi. So unless they wanted to drop out of the church altogether, they had to stay and face the music. Enter Paul's one word of conflict-management advice: forbearance. Some of us like to call this being subject to brothers and sisters in the Lord, meaning: 1) you are free to argue your view, but 2) you are also expected to defer to the collective wisdom of the community, and 3) the health of the whole church is more important than one person getting his or her own way.

Suggestion for prayer: *Picture someone in the church who is a thorn in your side. Pray for that person. For yourself, pray for the grace of forbearance.*

Saturday, October 10   Read Philippians 4:4-9.

A friend once remarked to me that he found it difficult to trust anyone who smiled all the time. He was reacting against a version of proper Christian demeanor that demands constant cheerfulness and backslapping jollity. Now this behavior may be the genuine expression of a personality. But it may also be compulsive. Anyone who has ever been exhorted from funeral pulpit or graveside not to cry or be sad about a tragic death will recognize what I describe.

The joy Paul recommends, on the other hand, is not rooted in the variations of human personality or disposition, but in Christ. It is a gift that transcends our glandular differences. It is the joy of Christian freedom. Those who trust Christ are put right with God apart from the demands of the law, any kind of law. Earlier in this letter, Paul depicts Christian life as free. That is, God has called us for a life of knowing Christ and the power of his resurrection—and of suffering for the gospel in the hope of our own bodily resurrection with Christ (see Phil. 3:8-11). We can forget keeping the rules as a way of being good enough for inclusion in the chosen people. We are already in. We are free. And that is a cause for joy.

This being true, I am free to practice a joyful *piety*—a good old word meaning an intentional and conscientious walk with God—without worrying about whether or not I am appearing to be conventionally *pious*. God does not require me to wear a stained-glass persona! And when I am secure in this freedom, I need not be threatened when disagreement within the church arises.

Prayer: *Lord, when life becomes grey and depressing and doleful, keep me aware that you are for me no matter what happens. Amen.*

Sunday, October 11   Read Matthew 22:1-14.

Matthew has reworked a parable of Jesus (see Luke 14:16-24) into an allegory of God's way with the covenant people. The characters in the allegory have direct historical counterparts that Matthew's audience of Jewish Christians would have immediately recognized. The king is God; the marriage feast, the Messianic age; the servants who are sent out, prophets such as John the Baptist; the invited guests who will not come, the Jews; the king's army, the Roman army which had besieged Jerusalem in the year 70; the inviting of street people to the banquet, the Christian mission to the Gentiles; and the close review of the guests by the king, the final judgment.

The daunting phrase is the last one in verse 14: "Many are called, but few are chosen." How are we to interpret it? The use of common sense may be best. Many hear the message of the kingdom of God, but only a few accept it. This affirms my personal responsibility to accept or reject the gospel.

And yet, the forcible removal from the feast of the man in the allegory who offended because he was not wearing a wedding garment disturbs us. We want more information to assure us of the fairness of the king's action. Was the fellow thrown out because he *could* have dressed appropriately but did not care enough to do so? Or did he find himself embarrassed before the king because he did not own a wedding garment? Yet more information is not available. So if we feel uneasy about the harshness of this last part, we can read Luke's version; or else we can consider that uneasy is exactly how Matthew intends us to feel.

Prayer: *Lavish God, we thank you that by calling us into your kingdom you have invited us to a banquet. Clothe us with your righteousness, that we may not be found wanting when crises come upon us. Amen.*

SUFFERING: ITS PLACE IN LIFE

October 12-18, 1987   **Douglas Bowling†**
Monday, October 12   Read Job 2.

Suffering is a part of the human condition

Why did God let my baby die? When is God going to heal my paralysis and get me out of this wheelchair? Where is a loving God when innocent children are dying from starvation? These are questions we have all heard. They are questions of agony.

In the second chapter of Job we have an answer: Suffering is a part of the human condition. "Shall we accept good from God and not trouble?" (2:10, NIV) This is neither the answer we want, nor the response we wish to hear. But let us remember that this statement came after Job had lost land, servants, crops, money and—his most precious possession—10 children. His words were not pious platitudes. He had been to hell and back. But he genuinely believed that the loving sovereignty of God could be trusted, that pain was as much a part of life as joy.

Acknowledging the normalcy of suffering reduces the anger we feel concerning its injustice. Owning pain relieves fear. Claiming the value of suffering leaves a quiet assurance that we can and will—by God's love and grace—survive and overcome.

Prayer: *God of love and mercy, I thank you for being present at every single one of my sufferings. Somehow that has made them bearable. Amen.*

---

†Minister, Washington Street United Methodist Church, Columbia, South Carolina.

Tuesday, October 13   Read 2 Corinthians 12:1-10.

Suffering produces a variety of responses

Ed wept at the graveside of his son, Steve, a handsome athlete who had died within minutes after an automobile accident. When I saw Ed four years later, much healing had taken place. He loved people more, was more gentle.

Fran and Bart lost their nine-year-old son to leukemia. It was devastating. I saw them ten years later. Fran was despondent. Bart said angrily, "I don't let myself remember those days!"

Ed had become "better." Fran and Bart had become "bitter." What was the difference? Suffering produces a variety of responses. Some people respond to suffering with *resignation*. When tragedy strikes, they withdraw from life. While such withdrawal produces a measure of safety, it rarely completely protects them from further suffering. And worst of all, it causes minds and relationships to atrophy.

Others respond to suffering with *denial*. It does not fit into their belief system to feel pain. What is most frightening about denial is that invariably the grief emerges later with far greater intensity.

Paul provides Christians with an *alternative* response to suffering. He says, "There was given me a thorn in my flesh. . . . I pleaded with the Lord to take it away from me. But he said to me, . . . 'My power is made perfect in weakness'" (NIV). Paul admitted that he was suffering and confessed that he was most displeased to be in pain. But he refused to resign from life because of it. He saw his suffering as an opportunity for growth. He believed God could use that suffering to make his witness brighter and better.

Prayer: *God of care, as we suffer we tend to withdraw into bitterness. Help us, through the pains and sorrows, to grow. Amen.*

Wednesday, October 14   Read 1 Thess. 1:1-10;
                                                              Matthew 22:15-22.

Suffering can result from faithfulness

It was during the 1960s. America was in the midst of social and racial upheaval. Jack Shea, 41, was a successful, high-paid oil executive with a major petroleum company. He was good at his job. Then things changed. After the assassination of President John Kennedy, Jack went through some tough self-examination. He realized that he had been a success in his business, but a failure as a citizen of Dallas. Jack Shea took the risk. He wrote an article that was picked up by *Look* magazine. He entitled it, "Memo about a Dallas Citizen."

Jack's article produced a rage in Dallas and brought him trouble in his job. His company demanded that he never put another word in public print without having it first approved by his superiors. To have agreed to such a policy would have been an absolute desertion of his faith and principles. He lost friends and felt like an outsider in his own city. He finally quit his job.

Jack Shea suffered because he was faithful. In today's reading in Matthew, our Lord was tested. His faithfulness to God brought him open animosity from the Pharisees. The Savior faced it directly: "You hypocrites!" he exclaimed. "Why are you trying to trap me?" (TEV) Jesus' faithfulness brought him suffering, too.

Being a Christian is not always a matter of being happy. Sometimes it is a matter of being true. And on occasion, that truth brings suffering with it.

Prayer: *Dear God, it is not easy to be loyal to you. Give us the strength to share in the sufferings of the cross of Jesus. Amen.*

Thursday, October 15   Read Ruth 1:1-19*a*.

Suffering sensitizes us to the hurts of others

This is one of the most moving stories in the Old Testament. Naomi loses her husband in death. Then her two sons die. Left with two foreign daughters-in-law, Orpah and Ruth, she makes the decision to return to her homeland. As they travel along, Naomi decides it is selfish to remove these young women from their native land, so she releases them. Orpah tearfully departs. Ruth commits herself to go wherever Naomi goes.

What motivated Naomi to release her daughters-in-law? It wasn't that she didn't love them. She did. That she wasn't interested in their future. She was. She was able to release them because of her own past pain. Her recollection of the death of her own husband and the loss of her sons sensitized her to the hurt these young women might experience in a strange land.

It is out of our own pain—as we face it, struggle with it, plumb its depths—that we begin to develop the resources that enable us to suffer with others. Almost always the people who work for the abolition of hunger, oppression, and prejudice are persons who have suffered.

If pain is a part of our past, we can celebrate it. The remembrance of suffering can empower us to turn our focus from ourselves toward others. Through this ministry of remembrance, we are enabled to see the hungry and *feel* their hunger; see the oppressed and *experience* their oppression. This inner identification can open whole new areas of ministry which work for God's glory and the good of others.

Prayer: *Creator of all, we have suffered. Assist us as we seek to turn that suffering around, to use it in ministry with others. Through Christ. Amen.*

Friday, October 16　　　　　Read Philippians 4:8-13;
　　　　　　　　　　　　　　　Psalm 146:1-2.

Suffering met with praise produces joy

A man was returning home from a conference on praise. Lulled by the monotony of the highway, he fell asleep at the wheel. His car went down an embankment and landed upside down below a bridge. He crawled from beneath the wreckage, unhurt. Noticing a crowd gathering on the bridge above, he crawled atop the overturned auto, looked up at them . . . and sang the doxology!

When Paul wrote the church at Philippi, he was imprisoned. Yet he said, "Fill your minds with those things that are good and that deserve praise" (TEV). It was not that Paul's life was pain-free. It was rather that he had learned—as had the driver of the overturned car—that suffering met with praise produces joy.

When we are ill or discouraged, if we begin to consider all the bad that can happen, we tend to feel worse. If we focus on all the good that *has* happened, we usually feel better. Giving thanks in the midst of suffering is not a denial of the reality of the pain. It is, rather, a Christian's affirmation that God's grace and love are larger than one's own personal suffering.

When I was a child, I remember singing an old gospel hymn entitled, "Does Jesus Care?" It listed a number of difficult situations which would try one's faith. Many years later, I experienced tragedy. The Sunday following a very sad funeral, I did not feel like attending worship, but I forced myself to go. The choir sang that old hymn. It reminded me of the many times that Jesus had cared for me. Because I had gone to worship to praise God—even though not feeling it—I was free to receive God's gift of joy.

Prayer: *O God, help us to find the joy that comes from praising you, even while we suffer. Amen.*

Saturday, October 17   Read Psalm 139; 146:5-10.

Suffering is never outside the knowledge of God

You cannot read Psalm 139 and believe you are outside God's awareness and love. The writer's phrases are beautiful beyond comparison: "You know everything I do"; "You understand all my thoughts"; "You are all around me on every side" (TEV). There are over 20 such affirmations in this one short psalm.

This psalm is important to us because it offers us a fourfold hope. First, it says that God knows us—knows us personally. We are not strangers (vv. 1-6). Second, it clearly states that wherever we are, God's love precedes us! God is with us and will not let us go (vv. 7-12). Next, there is an assurance in the psalm that our lives are not accidents of nature, that God created us and willed that we have purpose and meaning (vv. 13-18). The fourth assurance is that God is one with whom we may communicate. Our God is approachable, available, one to whom we may say, "Search me . . . try me . . . lead me" (vv. 23-24). These are words you speak to someone you trust.

Our belief that God cares about our suffering is based on much more than one psalm. The Bible says it in scores of other places. God's servants, who show concern for us, remind us of it. Our faith leads us to believe it. Sometimes the crisis experiences themselves serve as a reminder that God cares. While life is normal, God goes unnoticed. The crises bring to recollection the numerous occasions when God has been faithful.

Prayer: *Help us, O God, to tailor our faith to the magnitude of your goodness. May each of our problems fade into insignificance through the light of your presence. In Christ's name. Amen.*

Sunday, October 18   Read Job 19:25-26.

Suffering is only temporary for the Christian

Job suffered tremendously. Few persons I have known have experienced as much pain. Yet he worshiped God and did not break. He refused to recant his faith. How did he do it? Job says, "I know that my Redeemer lives, and . . . I shall see God" (TEV). Job knew that the pain and death in his life were only temporary. He was convinced that God would ultimately make things right. He was not sure that he would live to see it, but he was sure of God's victory in eternity.

In one of my first pastorates, I received a call early one morning. I was informed that a young mother in my congregation had been rushed to the hospital. A mild case of influenza had developed quickly into a life-threatening illness. When I arrived at the hospital another of my church members met me in the lobby with the painful message, "Carole has just died." Two days later, on my way to the funeral, I stopped at Carole's mother's home. I walked past the potted plants sent in love, the friends who had gathered there, and went back to the den. I took this saddened mother's hands in mine. I tried to say something comforting. She listened gently, then said, "Preacher, what in the world would I do without my risen Lord?" She knew that her suffering was only temporary. She counted on resurrection.

I don't know what is going on in your life. Maybe suffering is thundering down. Perhaps adversity seems years away. Just in case, think of Job's way of handling pain: Count on God's resurrection.

Prayer: *God of compassion, it is healing balm to know that in the end your love and power will wipe away every tear. Through Christ. Amen.*

TRAITS OF THE CHRISTIAN LEADER

October 19-25, 1987   **Perry C. Cotham†**
Monday, October 19   Read 1 Timothy 3:1-13;
Titus 1:5-9.

In my own church fellowship, today's scripture readings are often called qualifications for church leaders. *Qualification* is an interesting word. We have qualifications for a job, qualifications for surgeons, qualifications for beauticians and barbers, qualifications for airplane pilots. The word implies a minimum standard of fitness for the particular profession or task described. Qualification does not speak much of excellence, only to the barest minimum required for the job.

One might well read the lists of qualifications in the pastoral epistles and ask how any of these young churches could possibly have had candidates already meeting these qualifications.

Are these passages on church leadership to be discarded? Not at all. The passages should be examined in light of other New Testament texts on the subject of leadership. Additionally, these passages might better be viewed as listings of *descriptions* of Christian leaders rather than qualifications. "Look for this kind of person as your leader," the writer is saying.

In our study and meditations this week, we will reflect on some of the traits of God's leaders—both the few who are appointed to church office and the many who exert influence for good in both church and society.

Prayer: *Dear God, you have called me to serve you in my own way. Encourage me by the realization that no one ever completely measures up to your calling. Then discipline me so that I may devote myself to do at any given time the best I can. Through Jesus. Amen.*

---

†Free-lance writer and editor; former professor at David Lipscomb College; Nashville, Tennessee.

Tuesday, October 20   Read Ruth 2:1-13.

Kindness and gentleness are traits of a Christian leader.

The definition of a leader is elusive. We usually think of leaders as being those rare men and women who make their way to the top of some organization or institution. Even then we realize that those who appear on the organization chart to have the greatest authority may not be the ones who wield the greatest power.

God has a leadership role for each of us. A parent has great influence in the home. A businessperson can exert influence in the work environment. A student can exert influence in school. The essence of leadership is influence.

Today's reading relates the meeting of Ruth and Boaz. Ruth gained permission from Naomi to glean in the fields, and soon she attracted the attention of Boaz, a prosperous kinsman of Naomi.

Boaz obviously was a prosperous farmer who was able to hire a number of servants. In his kindness to Ruth, however, Boaz displayed a strong trait of godly leadership. Ruth was so moved by his tenderheartedness and generosity that she falls prostrate before him and asks, "Why are you so kind as to take notice of me when I am only a foreigner?" (NEB) Boaz then commends her for her venture of faith in a new land and a new religion and offers blessing: "The Lord reward your deed; may the Lord God of Israel, under whose wings you have come to take refuge, give you all that you deserve" (NEB).

Prayer: *Call us to remembrance, dear God, that the virtues of Christian leadership are not human achievements but fruits of your Spirit in our lives. Enable us to take the lead in being kind to one another, as you have shown kindness and forgiven us in and through Christ. Amen.*

Wednesday, October 21   Read Psalm 128.

A Christian leader truly fears the Lord.

To fear the Lord does not mean to be frightened by God. This is something most of us may have learned quite early in our Christian experience. We know that to fear the Lord means reverence and respect. And yet, how does that fear translate into ordinary attitude and action?

The psalmist provides an answer to this question in the parallelism of Hebrew poetry. To fear the Lord is to live according to God's will (v. 1). Fearing the Lord means to repudiate self-will. To listen to God's voice. To think and live by godly attitudes. To respect God's moral law. Those who take the lead in fearing the Lord become the Christian leaders of any generation.

Fearing the Lord and striving to discern and follow God's will is never easy. Leaders are made of flesh and blood, not marble and stained glass. Even the great leaders of biblical times were fallen, fallible, and frail. Moses was easily angered. David broke half of the Ten Commandments in that entire episode involving Bathsheba, and yet he is called a "man after [God's] own heart." Righteous Noah became drunk. Faithful Abraham was capable of both lying and risking his wife's chastity for his personal safety. Impetuous Peter could also lie for his own safety.

God's leaders know that disabilities need not disqualify and that human failures need not be fatal.

Prayer: *Dear God, teach us what it means truly to fear you. Lead us to know that when we think we are strong in our own strength we are the most pathetically weak of all people. Through our own acknowledged weakness, give us grace and give us strength. Through Jesus. Amen.*

Thursday, October 22   Read Mark 10:42-45.

A Christian leader devotes his or her life to the service of others.

Christian and secular understandings of leadership are not identical. In our text, Jesus introduced an altogether new style of leadership and expressed the difference between the old and new styles. Among the followers of Jesus, leadership is not synonymous with lordship. We are called to be servants, not bosses; slaves, not masters.

Thinking of leadership in a servant-mode is a difficult task. To link leadership with terms such as "servant" or "slave" seems ridiculous to us, because we are usually associating these terms with a person who has no significant position or power. No one would think of asking a waiter, a janitor, a taxi-driver, a floor-scrubber, "Excuse me, would you tell me what to do!" Yet that is at the very heart of Christian leadership—a leadership by the power of example.

All true leaders exercise power. But the power of the worldly leader is through authority and position, and the power of the Christian leader is through example and service. One style of leadership is fostered by pride; the other is rooted in humility.

But I believe Jesus' main reason for his teaching must have been related to the intrinsic worth of human beings. If human beings are the crowning work of God's creation, if God has endowed them with an eternal soul, then they must be served, not manipulated; respected, not exploited. It is in humble service that we are most like Jesus; though he was Lord of all, he became the servant of all.

Prayer: *O God, we look to Jesus as the ultimate example of leadership by servanthood. May we see him clearly. Amen.*

Friday, October 23   Read Matthew 22:34-46.

A Christian leader demonstrates both a deep level of love for God and a love for neighbor that is equal to his or her love for self.

Once the *Nashville Banner* ran a series of lessons on the Ten Commandments. Then the *Banner* sponsored a contest in which readers were asked to submit an eleventh commandment. A sampling of the entries might include "Thou shalt respect the universe and all creatures and things therein" and "Thou shalt not live thy life in ignorance." My personal eleventh commandment is "Thou shalt not take thyself seriously."

Jesus cites a great commandment which appears in today's text and twice more in the Gospels. Obviously, a Christian leader is one who deeply loves and respects both God and neighbor. Jesus linked the two kinds of love. To the extent that I strengthen my relationship with the Lord, then to that extent I enrich my relationships with other people.

A Christian simply cannot lead others without adhering to the love ethic. The maximum standard for loving the Lord is with all our heart, soul, and mind. This, no doubt, has created many interesting three-point sermon outlines, with preachers giving their personal meanings for heart, soul, and mind. Jesus means simply that we are to love God with all our energies and without reservation or conditions.

These words of Jesus, "Love your neighbor as yourself," follow closely. We *will* love our neighbor more when it fully impacts on us how much God loves and forgives us.

Prayer: *Dear God, take away our fear of risking to love so that we may devote our energies to loving you and loving our brothers and sisters, just as Christ has loved us. Through him. Amen.*

Saturday, October 24   Read 1 Thessalonians 2:1-6.

The Christian leader is a person of integrity.

In our readings for the next two days, we will learn a great deal from Paul about the traits needed for effective Christian leadership. Few, if any, are more important than integrity.

Clearly, Paul had been accused of insincerity. His enemies said that he was more concerned with making money from his converts than with presenting authentic teaching. Paul was being represented as nothing more than a preaching vagrant.

Paul's defense is masterly. He reminded his readers of how much he had suffered physically for his ministry and how boldly he had preached the gospel in a conflict-ridden environment. He claimed that his exhortation involved no falsehood and no guile. The word rendered "guile" originally had reference to catching by means of a bait; from this it was used of any cunning or deceitful effort to ensnare people.

Paul tells his readers that he also refused flattery and sought only to please God. A man or woman who seeks first and foremost to be a people-pleaser cannot be an authentic Christian leader.

Flattery is a symptom of insecurity. Furthermore, flattery and manipulation render leadership ineffective. There is a quote I have heard often, though attributed to various people, that is worth sharing: "I don't know the secret of success, but I do know the secret of failure—trying to please everybody."

Prayer: *Dear God, you know our thoughts and our motives better even than we know them ourselves. Inspire in all of us the desire to seek the truth, the will to love and respect the truth, and the courage to speak the truth in love at all times. Through Christ who is truth. Amen.*

Sunday, October 25   Read 1 Thessalonians 2:6-12.

As Paul continues his defense to the Thessalonians, he mentions several positive attributes of Christian leaders:

Non-authoritarian. Paul could have entered the city with great pomp and insisted on first-class treatment. How easy it is to abuse spiritual influence, especially by using such statements as "God is leading me to do this" or "The Lord wants you to . . ."

Kind sensitivity. Paul compares his behavior to that of a nurse among children. He had become one with them, giving them tender care and nurture.

Fondly affectionate. Paul and his companions had cherished such a deep regard for the Thessalonians that he now employs a most unusual word, found only here in the New Testament, to express this real depth of feeling. Paul's loving attachment to people is at odds with the notion that leaders must be coolly detached and emotionally distant from their followers.

Self-sacrificial. Throughout their stay in Thessalonica, Paul and his co-workers had been continually sharing themselves. Unless people can see in us an embodiment of the truth, then we are merely imparting facts and ideas without imparting life.

Diligent labor. Paul reminds his readers of the incessant toil undertaken with a view of imposing no burden on those to whom they preached. Adding industry to great ideals and vision is a hallmark of history's great leaders.

Enthusiastic affirmation. Christian leaders want only to bring out the best in their followers. They love and encourage as a parent would a child. They want others to reach their full Christian potential.

Prayer: *Prince of Peace, control my will. Transform me to become like you, and equip me to serve in your name. Amen.*

BLESSED ARE

October 26–November 1, 1987   **Peter van Eys†**
Monday, October 26   Read Matthew 5:1-12.

The Beatitudes offer a challenge to any reader. None can listen to their sheer beauty without being touched by their power of insight. We join a long parade of persons who have sought to understand them.

The Beatitudes are a part of that great body of work known as the Sermon on the Mount. Matthew has compiled many of the great teachings and statements of Jesus in a discourse that is unequaled in scripture. The Sermon on the Mount speaks of the Christian life and of the Christian ethic with a perspective that Jesus is more than just a prophet, more than just a teacher; he is the harbinger and embodiment of the kingdom of God.

We must realize the context of these words. Jesus is speaking from an understanding of Jewish thought and prophecy to persons equally versed. He offers an ethical standard based upon confidence in God and centered in the hope of salvation. The Beatitudes, as well as the entire text of the Sermon on the Mount, are incomprehensible without the transforming power of God.

To read these verses without God is either to laugh or despair; but to read these verses with God is to open one's life to a deeper communion and a vital faith.

Prayer: *O God, help us as we seek to grow through prayerful study of the Beatitudes. May we read with eyes that search, minds that seek, and hearts that embrace. Amen.*

---

†Minister, St. James United Methodist Church, N. Baltimore, Ohio.

Tuesday, October 27   Read Matthew 5:3.

The first beatitude is considered by many the cornerstone upon which the others are built. It speaks with timeless relevance, and we are compelled to give serious thought to it.

Both Matthew and Luke include this beatitude in their Gospels. However, there is a difference between the two that should not be overlooked. Luke writes, "Blessed are you poor" (6:20), speaking obviously in terms of material possessions, while Matthew qualifies his audience as the "poor in spirit." Our possessions often separate us from God. Our material wealth heightens our personal pride and removes us from the body of humanity. The poor understand dependence, and that may translate into a deeper understanding of God; for we are all needy persons before our Creator.

But the subtlety of Matthew's words is beautiful. To realize one's material poverty may or may not nurture one's relationship to God. But to realize one's spiritual poverty is to begin experiencing God anew. Our lives are journeys—journeys of the soul seeking the Maker. The poor in spirit are those believers who long daily to be closer to God, who desire to grow in wisdom, and who are the most faithful to the constant need for God's renewing grace. We are all the poor in spirit when we discover our souls yearn for God.

The benediction is most striking in its use of the present tense. To accept that one is poor in spirit is to participate in the kingdom of God. For the kingdom is experienced where created and Creator are truly bound together; and those who seek shall find.

Prayer: *O God, help us lay aside possessions and emotions that separate us from you. May we be as the poor in spirit, those who know their need to grow each day. Amen.*

Wednesday, October 28   Read Matthew 5:4.

"Blessed are those who mourn." As a local church pastor, I have found this particular beatitude the one most often cited. Death has no strangers.

Jesus realized that mourning in and of itself is not a blessed experience. Rather, the discoveries of the grief process give birth to that blessedness. Our natural tendency is to run away from or to deny feelings that are painful. We seek to avoid grieving because it hurts. However, those who embrace their sorrow find arms that sustain.

We assume that to give in to mourning is to be weak; and we want to be strong. Yet, Jesus taught that those who mourn find a strength far greater than themselves. The English word *comfort* is derived from the Latin phrase "with strength." As we experience the painful times of grief, we find the strength of God present with us; and we are strengthened by a greater power. To mourn is to admit our need for God and to allow God's healing presence to strengthen us.

For me, there is an additional viewpoint to ponder here: Blessed are those who realize they are sinners and mourn for their sins. Again, the power lies in our admission of our need. We do not have the strength to live in the midst of the world's temptations without God's help. The first step is to know and mourn our own sinful nature.

I was struck recently by the thought that *mourning* and *morning* are pronounced alike. Those who claim mourning discover the power of God and the light of a new day, just as surely as those who claim the morning.

Prayer: *O God, may we be able to accept our pain and our sinfulness, knowing that in our weakness we will find your strength. Amen.*

Thursday, October 29   Read Matthew 5:5.

Each beatitude brings to the reader's mind a different image. The majority speak of conditions that we would not wish upon ourselves; but only the third one seems to create a negative impression. Not many of us desire to be called meek in the contemporary sense. Somehow, we have taken the word *meek* to mean cowardly, weak, or without substance. But Jesus probably had a very different concept in mind.

Recently as I was driving the interstate system through Nashville and honking my horn profusely, I realized what meekness means. To be meek is to be non-aggressive. Blessed are those who stand humbly before the throne of God and courageously before the throne of Caesar without thought of personal gain. Blessed are those who do not take advantage of the privilege to enjoy human relationships but rest upon the promises of God. Blessed are those who place their hope in the Creator of all things, for they know that God provides for their needs. They are the meek.

The fruit of meekness is the realization that God indeed owns all creation. No matter how hard we work or how aggressive we become, we only possess that which God permits us. We are not due anything; we receive from a loving parent. Thus, as Jesus affirms, "Blessed are the meek, for they shall inherit the earth." There is no other way for us to receive than as heirs before God. Those who live non-aggressive lives before God and humanity reflect the deeper truth that without God we have nothing, but through God we have all we need.

Prayer: *O God, help us to be meek so that we may receive the richness of your love and mercy which has too often been hidden by our aggressiveness. Amen.*

Friday, October 30   Read Matthew 5:7.

The merciful are those who demonstrate mercy. The merciful have an inner feeling of love that is displayed through acts of mercy, each based upon the presupposition of equal dispensation. God is often characterized in scripture as a merciful being; but that mercy has a definite development through the Old and New Testaments.

The God of the Old Testament does not separate the concept of mercy from the act of mercy. Mercy does not exist without the act. Furthermore, that mercy is part of the experience between God and the chosen people. Through the covenant relationship, God's people may rightly call upon the mercy of God. Throughout the Old Testament, we find divine love manifested through saving acts of mercy.

The New Testament builds upon this theme. The ministry of Jesus also contains several acts of mercy: healing the sick, feeding the hungry, even raising the dead. Each is designed to offer wholeness to broken lives.

What is important to recall is the gift of mercy to the covenant people. In the Old Testament, the chosen were the people of Israel; however, through Jesus, God has established a new covenant open to all. Today, the merciful are those people who understand and accept the new covenant.

Again, the concept is not separate from the action. God's mercy is offered through the saving act of Jesus. Thus, we cannot fully comprehend God's mercy if we are not merciful. Blessed are the merciful, for they have entered into the new covenant with God. They know the gift of salvation in Christ—God's greatest act of mercy.

Prayer: *Dear Lord, stir our hearts to receive your saving grace and our place within your covenant people. May we know your mercy by being merciful. Amen.*

Saturday, October 31   Read Matthew 5:9.

The word *peace* has three basic meanings: the absence of conflict, being in a right relationship with God, and serenity of spirit and mind. I imagine that Jesus was speaking to each of these understandings as he uttered this particular beatitude. His day knew the horrors of war. His community realized the pain of separation from the Lord. His people felt the anxiety of troubled souls.

The present age has a similar situation. Peace is a benchmark word in our society but a sadly absent reality. Peacemakers are few and far between. Nevertheless, the challenge to some and the call to others is very clear. We are to be peacemakers in this world. We are to live as people who feel at one with God and who feel unique and important within God's plan. We are to trust in a Lord who knows, hears, sees, and delivers us from our problems. Then as we participate in God's peace, we are able to experience the pains of life in a healthy manner. Though our lives may be touched consistently by the harsh side of life, we will place ourselves in God's loving arms.

The greatest peacemaker was Jesus, whom we hail as the Son of God. Therefore, we find the key to fathoming this benediction in the person of Christ. Those who seek to be a part of the ongoing peacemaking presence of our Savior reflect the true nature of Sonship. When we accept the peace that God offers and in turn offer it to others, we transcend the world and claim status as children of God.

Prayer: *O God, in the spirit of your Son Jesus may we live for peace in the world through complete faith in your providential care. Amen.*

Sunday, November 1   Read Matthew 5:1-12.

A week has not permitted us opportunity to reflect upon all of the beatitudes in Matthew's Gospel. Nevertheless, I believe that we have managed to ascertain the thrust of their thought. Jesus is offering to any who would listen a new perspective on relating to God and to God's creation.

To close our week, I wish to consider these two words: *blessed* and *reward*. *Blessed* has been the common word linking the beatitudes, and it means literally "happy" or "fortunate." Those who came from the Old Testament tradition would have understood blessedness in light of material possessions as their due for righteous living, with an emphasis on the future. When Jesus spoke, he captured the sense of future and the relation of the faithful; however, the fruit of that blessedness lay in the kingdom of heaven rather than in material wealth.

Our text for today underscores the excitement our impending reward should generate. We who are blessed should rejoice. Our reward will be great, and we will join a host of faithful persons throughout history. Again, Jesus bases his understanding of reward on the rabbinic teaching of his day—that all are called to be righteous and are rewarded according to their toil. It is the latter statement from which he departs. God indeed rewards the faithful through the sacrifice of Christ, but it is a gift that we can never earn.

This reward motif is finally modified by the mystery that, even though Jesus speaks of a day when all will believe and claim the kingdom, those who enter the proper relationship with God through Christ are already participating in that kingdom.

Prayer: *O Lord, may we be your blessed people, manifesting today your kingdom which is to come. Amen.*

THE DAY OF THE LORD

November 2-8, 1987   **Donald C. Schark†**
Monday, November 2   Read Amos 5:18-20.

God's coming among us in triumph has long been the hope of many people. The prophet cried out to God, "Oh, that you would rend the heavens and come down" (Isa. 64:1, NIV), hoping that God's presence might set right the tumbled priorities of the world. Many today hope that the day of the Lord is near and that God might judge and change the lives of others.

Amos teaches that the day of the Lord is not a time when God merely confirms who and what we are and punishes those who live contrary to us. Rather, the day of the Lord is darkness and confusion, since the presence of God always brings judgment. Jesus, the eternal Word made flesh, brought judgment wherever he went. His measure of grace, justice, and mercy cast a long shadow over the bright treasures of false religiosity.

The mystic St. John of the Cross wrote that God's presence always brings a darkness that eclipses our own righteousness. In that darkness we are forced to examine our shortcomings without the option of exalting our own holiness by pointing to the sins of others. The day of the Lord means judgment, "pitch-dark, without a ray of brightness" (NIV), in which hope depends not upon our righteousness but upon the mercy of God.

Prayer: *O God of light, help us in your presence to find the glow of love that draws us to your mercy. Amen.*

---

†Pastor, Azalia-London United Methodist churches, Dundee, Michigan.

Tuesday, November 3   Read Amos 5:21-24.

The day of the Lord means repudiation.

God speaks in very strong language about the feasts, meetings, sacrifices, and songs of the chosen people. "I hate, . . . I despise, . . . I cannot stand, . . . I will not listen" (NIV). The people of Israel thought that naturally God would be pleased with their actions. They failed to see that God expected something else from the people called by God's name. Our priorities are not always God's. When we assume that they are, we run the risk of doing those things that seem religious but neither help others nor glorify God.

"It is a dreadful thing to fall into the hands of the living God," (10:31, NIV) writes the author of Hebrews, because God so often turns our priorities around and repudiates our best efforts. God challenges the way we treat others, just as he challenged the society in Amos' day.

"Let justice roll on like a river, righteousness like a never-failing stream" (NIV). Justice—treating others fairly and honestly. Righteousness—doing the "right" work of God, spending our time and resources to help others. Unlike feasts which exclude the world's hungry; assemblies which bar those who are different because of race, nationality, or sex; sacrifices void of self-giving; and songs which we sing in praise to ourselves, the works of justice and righteousness will never be repudiated at the day of the Lord.

Prayer: *Forgive me, Lord, for spending my life on those things that I think are important and ignoring what you know is important. Amen.*

Wednesday, November 4   Read Psalm 50:7-15.

The day of the Lord means an examination of our dedication to God. The psalmist's complaint was that the people of Israel sacrificed to God without becoming involved with the revelation of God. In fact, these worshipers began to suspect that God needed the sacrifice of bulls and goats and that they were doing God a favor by offering up these creatures. They thought that God needed them at least as much as they needed God.

God's reply, however, reminds them that they had gotten their relationship out of balance. "The world is mine, and all that is in it" (NIV). God does not need what we give. We gain no celestial bonus points by giving a large offering to God.

The psalmist tells us that the day of the Lord means a reevaluation of how we respond to the revelation of God's love in the world. Are our offerings merely an inconvenient kind of tax we pay in order to claim we are religious? If that is our attitude, it is no wonder, then, that we often give to God with the same enthusiasm that we give what is due to the Internal Revenue Service.

God seeks a response that is measured by our involvement with the offered revelation. God wants prayer and worship that spring from love and dedication. "Call upon me . . . and you will honor me" (NIV). The life of prayer and worship that acknowledges a dependence upon God shows that we are taking God seriously, that we are worshiping "in spirit and in truth" (John 4:24, NIV).

Prayer: *Help me, O God, to love you with all that I am. I offer not parts of my life but my whole self to you. Amen.*

Thursday, November 5   Read Matthew 25:1-13.

The day of the Lord involves preparation.

Jesus' story of the ten maidens is not about a lack of faith. All the women believed that the bridegroom was coming; all of them brought their lamps; all of them went out to meet him; all the women were sleeping. But only five were prepared for the long wait that occurs between the beginning of faith and its fulfillment.

The bridegroom catches us unprepared when we allow our faith to become a once-a-week ritual. He catches us unprepared when we shun prayer, Bible study, and meditation, thinking that they have no value in our very practical lives. We are caught unprepared when we think that giving to the poor, speaking a word to the lonely, offering comfort to the sorrowful, or trying to love our enemies is a waste of time.

We never can know when we may experience the day of the Lord, for God comes to us not just at the end of time but in time—in the faces of our spouse and children, in the hunger of the starving, in the wounds and suffering of the afflicted. Because the day of the Lord is every day, we have the opportunity always to show the depth of our preparations.

The five foolish virgins, searching for what God had already given, missed the day of the Lord. As we believe that each day will bring with it the opportunity to greet the Lord in whatever guise, we can be prepared to light the way into the hearts of others.

Prayer: *O God, who comes to me each new day, let me be prepared to meet you. Amen.*

Friday, November 6   Read Matthew 24:45-51;
                                                        25:1-13.

"What did you expect?"

The question is asked of us by those who see our disappointments. Sometimes we expect too much and constantly feel
disillusioned and without hope. But the day of the Lord involves
expectation. In both parables in today's reading, expectation is
the theme. The wicked servant did not expect his master to
return, at least not for a very long time; and he took advantage of
the absence in order to satisfy his own greedy desires.

The virgins, on the other hand, expected the bridegroom to
appear even though he was delayed beyond a reasonable hour.
They lived not just for the moment but with the future in mind.

Expecting the day of the Lord helps keep our faith alive in the
same way that our great expectations enthuse us and make us
conscious of time itself. Having something to look forward to
keeps us alert, alive, and active.

Do you expect the Lord to be present with you today? If so,
then this day can become an opportunity for learning, for service, and for fellowship. Because I expect to experience the
Lord's presence, I cannot live like the wicked servant, abusing
and mistreating others. But I can live like the virgins who were
ready to lift their lamps high, to sing, and to dance because the
bridegroom was coming among them.

Prayer: *O God of great expectation, keep my heart alert to your
coming. Let me celebrate each day as the day of your visitation. Amen.*

Saturday, November 7 Read 1 Thess. 4:13-15.

Death is not something we live with consciously every day, yet psychologists tell us that death colors all that we are. In subconscious ways people grapple with their own mortality, and this struggle affects what we do and how we live.

The day of the Lord, though, means hope to those who are dying. In other words, it offers hope to all people. The apostle Paul wrote to the Thessalonian church about death because many troubled believers there wondered about their loved ones who had died. Had they in their deaths missed the coming of the Lord? Paul tells them that they needn't be ignorant or hopeless about the afterlife. The day of the Lord encompasses both death and life, the present and the future.

Walter was 89 years old and dying. We talked in the hospital about what lay before him. His children were grown, and his wife had preceded him many years ago. For Walter, life was the future; he was ready to let go of the past. "God has been faithful to me for 89 years," he struggled to say. "God has never let me down." Every day had been a day of the Lord for Walter, and the hope he possessed told him that the day of the Lord would continue—world without end. Amen.

We do not grieve like those who have no hope. We live in the day of the Lord, a day which stretches far beyond the limits of death and time.

Prayer: *O God of hope, make this a day of your presence, and let me rejoice in the hope which you give. Amen.*

Sunday, November 8   Read 1 Thess. 4:16-18.

Most people imagine the day of the Lord as a time of divine punishment, a fiery judgment upon a wayward world, Armageddon and the end of life.

The apostle Paul, though, in his letter to the Thessalonians explained the day of the Lord as a time of reunion, a meeting with long-lost loved ones and, more importantly, an invitation into the presence of God. Contrary to those who looked for the ruin of mighty empires and all the enemies of God, Paul spoke gloriously of the coming of the God who loves us. He meant this teaching to encourage the church. "So then, encourage one another with these words" (TEV).

The day of the Lord means comfort. Although we may tremble at the thought of meeting God, although we may be overcome by a sense of our own unworthiness and guilt over things done or undone, the day of the Lord means that God will comfort the people.

God is not pitted against us but is actually for us, is on our side. This hope inspires us. God has not abandoned this planet but will fulfill, and indeed is already fulfilling, the promise to "make all things new" (Rev. 21:5).

When we teach the illiterate to read, volunteer at our community cancer society, walk to raise funds to ease world hunger, we experience and share the comfort of the day of the Lord. And like the apostle Paul, in these actions we may hear, ever so faintly above the din of a sinful world, "God's trumpet call" (NEB).

Prayer: *O God of comfort and encouragement, open my ears to hear your call, my eyes to see the needs of others, and my hands to do your work. Amen.*

HUSH . . . GOD IS NEAR!

November 9-15, 1987   **Roy W. Hall**†
Monday, November 9   Read Zephaniah 1:7.

Put your ear to the ground, scan the horizon, listen to the sound borne along by the wind. Above all, get ready for God who swiftly approaches! This is the message of Zephaniah. He lived in Jerusalem, and perhaps the hustle and noise of city life led him to call for silence. The Hebrew word is literally *hush*.

What is at work in such a command? Is the major emphasis upon a God who is going to sneak up on us and catch us unaware? Does God suddenly peek around the corner to surprise us with our hands in the cookie jar? Maybe.

But then again, maybe the main stress is not on the prophet's perception of God but in the former's insight into human nature. Could such language amount to a commentary on our persistent refusal to recognize the advent of God in our midst? Recognizing the divine requires readiness, attentiveness, discipline, and quietness. But who has the time to listen for God with the telephone continually ringing or the television blaring? Who can be ready for a meeting with God when we have to hustle to our next appointment?

But the prophet's words are timely. To what end is our rushing, straining, noisy, hectic existence if we do not discipline ourselves to be ready for God's appearing among us? Now hear this: God is always coming! Be quiet. Listen. Already God is very near.

Prayer: *Dear God, help me to be quiet now, very quiet, and to prepare my spirit for your appearing. Amen.*

---

†Pastor, Scottsboro Cumberland Presbyterian Church, Scottsboro, Alabama.

Tuesday, November 10   Read Zephaniah 1:12-18.

Zephaniah announces the approach of the fearsome "day of the Lord." The concept of such a day did not originate with him but developed gradually in prophetic thought. It seems to have originated in the people of Israel's conviction that God had fought with them in the battles resulting in the conquest of Canaan. Eventually the prophets looked forward to a final, decisive, apocalyptic battle in which God would overcome all foes and establish righteousness and justice on the earth.

The day of the Lord is pictured as a day of darkness, distress, panic, danger, and ruin. The prophets employed such negative imagery to stress just how seriously God regarded the covenant demands. A striking feature emerged in the concept: namely, Israel herself would be called into account on this day.

This latter idea is central in Zephaniah's prophecy. It does not spare Israel in its warnings. It is intriguing to consider that the prophet was very likely of royal descent. With justifiable pride he traced his lineage back to Hezekiah (1:1). This raises an important question: Can we live close to sources of power and authority, perhaps living as beneficiaries of the same, and yet remain courageous enough to proclaim the judgment of the Lord? As we look around us today and witness the ways in which justice and righteousness still go lacking, the question takes on a much-needed urgency.

Suggestion for prayer: *Think of those ways in which privilege may prevent us from being obedient to God. Then pray for courage to live and speak faithfully for God.*

Wednesday, November 11   Read Psalm 76:1-6.

Psalm 76 is a hymn which celebrates God's ultimate triumph over pagan might. Scholars point out that verse 3 probably refers to a symbolic pantomime in worship. At some point in the service, the liturgists actually broke arrows and swords and burned shields as a dramatic object lesson for the gathered faithful.

The thought of destroying weapons of war in an act of worship may strike a deep and responsive chord within us today. As I write, the hottest toy items in the local department store are Rambo-esque toy machine guns, machetes, and so on. There is even "shrapnel" candy available when it comes time for a break in the play. In the non-make-believe world, armaments pile higher and higher all around the globe. Taken together, these facts point to the dark, aggressive side of our human nature.

Hymns, of course, are sung prayers. Psalm 76 is a prayer of acknowledgement that God has the power to overcome the world's death-dealing ways. The symbolic pantomime appealed to that place in the worshiper's heart where confirmations come that good is stronger than evil, that love is more powerful than hate, and that God's good design for the world ultimately cannot be thwarted. All that is within us which opposes God can be broken by divine power. The next time we attend worship, Psalm 76 may remind us that prayer should be offered for God to overcome the aggression within each of us.

Prayer: *Lord, in this quiet moment help me to allow you to break those weapons at my disposal which I use against those whom I perceive to be enemies. Amen.*

Thursday, November 12   Read Psalm 76:7-12.

Today's reading views the purpose of God's triumph, God's destroying the weapons of destruction and stunning into motionlessness the warlike. This shows God's concern to "save all the oppressed of the earth." (v. 9). A particularly appealing part of the hymn is found in verse 11. The psalmist invites Israel's neighbors to join in bearing gifts to God and in acknowledging God's plan. This openness to other peoples reveals the psalmist's view that God's deliverance is intended for the whole world. The oppressed are not only Israel but also foreigners who are unable to live in peace and justice, given the godless powers at work in the world.

Who are the oppressed today? We are able to identify those who are poor, hungry, and without human rights in all parts of the world. And it is never far from our memory that the whole world lives under the nuclear shadow. All humanity is oppressed.

It is no longer responsible, if it ever was, to seek peace, justice, and safety only within our own borders. The world is truly a global village, and we all share the seemingly unsolvable problems which make for contemporary oppression. Is our understanding of God's aim sufficiently broad so as to seek not only our own welfare but that of all other people? It is a most urgent question. Today, let us pray for world leaders who seek peace and justice and pray that we may foster those attitudes which stress our commonality as members of the human family, including our common dependence on the transcendent One who wills salvation for all the people of the earth.

Prayer: *God, grant us to see the world as one human family which you love and are seeking to deliver. Amen.*

Friday, November 13 Read Matthew 25:19-30.

Scholars distinguish several settings for the parable of the talents. When Jesus first uttered these words, it is probable that they had reference to his dispute with the Pharisees. The latter were guardians of the divine revelation, but like the third character in the story, they had buried the grace that is within the law beneath a mound of deadening legalism. The parable points to a style of religious life that emphasizes safety rather than risk. And yet it is only in risking that we receive a return on what God has given us.

It is not through rational argument that such a deep truth is made clear to us, but through consideration of the life and words of Jesus. He risked association with sinners and publicans. He risked telling the story of a "good" Samaritan. He risked going home with a man like Zacchaeus. He risked confronting the demonic powers head-on. He risked entrusting the church to frail human beings like Peter and like us.

A movie from a couple of years ago was entitled *Risky Business*. It would be hard to find a better title for a sermon on the central thought in this parable. The Lord has blessed us abundantly. We are the recipients of God's love and grace. And to what end: that we should play it safe? Hardly. As long as there are sinners and publicans, spiritual lepers, demonic forces and the like in our world, we are compelled to risk setting God's love loose in our own words and deeds. Seeking a right standing with God through playing it safe will inevitably fail to yield a return on what God has given us.

Prayer: *O God, we believe you call us to an exciting adventure—and yet we sometimes feel bored. Could it be that we are unwilling to risk? If so, please free us up. Amen.*

Saturday, November 14   Read Matthew 25:14-18.

A second setting of the parable of the talents was in the life of the early church at the time of Matthew's writing. Several years had passed, and scholars suggest that the phrase, "Now after a long time" (v. 19) reflects the experience of waiting for the Lord's return.

Have you had to wait for someone or something lately? Perhaps you've had to wait for an elevator or in the doctor's office or for your car to be repaired. Most of us do not like to wait. Waiting may make us feel stymied or helpless. One way to cope with waiting is to find a way to keep busy. We may twiddle our thumbs while waiting for an elevator or punch the button again as if that will speed up matters. We pass the time in the doctor's office by reading from a whole array of magazines. We go for a doughnut while the engine is being tuned.

Clearly, the challenge of the parable to the church is to keep busy. It is precisely in putting the gifts of God to use that our flagging spirits find new buoyancy. Isn't it true that if we are busy with acts of faith, hope, and love that the problem of waiting recedes into the background? Who has time to worry that the owner is not yet back when there are wounds to be healed, hungry persons to be fed, lonely ones to be visited, and interest to be returned on what the owner has entrusted to us?

Prayer: *O God, help us to see the many things we can do this very day to return interest on your love. Amen.*

Sunday, November 15   Read 1 Thess. 5:1-11.

Once again we encounter the question about our Lord's return. It will not satisfy everyone, but Paul offers no astrological timetable. Instead, Paul emphasizes the importance of readiness and appeals to the image of the thief in the night, a picture given by Jesus (Matt. 24:43-44; Luke 12:39-40), in order to make a point.

It is noteworthy that the passage actually stresses not the future but the present. Notice Paul's language: "You . . . are not in darkness" (v. 4, TEV); "all of you are people who belong to the light, who belong to the day" (v. 5, TEV); and "we belong to the day" (v. 8, TEV). We are to encourage one another not by being preoccupied with the future but by claiming who we are now, in the present. Our ultimate preparation for the advent of the Lord is to be what we already are—sons and daughters of God.

Who am I? Who are you? There are a good many voices in the world devoted to telling us what we are not. Thank God for the gospel which tells us who and what we are! This is the good news: you are a unique human being of infinite worth and value, a child of God. God does have a timetable. History is moving toward a consummation of God's choosing. But we do not have to wonder what our standing will be in that day (v. 9). Because of the gospel, we already know. Our part is not to scan the skies but to live as those who know themselves to be children of grace: sensitive, aware, open, responsive, and responsible—now!

Prayer: *O God, throughout this whole day help me to celebrate who I am—your child. Amen.*

THE GOOD SHEPHERD

November 16-22, 1987
Monday, November 16

Nancy Carol Miller†
Read Psalm 80:1;
Jer. 23:3-4; Heb. 13:20.

The Bible offers a variety of images of God. God is described as, among other things, father (Luke 11:2), mother hen (Matt. 23:37), king (Ps. 24:7), and host (Ps. 23:5). But in the scripture passages for this week, the dominant divine image is shepherd.

For the people who lived in biblical times, sheep provided food, drink, clothing and even covering for their tents. Since the people depended so much upon their sheep, the shepherd's work was a matter of life and death. Thus, it is not surprising that throughout the Old and New Testaments God is pictured as a shepherd tending a flock.

When the Israelites are downtrodden and afflicted, God, the Shepherd, guides and comforts. Sometimes Yahweh calls on a people or a leader to mind the sheep. Still, when those human representatives fail in their shepherding, God stands by as protector of the lost and the vulnerable.

In the fullness of time, God sends Jesus to take care of the flock. This Good Shepherd is willing even to lay down his life for the sheep. And in the Gospel of Matthew, God's final judgment is described in shepherding terms: God separates the sheep from the goats.

The biblical image of God as shepherd is a word-picture reminding us of God's constant care.

Prayer: *O Divine Shepherd, we give thanks for your constant care. Amen.*

---

†United Methodist minister (Minister of Discipleship), West End United Methodist Church; attorney; Nashville, Tennessee.

Tuesday, November 17   Read Psalm 23.

Probably more Christians can recite the twenty-third psalm than any other Old Testament passage of scripture. Even those of us who grew up without a tradition of memorizing Bible verses have this psalm written on our hearts. Though months or years may go between readings, these words emerge from the deepest recesses of our memories. They seem to come again when we feel displaced or in need of a safe, secure place.

Psalm 23 is written in the first person singular:

> The Lord is *my* shepherd.
> *I* shall not want.

As a child I thought the song was sad, reflections of a person totally alone except for God. But the image of the shepherd contradicts the voice of a lone pilgrim driven by godly devotion. A shepherd cares not for a single animal but for an entire flock. In the same way, God cares for us, not just as individuals but as a people.

Nor is the shepherd portrayed here as one who drives the flock anywhere. Unlike Western shepherds, those from the ancient Orient lead their flocks. And so the psalmist says:

> He leads me beside still waters;
> He restores my soul.

God the Shepherd leads a people into a future of restoration and hope.

Prayer: *God, teach us to live by trust, knowing that we are part of a flock and that your staff will comfort us. Amen.*

Wednesday, November 18   Read Ezekiel 34:20-24;
                                                  John 21:14-17.

The prophet Ezekiel wrote during one of the lowest times in Israel's history—the Babylonian exile. It was a time of enormous confusion and uncertainty. Would they ever return to Jerusalem? The flock of Israel felt abandoned, like sheep without a shepherd.

In this passage, God promises to send the Israelites a shepherd. The one they are promised is David, who will rule at last over a united Israel. But this shepherd-boy-turned-king will not be an absolute ruler. He will be subject to the will of God, an "undershepherd" to Yahweh, sent to care for the flock.

One chilly night, twelve-year-old Trevor and his parents were watching a television news report on the plight of those who live in the gutters and doorways of New York City.

Trevor looked at his parents in disbelief. "Do people really live like that?"

"I'm afraid so," his father replied. "And not just in New York. There are many homeless people right here in Philadelphia."

"We've got to do something," the youngster insisted. "We can't let this go on."

With the help of family and friends, Trevor began taking food and blankets and a word of hope to Philadelphia's street people. And now, thanks to an impractical little boy, a shelter has been opened.

When asked by curious TV reporters why he helps the homeless, Trevor responded, "Because it's not right to be greedy."

History shows that God has called all kinds of shepherds. And Trevor's story follows the scriptural witness that "a little child shall lead them."

Prayer: *God of all grace, empower us that we might be true shepherds to your lambs. Amen.*

Thursday, November 19   Read Ezekiel 34:11-16.

By the early 1800s some members of the Cherokee tribe had moved from their original home in western North Carolina and settled in northwest Georgia. A treaty with the United States guaranteed them certain land there. Soon they began farming the land and building a community. They developed their own alphabet and began publishing a Cherokee newspaper. They also opened their own schools.

When gold was discovered on their land, however, the fate of the Cherokee changed. In 1838, Georgia's legislators persuaded the U.S. Congress to uproot the eastern tribes and remove the Cherokees from their homes and farms by force. The military herded 17,000 Cherokees into concentration camps, then forced them to march to Oklahoma during the winter of 1838-1839. Over four thousand men, women, and children died on the long exodus. This removal, one of the most disgraceful acts in American history, was given a name by the Cherokees, *Nanna-da-ul-tsun-yi* ("trail where they cried"). The history books call it the "Trail of Tears."

In every generation, God's precious lambs are brutalized by human shepherds who prey on the flock. This prophet likens them to wolves in shepherd's clothing.

As this passage promises, when human shepherds fail, God stands ready to reemerge as the Divine Shepherd, vindicator of the downtrodden. God will gather the flock, no matter how widely scattered, and lead them to graze on justice.

Suggestion for meditation: *Spend a few moments thinking of modern flocks who are being ravaged by wolves in shepherd's clothing. Lift them to God in prayer.*

Friday, November 20   Read Mark 6:30-44.

The true Shepherd is Jesus himself, caring for a people who are "like sheep without a shepherd."

This text reveals the attributes of a good and faithful shepherd. Note that Jesus and the disciples have just returned from the wilderness, where they had gone for prayer and meditation. Apparently Jesus knew that in order to carry out his shepherding tasks, he must take time to listen to God.

Next, note that Jesus' compassion moves him to preach to the crowd. But he doesn't stop there; he also feeds the entire crowd with only two fish and five loaves of bread.

As a community of faith, we would do well to follow this example of the good shepherd as one whose life is marked by a balance of praying faithfully to God, witnessing to the faith, and feeding those who are hungry. In my own city, I have seen a ministry that invites persons to try. Community Care Fellowship is a day-shelter for persons who live on the streets. It is a place where time is set aside every day for prayer and where spiritual counseling is available for those who want it. It is a place where one can talk about God without apology.

But Community Care Fellowship does not stop with attending to the spiritual needs of the homeless. It is also a place of hospitality, where one can find a warm place to sit, a hot cup of coffee, and a bite of lunch. In addition, staff members and volunteers also advocate for changes that can help alleviate the suffering of those who have no address.

Prayer: *Good Shepherd, it is easy for us to close our eyes to the sufferings of the poor and even to shut you out by staying busy. Give us the courage to seek after balance and wholeness in Christ. Amen.*

Saturday, November 21   Read John 10:11-18;
                                              1 John 3:16-18.

In this passage from the Gospel of John, Jesus compares himself with "hirelings" who are paid to watch over other people's flocks. The hireling doesn't really care about the sheep; it's just a job. At the first sign of trouble the hireling runs away and leaves the sheep to be slaughtered. In contrast, we are Jesus' own flock, and he cares about our welfare. In the end, the Good Shepherd Jesus even lays down his life for us.

Sometimes those who follow Jesus also are called to lay down their lives for the sheep. The lives and deaths of the saints attest to that. What makes it possible for some to make that ultimate sacrifice? Perhaps it's a profound sense of connection with all of God's creation. Shug, an aging blues singer in Alice Walker's novel *The Color Purple,* describes that feeling:

> But one day when I was sitting quiet and feeling like a motherless child, which I was, it come to me: that feeling of being part of everything, not separate at all. I knew that if I cut a tree, my arm would bleed. And I laughed and I cried and I run all around the house. I knew just what it was. In fact, when it happens, you can't miss it.*

Only those who know that the fates of all the sheep are mysteriously intertwined can voluntarily lay down their lives as Jesus did.

Prayer: *Eternal God, we are grateful that you sent a Shepherd so connected to us that he was willing to die on a cross. Amen.*

---

*Alice Walker, *The Color Purple* (New York: Harcourt Brace Jovanovich, 1982), p. 167.

Sunday, November 22   Read Matthew 25:31-46.

My very first divinity school field placement was in prison ministry. Another first-year student and I began visiting a woman named Hannah incarcerated at the maximim security psychiatric hospital. The warden had tried to discourage us from visiting Hannah by bringing out a rather large cardboard box containing the arsenal of weapons she had fashioned from an array of everyday items she had in her cell and by telling us Hannah had killed five people.

One morning my clock radio blared the news that a friend of Hannah's had hanged herself while being held in solitary confinement. So I went out to see Hannah—to console her, to minister to her in her time of grief. As we talked about the circumstance of her friend's death, I found I was consumed with grief and anger. But Hannah knew prison suicide was a commonplace thing; the scars on her wrists were constant reminders of her own attempts. Hannah patiently listened and shared my grief. This notorious prisoner unexpectedly became my pastor.

Part of the reality of the incarnation is that Jesus can be found not only as shepherd among the flock but in the faces of "the least of these." As Henri Nouwen points out, when Jesus says in Matthew 25, "I was hungry and you gave me food, I was thirsty and you gave me drink, I was a stranger and you welcomed me, I was sick and you visited me, I was in prison and you came to me," Jesus is inviting us not only to help, but to discover God.*

Prayer: *Loving God, give us eyes to see the Christ in the faces of the hungry, the lonely, the sick, and the imprisoned. In the name of Jesus. Amen.*

---

*Henri J. Nouwen, *Creative Ministry* (Garden City, New York: Doubleday and Co., Inc., 1978), p. 83.

November 23-29, 1987   **Fred L. Beck†**
Monday, November 23   Read Isaiah 63:15-19.

Even as we hear the ancient prophet's cry, a similar sound rings in our own ears. We hear ourselves and others ask, "Why, God, are you acting this way toward us?" "Why, O Lord, do you make us wander from your ways and harden our hearts so we do not revere you?" (NIV) The cry of the present resonates with the past. The plea is for God to once again enter the scene and set things right, and to do it in such a way that everyone will recognize what is being done.

This is, of course, a faith concept devoid of grace and short on mercy. It depends on humanity's righteousness, but humanity is sinful; its "righteous acts are like filthy rags" (Isa. 64:6, NIV). From time to time we will hear the plea, "What did I do to bring such trouble to myself? What can I do to get God to relent? I've tried to be a good person, yet God does this to me."

Answers are not easy when this expectation is held dear. But there is hope in the words of the prophet, for he repeats, "But, you are our Father." This may be a cry of submission to a disciplinarian authority. But it may be an affirmation of assurance that, no matter how troubled or painful life may be, God knows and cares. It is ours to seek such a caring God.

Suggestion for prayer: *Give thanks that Jesus revealed the true God to us as one who always cares.*

---

†United Methodist minister serving as Chaplain at Alton Memorial Hospital, Alton, Illinois.

Tuesday, November 24   Read Isaiah 64:1-8.

"We are the clay, you are the potter; we are all the work of your hand" (NIV).

This verse, which inspired Adelaide Addison Pollard's hymn "Have Thine Own Way, Lord," can be interpreted two different ways. It can be viewed as grim resignation, which seems to be the tone of the prophet. He describes the despicable situation of the people as "unclean." "All our righteous acts are like filthy rags; we all shrivel up like a leaf, and like the winds our sins sweep us away" (NIV). He seems to hold God responsible for this lack of faith because "you have hidden your face from us" (NIV).

But the prophet continues a plaintive plea for God to relent and forgive. The verse becomes the submissive prayer of the penitent. We can almost hear the prophet say, "Here we are, Lord. We yield our wills to yours. Take our lives and reshape them, for we are moistened clay and you are the potter."

But they were more than lifeless clay. The people's plea for mercy was tied to God's demand for faithfulness. While we recognize that God is rich in mercy, there is still the demand for faithfulness laid upon us. The shaping of our lives in love and mercy, joy and peace, is accomplished when we are receptive, willing, and faithful material in the hands of the Potter.

Suggestion for prayer: *Give thanks for God's mercy that grants renewed opportunity for the reshaping of our lives.*

Wednesday, November 25   Read Psalm 80:1-7.

Psalm 80 is a lament. A sense of despair hangs on the words. The "Shepherd of Israel" is admonished to action on behalf of the people. "Come and save us. Restore us . . let your face shine upon us, that we may be saved" (NIV).

Prayers appear useless to a seemingly angry God. The people have been baptized with bitter tears and have given both neighbors and enemies food for scorn and laughter.

Hidden in this psalm, and in all laments, is a faith in God. In the face of despair, where it seems that God has turned away from us, to pray for salvation is an expression of faith and hope.

Some call this bargaining. The implication is that we turn to God in desperation. And it may be so. Praise be to God for any who in desperation cry out and find the great and good Shepherd present to hear and to respond with presence and grace.

Does grace given to the despairing, who make promises for future faithfulness, bring broken promises and further despair? Perhaps. But there is also the hope that the despairing may find the light of God, that the promises made will be kept, and that God will be truly blessed through their lives.

Some who read this may themselves have experienced the reality of God's love and grace out of a sense of despair. May many more.

Suggestion for prayer: *Give thanks for God's love and care expressed in times of despair.*

Thursday, November 26   Read 1 Corinthians 1:3.

The text for today is brief but filled with great meaning. To give thanks is to reveal much about one's outlook on and approach to life.

Thanksgiving is stricly a voluntary attitude. To give thanks is a choice we have made, a choice that has grown out of a sense of gratitude to God and others.

Gratitude is in part a learned attitude. As children, we were taught to say thank you. Maturity allows that learned attitude to blossom into one of still greater meaning. We recognize that all life is a gift from God. Our innate talents, skills, and abilities are given by God. With gratitudes' guidance, these gifts develop into tools to be utilized for good—for ourselves, our families, our church, our community and world.

Thanksgiving can also produce joy as we learn to appreciate that which we receive in daily blessings. Like Paul, we may learn to be content in whatever state we find ourselves (see Phil. 4:11). In this contentment we find that gratitude becomes a constant factor giving everything in life worth and meaning.

Thanksgiving teaches us to share. Selfishness and gratitude cannot be compatible. The grateful find ways to share. In multiplied ways, our gratitude spills over into the lives of those around us, and, like everything contagious, begins to be seen in others.

Paul said, "I give thanks . . . " Let us be like-minded.

Suggestion for prayer: *Give thanks today for that which normally you take for granted.*

Friday, November 27   Read 1 Corinthians 1:3-9.

Paul reminds us that gratitude in the face of hardship or plenty is a good thing. There are thousands who spend their days in solitude, alone, in nursing homes or homes for the aged, in slums or on the streets. How thrilled these folks would be to hear someone say to them, "I give thanks to God for you always."

These words of thanks for others might well express a greater sense of thanksgiving than those for material things such as food and home. To say to a son or daughter, "I thank God for you," could be an expression of love that might restore a broken relationship. Spoken to a mother or father, these words could lift their spirits for another day. In a similar vein, when spoken in a church setting, these words can do much to strengthen the bonds of faith and love.

Paul expressed thanksgiving for the grace given in Jesus Christ and how, through this, the Corinthians had been enriched in every way. Praise was given for those to whom Paul wrote and to God, who in and through Christ had made their lives more complete. This is a proper combination for the thanksgiving we are called to share.

Devotional exercise: *Say to others around you, "I thank God for you," adding whatever reasons you feel within your own self.*

Saturday, November 28   Read Mark 13:32-33.

"Be on guard! Be alert!"

These words of warning flash in our minds like the lights of police and emergency vehicles. We are startled to attention. We are warned that we do not know the day or hour when the Messiah will return. Since that day and hour is known only to God, our responsibility is to watch. But watching and waiting are passive, and Jesus was not a teacher of passivity. We are called to do more than merely watch in dullness.

Jesus' call to alertness must certainly reflect active goodness. Paul encouraged the Thessalonians to be about doing good as they waited (see 1 Thess. 5:1-11). This encouragement extends also to us.

Our alertness will reveal to us a more meaningful expression of our faith and hope. We will look around us and see fields ready for harvest. Like the army of Gideon, we will drink of refreshing water for our souls and exhibit a watchful eye for that which threatens our faithfulness. Active waiting and watching is invigorating. Good things are being done, the faithful are increased, and the Lord God is praised for daily blessings.

Some warn, "Watch for signs of Jesus' coming." No, watch instead for signs of his presence among us and for opportunities to extend that presence in kindness and justice, in love and peace.

Suggestion for prayer: *Thank God for opportunities to do good today, and ask for guidance in doing it.*

Sunday, November 29 (Advent begins)
Read Mark 13:34-37.

"Watch!" The passage ends with this instruction.

There is a strange dichotomy in watching. On the one hand, when we watch in anticipation of punishment, our feelings are those of dread and fear. We rue the day and time that we must face our punishment. We may even work to delay that time as long as possible. Not knowing when it will come influences all we do, for the anxiety affects our whole being.

On the other hand, watching for something that promises joy and blessing fills us with a different form of anxiety. We cannot wait for its coming. We would bring it more quickly if we could. We make preparations over and over for that occurrence or we pester those who are doing so, for that great day holds so much joy in store for us.

Both kinds of waiting are implied in the words of Jesus as Mark records them, though the side of warning seems more prevalent.

Nevertheless, the person who watches, who makes adequate preparations, who anticipates the return of the master and the joy that will be shared at that time will lay aside dread. Like the faithful in the parable of the ten girls, those who watch and wait in joyous anticipation will welcome the hour of the return, no matter how late. They have made their preparations and can rejoice that the master is once again present. In God's grace the dread is turned to joy, the fear to peace.

Suggestion for meditation: *Watch for the joy and peace that the grace of our Lord Jesus Christ gives at his coming.*

SHALOM THROUGH THE WORD THAT ENDURES

November 30–December 6, 1987   **Cecilio Arrastía†**
Monday, November 30   Read Isaiah 40:1-2.

Isaiah reminds us our comfort is hidden in God's love. Comfort is a gift from God. There is only one way to end our desperation and anxiety—through God's forgiveness. Our consolation is rooted in God's acts.

However, the text also tells us that the grace that makes our comfort possible is costly. Judgment—which is painful both to the Creator and to the creature—is part of this healing process. The cross is still at the center, representing both judgment and forgiveness.

Consolation comes after suffering. Beyond our suffering and hopelessness is forgiveness, which marks the beginning of our comfort and the awakening of hope. Our frozen horizon melts away, and a new future beckons us, full of peace and serenity. "Tell them they have suffered long enough," God says (TEV).

The word *comfort,* from Latin, means "with strength, with energy." This energy comes from God. It is God's grace working in us in the midst of tragedy and depression. It is Paul knowing that God's grace is all he needs: God's grace is enough. More than the power of our intellect or the resources of our organizations, God's energy is the deciding factor.

Prayer: *O God, give us enough wisdom and humility to realize that without your power and forgiveness we will never have comfort. In Christ's name. Amen.*

---

†Associate for Resources and Service, Evangelism Program, Presbyterian Church (U.S.A.), New York, New York.

Tuesday, December 1   Read Isaiah 40:3-5.

There is a connection between the disclosure of God's glory and our actions.

God's revelation begins with a voice. In the beginning there was chaos and darkness. God spoke and cosmos (order) came into being. "In the beginning was the Word . . . and the Word was God" (John 1:1). "A voice cries," says Isaiah. "In the wilderness prepare the way of the Lord."

The desert is the scene of struggle, formation, vocation. It is in the wilderness where God has to struggle with humankind. In the desert our sinfulness and our idolatry are obstacles to the disclosure of God's glory. The desert is the arena of our rebellion and eccentricity. The wilderness is a symbol of our solitude and loneliness, because there we have deserted the Lord. We have made idols, right there. So, the voice cries out *from* the desert, where God is; and *to* the desert, where we are fighting against God.

The desert will be transformed. Moreover, the whole land will be changed in order to see the glory of the Lord: valleys will be filled; mountains will be leveled; hills will become plains; and the rough areas will be made smooth.

And then the glory of the Lord will be seen. Glory means substance, majesty, richness, fullness. The poverty of our arid desert will be transformed into the richness of God's glory.

Prayer: *O Lord, clear our eyes so that we can see thy glory, and redeem our nothingness with thy fullness and substance. Through Christ we pray. Amen.*

Wednesday, December 2   Read Isaiah 40:6-8.

The voice continues. The desert has been cleared, but that is not enough. The word is needed; the message must be proclaimed. In the beginning, the Word. At the end, the Word. Nothing happens apart from the Word. But the question comes back, "What message is going to be proclaimed?" It is not just any message, a secular ideology, a dry theological dogma, an abstract philosophical theory. It must be specific, clear, concrete.

The answer is dramatic. It is a contrast, a vivid contrast, between the weakness, the fragility, and the transitory character of humanity and the solid, massive, impressive nature of God's Word, which endures forever. What an analysis of what we are; what a description of who God is! We are grass; God is wind, breath. God is *ruach:* unpredictable, powerful, free, mysterious. Sometimes God is music, like the wind. Sometimes God is a shaking, dreadful noise. But God is always sovereign. While we fade and grow old and weak, God and God's Word endure forever.

The existential implication of this dramatic contrast is easy to detect. We live by trusting in our own weakness and fragility or by depending on God's endurance and eternity. We are victims of our own nonsensical decision, or we are granted the power of the Word and the power of God to transform our reality into something different and positive. We either live looking at our future from our present—the doubtful present of grass—or looking at our present from God's future—the future of One who endures forever.

Devotional exercise: *List five weak spots that you see in yourself. List five virtues that you see in God, as they are revealed in Jesus Christ.*

Thursday, December 3   Read Psalm 85:8-13.

"I am listening to what the Lord God is saying" (TEV). Without our listening, the word loses its edge, its sharpness. In Hebrew, *listen* is equivalent to *obey*. It is not an acoustic experience but a volitional one. It goes beyond the eardrum; it touches the will. The goal of God's word is to enlist the obedience of the listener. More than rhetoric, listening is ethics. Christ, who is the truth, is also the way.

Listening includes a concrete and big "if." There will be peace and healing, "if we do not go back to our foolish ways" (TEV). The spoken word demands a radical change. A radical love expects a radical obedience. Without our listening, our ways remain foolish, childish. Maturity and growth come as a result of our listening—our obeying—the word of God. Because of this, hearing the word and Bible study are not part of the entertainment program of the church—they are the life of the church. We do not preach on Sunday to *fill* part of a worship service. We preach because without the proclaiming and the hearing of God's word our lives will be *empty,* will never be *filled.*

The end of the discourse is magnificent—the most beautiful and poetic description of what shalom is all about. It is a symphony of hope and health.

—Love will meet faithfulness. What a friendship!

—Righteousness and peace will embrace. What a marriage!

—Our loyalty growing up from the earth and God's justice coming down from heaven. What an encounter!

Prayer: *God, mine is the prayer of the holy one, St. Francis: Make me an instrument of thy peace. Amen.*

Friday, December 4   Read 2 Peter 3:8-15*a*.

Peter's discourse is about God's power and God's freedom. Power used in God's own time frame—in God's own *kairos*. The highest expression of our wisdom is to live within God's timetable. Many of our anxieties will disappear if we stretch our dreams and projects to fit them within the projects and dreams of God and God's "calendar."

Sometimes, we identify God's patience and slowness as failure to deliver, to fulfill. The answer to our confusion is found in God's patient nature. God is giving us time, just "because he does not want anyone to be destroyed, but wants all to turn away from their sins" (TEV).

In the midst of God's patience there is no room for doubt. "The day of the Lord will come." At God's own time. In God's own way. Surrounded by mystery, in the thick of darkness, God will come.

People will look at this day of the Lord from two different perspectives. Some will see only destruction, and they will despair. It will be the end of everything, the ultimate, the *omega* of history and hope. For those who have lived in holiness, there will be another day; not a twilight but the dawning of a new age. And righteousness will be at home in this new day.

There is a connection between our perspective and our life-style. Holiness, integrity, commitment will be the heart of the equation. Without these, we will be blind to God's disclosure. Darkness and despair will be at the end of the tunnel—a long journey into the night. Purity of life will usher us into a new day, a new dawn.

Prayer: *Lord and Savior, help us, we beseech thee, to keep our eyes opened to the light of the new day. Help us to wait with holiness of life. Amen.*

Saturday, December 5   Read Mark 1:1-3.

"The Good News about Jesus Christ, the Son of God" (TEV). Just like that! The Good News, Jesus Christ, the Son of God. Christ *is* the good news of God—the gospel—the Word.

Then the writer of the oldest canonical Gospel looks back. It is true; our future is hidden in God's past. What God did is the promise of what God will do. God does not improvise; God plans ahead. God's salvific project has continuity. Now, in Christ, the time is fulfilled; the promise becomes a *fait accompli*. No more waiting. God is with us.

The plan is clear. The Lord has promised a messenger to prepare, with the power of the word, a way for the Lord. The messenger is not the Lord, but one who points to the Lord. The final and redemptive act belongs to the Lord—is the Lord. Whatever the messenger does is preparatory, prologue. The epilogue belongs to God—the writer of the script.

In a sense, the church should be like John the Baptist. It is a finger pointing to God. It is not the kingdom, but it is the anticipation of the kingdom. As John did, the church must: negate self, be humble, dress in humility, proclaim the Good News.

The image of the shouting desert prophet is a challenging one. A silent church is a negation of the Christ who shouted love, justice, peace, equality. The proclamation is not our own choice; it is given. "Get the road ready for the Lord" (TEV). Not for an ideology, not for a structure, not for a utopia. Just this: get ready for the Lord!

Devotional exercise: *List three noisy shoutings that the church must engage in today. Then pray for power and determination to really shout in the name of Jesus the Christ.*

Sunday, December 6   Read Mark 1:4-8.

From the spoken word, to the dramatized word. The turning point—from words to action—is two verbs. And the verbs are action verbs in present progressive: *preaching* and *baptizing*.

Both actions are sacramental actions. The word gives meaning and light to the sacrament. The sacrament provides the word with flesh and substance. The word is a spoken symbol, while the sacrament is an acted one. To separate the word from the sacrament is to hurt both. Theological and liturgical aberrations arise when this separation takes place.

John's message was radical and straightforward. "Turn away from your sins and be baptized" (TEV). These are concrete actions. If we act, we will receive the benefits of what God has already done. "God will forgive your sins" (TEV). This future tense, in a sense, is a past tense. The question mark is on our side, in our disposition to really repent and be baptized. But let us be very clear and keep everything straight. This is not a commercial transaction. God is not waiting for our repentance in order to give the Son. This forgiveness is a matter of our appropriation of God's redeeming action. The battle is already won; we just enjoy the taste of victory and rejoice. Even before getting home, the lost son had been forgiven. His return made actual something that was potential.

The response to John was rewarding. Many heard, believed, and were baptized. What a refreshing sight for churches that are shrinking in membership and decisions for Christ. What a challenge!

Prayer: *Lord, help us to preach with enthusiasm and clarity and charity. Help us to be obedient and constant in our daily life. In Jesus' name. Amen.*

PREPARING FOR NEW LIFE IN CHRIST

December 7-13, 1987   **Marian "Shug" Yagel**†
Monday, December 7   Read Isaiah 61:1-4.

God's announcement of preparation

These words from Isaiah reach into the furthermost nooks and crannies of our selves: "The Lord has anointed me to bring good tidings to the afflicted!" These powerful words bring hope like those of a doctor comforting a patient after long hours of critical surgery and illness: "You are going to *live*."

As you reflect on your own "afflictions" and those of whom you love, what does God's good news bring to you? If you allow the haunting memories of brokenheartedness, bondage, and grief to rush to the surface, can you bathe them with the hope of God's promise "to raise up the former devastations"?

The hope with which Isaiah's proclamation floods our souls should be solid, very much like the kind which inspired confidence and expectation in the hearts of the Jews as they returned to Jerusalem. Yes, their exile was over. No, their lives would not be easier. Now life would be filled with *possibility*. The same is true for us. It took hundreds of years for the words of God's prophets to be fulfilled in Jerusalem. In Isaiah a new generation was called to expectation and new birth. Let us begin our preparation for new birth with this prayer:

Prayer: *Almighty God, we are an impatient people. We often lose sight of the foundations you have laid for us, and hence, forget to lay the foundation for future generations. Prepare us now for your eternal plan. Prepare the world, through us, for future generations. Amen.*

---

†Minister, Kern Memorial United Methodist Church and Nancy Webb Kelly Children's Church, Nashville, Tennessee.

Tuesday, December 8   Read Isaiah 61:8-11.

God's preparation through new life

Yesterday we read that new life has visible signs: "a garland instead of ashes, the oil of gladness instead of mourning, the mantle of praise instead of a faint spirit; that they may be called oaks of righteousness" (Isa. 61:3). Today we learn that God's promises are fulfilled *even as they are spoken:* "My soul shall exult in my God; for he has . . . covered me with the robe of righteousness."

New life—our new life—breaks forth *even as we pray.* Prayer *is* preparation for new life. It is often with great timidity that I thank God in advance for answering my prayers. Yet I have learned that it is just this sort of faith that is the richest soil for new birth. Every Sunday morning I stand before a congregation, ninety percent of whom live below the poverty line. Fifty percent of these folks are children who have grown up in the oldest, most crime-filled and delapidated housing project in East Nashville, Tennessee. Were it not for the expectation that "as the earth brings forth its shoots . . . so the Lord God will cause righteousness and praise to spring forth before all the nations," we could not pray at all. Yet at Nancy Webb Kelly children's church we pray the Lord's prayer with anxious hearts and eyes filled with great expectations. "All who see them shall acknowledge them, that they are a people whom the Lord has blessed."

As you prepare for new life in this Advent season, thank the great God Almighty in advance for the many blessings which will meet you in the days ahead.

Prayer: *Great God of salvation, I thank you today for all that tomorrow promises to bring. I thank you for courage, hope, and power to live life in your name. Amen.*

Wednesday, December 9 Read John 1:6-8, 19-23.

Witnessing to new life

The hardest aspects of witnessing to new life are the questions people ask and the answer we think we should give. We are told in the Gospel of John, "There was a man sent from God. . . . He came for testimony, to bear witness to the light, that all might believe *through* him" (italics mine). How does the author know John the Baptist was sent from God? How does he know "he was not the light"? The answers to these questions are one and the same: The author of John doesn't *know*—he *believes*. The Gospel of John is a witness to new life received as the result of belief.

We are both victims and purveyors of a world that has largely forgotten the experience of *verisimilitude*. Something which has verisimilitude is something which seems perceptibly true. It cannot be proven by scientific method nor formulated in cognitive terms. It is experienced, it is witnessed; it can only be testified to through personal encounter.

New life—our new life, the new life in Christ, and new life for the world—can be witnessed, but only by the cooperative interaction of our own experiences. To witness truth, then, is not to prove an hypothesis but to state a belief; to describe an understanding based on personal experience. The author of the Gospel of John saw something of John the Baptist which caused belief in the Baptist's words. In the later-encountered Light, the author's sense of verisimilitude was further confirmed in the life and teachings of Jesus.

Prayer: *God, we witness your creation and, so, witness you. We witness the fulfillment of prayer and, so, witness your power. We witness the power of your story as witnessed by others and, so, witness your Son. Thank you, Lord, for prayer, story, and belief. Amen.*

Thursday, December 10   Read John 1:25-28.

Baptism as new birth

Until you are baptised to new life, it will always be true that there "among you stands one whom you do not know." Very much like a dream that is never lived out, Jesus hovers close by, shaping your regrets and awaiting permission to shape your life. In baptism we *put on* Christ, or better yet we *live in* Christ. We are born to a whole new way of being in the world. The stranger we did not know becomes the Divine Inspiration we could not manufacture.

Baptism is a strange and wondrous sacrament. Its power overcomes the conceptual helplessness of the infant and transcends the conceptual analysis of the adult—the soul is touched for God's purpose and God's alone.

Are you one of the many Christians who worry and wonder as to the method and effectiveness of their own baptism? If you are, take this time to think for a moment: Were you baptized as an infant? adolescent? adult? How were you baptized: sprinkling? pouring? immersion? Whatever the method, whatever the age, its purpose was the same: that you might have new life in Christ.

If you are practicing the Christian life this day, even to the extent that you are reading this text, then God's preparations for new life through you are well in motion. *You* are part of God's advent in the world. You are no stranger to our risen Lord. Take this time to praise God for the movement Christ has wrought in your life through endless new birth!

Prayer: *God of our Savior, you are a gracious God. You bring forth new life in us all. Prepare my heart now for your continued rebirth, that I may rejoice with each new day of creation. Amen.*

Friday, December 11   Read 1 Thess. 5:16-18.

New birth as new life

Spiritual development is no easy task for even the most agile of thinkers and the most trained in the spiritual arts. This is true because spiritual growth always entails new life. And new life can only be learned as it is lived. There are no familiar roads to the kingdom of God.

Paul must have been a wonderful mentor for just this kind of pain of confusion and disorientation. He had listened to enough stories about the journeys of others. He had examined the importance of each of his own spiritual steps. He realized that while every journey is markedly unique, each also involves the common discovery of certain survival precepts. These precepts become the tools for a fulfilling religious experience.

For this reason Paul ended the majority of his teaching letters to the early churches with moral counsel consisting of several ethical injunctions. Today's scripture lesson, as well as tomorrow's, consists of these teachings designed to ease the loneliness and disorientation that often accompany the lives of spiritual sojourners.

"Rejoice always, pray constantly, give thanks in all circumstances." Paul is reminding the early church of the posture in which grace will always prevail. As followers of Christ, we can expect that it is God's will that we reside in happy relationship with him. Furthermore, we can expect that in whatever pain we find ourselves, we can find comfort through times of rejoicing, prayer, and thanksgiving.

Prayer: *My God and Redeemer, I seek your laughter as my own, your prayers for me as my prayers for myself, and your glory as cause for much thanksgiving. Amen.*

Saturday, December 12   Read 1 Thess. 5:19-24.

New life as discernment

Today's lesson is a continuation of yesterday's. Where verses 16-18 deal with one's spiritual *posture,* verses 19-22 deal with one's *utilization* of spiritual opportunity.

Paul begins, "Do not quench the Spirit," in either yourself or another. Only in freedom from rigid expectations and beliefs can the full benefits of spiritual growth be gained. Further, one must "not despise prophesying" by others, nor should we ourselves avoid speaking truth as we see it. In Paul's time, prophecy was a primary source of information about God. To put one's self apart from such activity of the Spirit was to place oneself in spiritual peril.

This is true today. Many people are afraid of, or unwilling to hear, modern prophets. As a result we fail to develop skills for discerning the differences between real and false prophets. If we are to be born anew of the Spirit, we must have ears that will hear and minds that will make usable and accurate judgments about what we have witnessed. Only then are we able to truly "abstain from every form of evil" and "hold fast what is good."

Today's lesson concludes with a blessing from Paul that reminds us that it is only through God that we can acquire holiness. We are further reminded that holy perfection involves our total selves: our spirits, souls, and bodies. This requires knowledge of who we are *in the world.* Because God "is faithful," we can trust that God will sanctify us, for we are called to God by God's choice, not our own.

Prayer: *Lord, God, and Savior/Parent/Healer of us all, grant us all discernment in matters of spiritual worth. Keep us ever strong and open to your movement in the world. In Jesus' name we pray. Amen.*

Sunday, December 13   Read Luke 1:46*b*-55.

The Magnificat: Discernment as faith

In more recent Christian history we have translated "Mary's Song" with the image of a glowing peasant girl so moved by the Holy Spirit that she could sing unambiguous praises in the midst of what is treated as a planned pregnancy. While it may be true that every young Jewish girl was raised with the hope that she might someday birth the Deliverer of Israel, it is also true that a young woman expected to do so within the security of customary marriage and family practices. Mary may not have been surprised at her condition, given the ample warning from the angel; but surely she was amazed!

Mary surely was relieved by the realization that Elizabeth shared her understanding of God's purpose in her life. In sheer joy, she utters the words of her ancient mentor Hannah: "My heart exults in the Lord; my strength is exalted in the Lord. My mouth derides my enemies, because I rejoice in thy salvation" (1 Sam. 2:1). Hannah's words become a powerful expression of a prophetic story in its unfolding.

I am deeply touched, and awed, by Mary's capacity to trust God and her own understanding of God's work in her life. While we tend to read the biblical stories with retrospective clarity, I would imagine that Mary's experience was as confusing and befuddling as our own *when it was happening*. Mary offers a living example of spiritual discernment and the indispensable place such discernment has in building a life of faith. Mary witnesses to the spiritual truth which moves us through this Advent season: it is in acts of faith that new life is born.

Prayer: *God Almighty, we stand before you as potential bearers of your Light and Life in the world. Grant us faith that we might parent a new generation of faithful followers. In Jesus' name we pray. Amen.*

GOD'S SURPRISING CHOICES

December 14-20, 1987
Monday, December 14

Martin Pike†
Read Romans 16:25-27.

"One of these days you will understand" is an overworked line. It is a line that I have received with chagrin and dished out with relish. The one who speaks it implies that the recipient lacks something—age, experience, wisdom. That line closes the door on whatever conversation is underway. The implication is that before the discussion can continue one must age ten years, experience excruciating pain, or suffer a terrible loss.

In the process of disciplining my children, I was often aware that the validity of my actions was being questioned. "One of these days you will understand," I would say. And that would be the end of it. Now that my children are mature, they sometimes dredge up one of those incidents. By the grace of God the wound has healed, and we laugh about what at the time seemed a tragedy. But more often than not, I, the very one who said, "One of these days you will understand," am the one to whom understanding has come. Even though its arrival has been somewhat delayed, it has come as a much-needed blessing.

Paul speaks of a mystery kept secret for long ages but ultimately disclosed by the grace of God in Christ. For those who wait with patience the reward is sure. That is what Advent is all about: waiting with patience.

Prayer: *O God, your gracious love exceeds our understanding. In the gift of your Son the mystery is revealed. Let us wait with patience for his coming. Amen.*

---

†Minister, First Christian Church (Disciples of Christ), Kingsville, Texas.

Tuesday, December 15   Read Psalm 89:1-4, 19-24.

More than once I have discovered that enthusiasm for a project in its initial stages is not always sufficient to bring it to a successful conclusion. Brainstorming, goal setting, and strategic planning can be fun. The heart literally sings as some noble venture is contemplated. Ultimately there comes a time when the idea has to be translated into action. It is at this point that enthusiasm begins to reveal its character.

There were moments during one such venture when a friend's support was put to the test. We had planned our project carefully. We looked forward with enthusiasm to its completion. Temporary setbacks, harsh criticism, widely expressed doubts came at us. It became evident that some of our goals would not be attained, and hoped-for results would be less than expected. But my friend was as good as his word. He was faithful. He stuck by me to the end.

In retrospect, I came to understand that the most significant thing that happened was something we had not planned. The adversity through which we passed strengthened the ties that bound us together.

So it was that when God enlisted David to lead the people of Israel, God assured him, "You can count on me." David's human frailty put God's patience to the test again and again. Even so, God did not forsake him. At the end, David summarized his experience: "I will sing of thy steadfast love, O Lord, forever; with my mouth I will proclaim thy faithfulness to all generations." In spite of his trials, David came to bless the tie that bound him to the love of God.

Prayer: *O God, I, too, have put your love to the test. You have been faithful in every circumstance of life. Make my love as constant as yours. Amen.*

Wednesday, December 16　　　　Read 2 Samuel 7:8-16.

David never dreamed of becoming a prince. He was a shepherd boy. Years later, this shepherd boy who did become a prince was reminded of the humble background from which he had come. It was Nathan who brought the reminder. "I took you from the pasture," said the Lord of Hosts, "from following the sheep, that you should be a prince over my people Israel."

It is not unusual to discover that many of the tasks that need doing in the world are done by people who, like David, never dreamed of doing them. Like David, first one and then another has been called from the ordinary to the extraordinary. The entire biblical record seems to reflect such a pattern. God reaches down into little backwater towns like Nazareth, touches the unknowns, and calls them into service.

In the life of the church I continue to be amazed by the manner in which God enlists people I have overlooked or given up on. It seems God has a way of reaching out to shepherds, fishermen, tentmakers, tax collectors, and the Marys and Josephs of the world.

It was to David's credit that he sensed the hand of God at work in his life, as did Mary and Joseph in their own time. This insight was helpful in all that followed.

One difficulty that most of us have is not unlike that of those heroes. We find it hard to believe that God may favor us with a special invitation to servanthood. Like little children who dream about what they will be when they grow up, we do not often consider that God may have a suggestion for us. If God took David from the pasture, from following the sheep, might not any one of us be eligible for service?

Prayer: *O God, let us be ready to serve you when you call our name. Amen.*

Thursday, December 17   Read Luke 1:26-30.

Luke's account of the birth of Jesus tells us that angels appeared to Zechariah, to Mary, and to the shepherds. In each instance they found it necessary to calm the fears of those to whom they were sent. Apparently angels are instructed early in their training to initiate their conversations with, "Do not be afraid." God seems to know what strikes fear in our hearts.

There is something strange about this. Most angels are the harbingers of good news. They tell us that God has picked us out from all the rest or that a child is born or that someone we were afraid we would never see again has risen. I'm not sure why they always find it necessary to reassure us that they mean no harm, but they do.

It may be that so much of the time good news doesn't sound like good news when we hear it. Sometimes it sounds as if another burden has been added to our already overloaded schedule. Or that we are going to have to do something that we do not think we have the ability to do. Or that we will be required to go see someone we are not sure really wants to see us. Angels can be kind of pushy.

When someone asks me if I'm ready for Christmas, it is not so much presents, trees, carols, and turkey and dressing that I think about, but angels. This is the season when they are out in force. The chances are good that when we least expect it, breaking the deep silence of our souls, we will hear these words, "Do not be afraid." What comes next will probably be different for each of us, but the tidings they bring will be good news. You can count on that. Mary did.

Prayer: *O God, transform our fear into faith. Amen.*

363

Friday, December 18   Read Luke 1:31-33.

My friend was asked to undertake a very demanding project. It would be time-consuming and would involve him in a controversy for which he had little appetite. "Why me?" he asked. He called off the names of a half dozen people whose relationship to the aforementioned project was far closer than his own. He lifted up their qualifications and the resources they had available that ought to have made them far more likely candidates for that call than himself. "Why me?" he asked.

Of course, I could not answer him. I did remember how, in the sixth month of a year in the long ago, the angel Gabriel was sent to a city of Galilee named Nazareth. Gabriel's assignment was to enlist the help of a young virgin who was betrothed to the village carpenter. I have often wondered about the wisdom of God's choice. In the light of history, I know the right choice was made, but at the time even Mary surely had her doubts. Like my friend, she was not put at ease by the introducton, "Hail, O favored one, the Lord is with you!" (v. 28) Luke tells us that she was "greatly troubled at the saying, and considered in her mind what sort of greeting this might be" (v. 29).

Though it took my friend a bit longer than it took Mary to respond affirmatively, he did. Like Mary, he also came to know something of the agony and ecstasy of every venture that bears the mark of God. Though neither of them sought to be chosen, both discovered that those whom God calls, God also sustains.

Prayer: *O God, help us to remember that your choices are always sustained by your love. Amen.*

Saturday, December 19   Read Luke 1:34-37.

"How shall this be?" was Mary's response to the angel who came to her. The angel told her not only that she would bear a son but that he would be great, and that of his kingdom there would be no end. To become the mother of a son was cause enough for astonishment, but to be the mother of an heir to the throne of David was beyond her wildest dream.

Mary's question is one that has confronted every noble vision. Every significant achievement in the history of humankind has had its beginning in this very question, "How shall this be?" Whenever the hope of peace has been lifted up in time of war, it has seemed the impossible dream. Whenever someone has mentioned reconciliation for healing the wounds of broken human relationships, there has been the question, "How shall this be?"

Later on, Mary's son would be asked this question too. "Lord, how can we feed so many with so little?" "Lord, sinners that we are, how can we be saved?" "Lord, how can it be that the lame will walk, the blind see, and the dead be raised?" "Lord, how can a person be born again?" "How can it be?" How *can* it be?

In the long ago, the angel reassured Mary, "The power of the Most High will overshadow you." This was the answer then; it is the answer now. For every person who senses the call of God to some high mission and who prayerfully asks, "How shall this be?" the answer is sure: "The power of the Most High will overshadow you."

Prayer: *O God, we know that we live beneath the shadow of your grace, mercy, and power. Help us respond to life's highest hopes and noblest dreams with faith and courage. Amen.*

Sunday, December 20   Read Luke 1:38-45.

As a boy I was quite shy. In the classroom I would do whatever I could to avoid being singled out by the teacher. When those who knew the answer to a question were asked to raise their hands, I would try to hide behind the person whose desk was in front of mine. Though I might raise my hand, I would do it in such a way as to insure that the teacher would not see it and would call on someone else.

But God is as likely to call on someone who is trying to hide as someone who is seeking to attract God's attention.

Luke's account of Mary's confrontation with the angel Gabriel tells us something about the process God uses to enlist those called into divine service. If you are a peasant girl betrothed to the village carpenter, the odds for being called to history's stage center might seem remote. Apparently God was not as interested in Mary's self-assessment as in the fact that she possessed the qualities essential to an act of surpassing grace.

I think of humble people I have known who have been called out of life's fringes and shadows into meaningful discipleship. For the most part they have been quiet, unassuming people who never imagined they possessed gifts that might be used for divine purposes. All of them have had something in common with Mary. Like her, when the call to servanthood came, their response was, "Be it unto me according to your word." Is there the possibility that you, even as you read these words, sense the tug and pull of God, calling you to take a step beyond where you are into the unknown, for Christ's sake?

Prayer: *Lord, give us the courage to move beyond our hiding places into servanthood. Amen.*

A TIME FOR FEELING GOOD

December 21-27, 1987 **Robert N. Zearfoss**†
Monday, December 21 Read Isaiah 61:10-11.

On this first day of the winter season when our thoughts are leaning toward Christmas, this scripture encourages us to affirm that even as the buds of spring lie dormant, ready to come forth in the new season, in like manner justice and goodness will emerge in the future. Whenever we witness the oppressing burden of injustice, we will work with the Eternal toward that day when fairness and compassion will prevail. Even captivity in a barbarian land could not destroy that spirit for Isaiah. The elements of trust and hope still existed. Something better was yet to come.

In addition to the imagery of buds of hope, the metaphor of a wedding is used by the prophet. It shows that the future has an element of joy in it. The garland of the groom and jewels of the bride symbolize the hope that a better world environment is in process. No matter how gloomy the external conditions at the time, the wedding party approaches the event and their surroundings with anticipation. Marriage in all ages implies dreams to be realized in the unknown years ahead.

Such is the mood available to us this winter as Christians prepare to celebrate the birth of Jesus. Amid rumors of war and threats of annihilation there are those who continue to build faith-filled lives.

Prayer: *God, it is helpful to us to recall Isaiah's faith in the future. Renew our anticipation. Amen.*

---

†Minister Emeritus, First Baptist Church, Evanston, Illinois.

Tuesday, December 22   Read Galatians 4:4-7.

Here, for the first-century Christians living in the Middle East, the coming of Jesus is presented in terms of an inheritance. Relying on an orderly, legal, historic procedure, Jesus the Christ is received as a gift only when maturity has arrived. The time had come for God to give to the world One who would change the perspective on life's meaning.

This idea of an inheritance is a good one. Its benefits are not to be ours until we have matured enough to appreciate its subtleties. Compare, for example, our nostalgic remembrance of the Christmas season with our present adult ability to search for the deeper, more mystical meaning of the Nativity.

When the time had fully come, Jesus was born. The terms had been met. Deliverance was at hand. So it is with us. The Gift has been delivered. Our hearts are full. We search for new ways to express our joy and the depth of our hope. We can almost echo the words of the psalmist, "My cup runneth over" (Ps. 23:5, KJV). We can take the accumulated expressions of our heritage and place them like a transparency on the computerized, media-oriented culture in which we live. We accept the traditional calendar observance of this Christmas with the deeper understanding that we are now mature enough to receive the treasure of God's love for the world.

Prayer: *Dear God, thank you for placing us within the fullness of time that we, too, might be presented with the treasure of Jesus, the babe of Bethlehem. In his name we pray. Amen.*

Wednesday, December 23   Read Psalm 111.

All rhythmic works of poetry are labors of love, and in this instance the psalmist has sought to express his joyful love in a unique framework. If we were to read the Hebrew words, we would see that the first word of each phrase begins with the next letter of the alphabet. We call this an acrostic. It is not easy, believe me. Try writing a letter that has each succeeding sentence start with the next of the ABCs.

A friend of mine has the practice of recalling the words to hymns she knows as she drives around the city. She tries to choose them alphabetically. For example, she picks "All Hail the Power of Jesus' Name," "Breathe on Me, Breath of God," and "Crown Him with Many Crowns." She tells me that it is not easy to find hymns beginning with the letters r, q, x and z. Try it sometime.

In this psalm, out of the realization that goodness and truth pay off, a bud of hope emerges. Any look at what the goodness of God produces will confirm this. No matter how much violence, greed, or destruction we see, there is still an overwhelming harvest of creativity and truth that can be identified. We can sing with the psalmist, "Great are the works of the Lord."

We nurture the buds of our hopes by remembering the ways in which God is consistent. There are certainties of faith that prevail even when uncertainties exist. So let us sing the carols that we cherish so much.

Prayer: *O God, as we receive renewed resources of hope at this season, structure our thoughts so that they become sonnets of praise to your glory. Amen.*

Thursday, December 24

Read Psalm 111:1;
Luke 2:22, 27.

The lectionary texts for this week bring us readings that focus on scenes other than the actual birth of Jesus. Isaiah speaks of wedding garments, marriage, the new sprouts that spring up in the new year, and the restoration of the new Jerusalem. The psalmist encourages us to count evidence of happiness, while the advice to the Galatians affirms our legal inheritance of God's promise through Jesus. The text in Luke reports an event often overlooked involving two elderly people in the Jerusalem Temple who see the infant Jesus.

Fortunately, we are familiar with the stories of the birth of Jesus. We know what it means to remember the Incarnation. In a community saturated with carols, oratorios, unusual lights and colors, we shall be content to count the ways that our faith is an affirmation of the coming of the Messiah.

The psalmist gives wing to our intentions by telling us where he finds an opportunity to express joy. "With all my heart I will praise the Lord, in the company of . . . the whole congregation" (NEB). When we enter the traditional services of Christmas worship, we give expression to our sense of God's presence in this world. We take a clue from Isaiah when he unashamedly says that he rejoices in the Lord and he does it with all his heart. So, it turns out, the lectionary texts prepare us for what is as yet unspoken, the hallelujah on Christmas eve.

Prayer: *God of the cradle and of the cosmos, we who sense our finiteness want to thank you for coming into a world that needs the Spirit of Jesus so much. Let our hallelujahs be reflected in the way we live. Amen.*

Friday, December 25 (Christmas)
Read Luke 2:22-28, 32-35.

In bringing the baby Jesus into the Temple a few days after the birth, Joseph and Mary were doing what was customary. In doing the expected, they experienced the unexpected! A devout man, Simeon, was present and with joy recognized the child as a sign of God's deliverance for all people.

The surprised parents let Simeon hold the child for a moment. "He took him in his arms . . . and said . . . 'now thy promise is fulfilled' " (Luke 2:29, NEB). Then this man sang what was his own song, a psalm of praise to God. He sang of the promise fulfilled and of a light that would bring new faith to the world.

Then elderly Anna came along, a woman who came from the tribe of Ashar (which means "happy"), and she also saw significance in this presence of Mary, Joseph, and the baby. In what could have been quite ordinary, Anna saw a unique meaning in that religious setting. Luke records that "the child's father and mother were full of wonder at what was being said about him" (NEB).

On this Christmas Day, as we complete that which is expected, we are urged to listen attentively and to look with open eyes at the customary events of a great holy day. There is miracle here if we are but sensitive to it. A conscious effort to sense wonder in the commonplace may reveal to us new aspects of rejoicing that we did not anticipate. As we accept the heritage of our faith, it may even happen that those who are elderly may give us a new look at the Christmas event.

Prayer: *God of creation, come into our celebration and let the light of your Son be central to this day commemorating his birth. Amen.*

Saturday, December 26　　　　Read Luke 2:36-38.

Consider for a moment on this day after Christmas these words about Anna, a widow, eighty-four years old. She came into the Temple in Jerusalem at the time Simeon was making his prophecy about Jesus. Anna thought herself fortunate to be at that place at the precise time when this happened. She gave thanks and then "talked about the child" (NEB).

During our own holiday season it would be good for us to "talk about the child." It is true that we sing carols and bring out treasured ornaments to recapture the delight of Christmas. We also bring and receive gifts, usually wrapped in colorful paper. Our conversation is rich with talk about other Christmases that had a poignancy all their own. It would be good for us also to talk specifically about the child Jesus. It leads us to consider the welfare of those around us and to have a new sense of wonder born out of tradition.

Anna talked about the child to all who were on the lookout for the liberation of their country. She talked about this baby who thirty years hence would bring truth and freedom in a new way. "When this baby becomes a man, watch out!" she might have said. "Things will change because of him."

Imagine being eighty-four! On top of that, try to imagine yourself looking at the current crop of babies and youngsters and anticipating what is in their future three decades hence. May those who know about Jesus never stop talking about the liberation and the peace that can come through him.

Prayer: *O God, thank you for those who have told the story of Jesus to us. Help us to tell it well today. Amen.*

Sunday, December 27   Read Luke 2:29-32; John 1:1-4.

"Now, Lord, you have kept your promise, and you may let your servant go in peace" (TEV).

These words of Simeon have been set to music and, known as the *Nunc dimittis,* are part of the service of Evensong in the Anglican Church. A contemporary hymn, "O Gladsome Light," written by the poet laureate Robert Bridges, was inspired by Simeon and his song. In retrospect, on this Sunday after the Christmas event, it is good for us to think about a song given shortly after the birth of Jesus. Giving promise of the future, it speaks to all who continue to express a radiant, joyful faith throughout the year. Simeon's *Nunc dimittis* echoes in our ears.

There come moments in life when it is possible to say, "Well, now I've seen everything!" While Simeon is saying something much more profound than that, his feeling of fulfillment is impressive. We, too, can possess a fragment of Simeon's peace as we, enriched by the warmth of Christmas, face the future. There is a budding of hope, an unfolding of joy, that brings a balm to our Christian witness.

The light of the world is available. Like the psalmist, Isaiah, and Simeon, we can say, "Our hearts are full." We shall seek continual sensitivity to the spiritual insights of Jesus that will give new meaning to the events of the winter. With Isaiah we can assert that the buds of springtime are not far away.

Prayer: *Creator of Christmas, Source of all significant revelations to humanity, open our minds and hearts to your presence in this bountiful world. Send us forth refreshed by our expectations in your Son, Jesus, our Lord. Amen.*

THE LIGHT OF GOD

December 28-31, 1987   **John O. Gooch**†
Monday, December 28   Read Isaiah 60:1-7.

The light of God leaps into the sky! A new age dawns out of the darkness of the old! Jerusalem is called to reflect to the world the brightness of God's new light.

The light leaps into the dark sky. That was the good news the prophet brought to Jerusalem at the end of the exile. This passage begins with the image of Jerusalem as a woman, crushed and broken, living in desolation. The call to her is to rise and reflect the light, because the light of God has broken upon her and a new life has begun. Because God's light has shone on Jerusalem, the nations will come, giving glory to God.

Jerusalem is next seen as a mother, watching her children returning home. The brightness of the light is reflected by the sea, coming back in thousands of fragments and sparkles of glory. It is reflected in the eyes and on the faces of the exiles returning, singing the praises of Yahweh. It is reflected in the wealth of the nations flowing to Jerusalem.

In response to the glory of the light, offerings flow to the Temple. Camels, on their own, come bearing gifts. Rivers of sheep come voluntarily to be sacrificed. Wealth pours out of Sheba in a measure its queen could only have dreamed of!

The outpouring of gifts is a natural response to the light and glory of God.

Prayer: *O God, give us the grace to reflect your light, the joy to sing your praise, and the freedom to pour out our gifts to give glory to your name. Amen.*

---

†United Methodist minister; free-lance writer and editor; Webster Groves, Missouri.

Tuesday, December 29   Read Psalm 72:1-7.

The light of God shines in justice and righteousness. This is one of the "royal psalms," a collection of prayers for the well-being and long reign of the king, and the only one to emphasize the king's duty to the poor. The theology which undergirds the psalm is the covenant between Yahweh and Israel. The king, too, is a part of the covenant, and his relationships to both Yahweh and the people are determined by covenant obligation. If he rules with justice and righteousness, then he will take up the cause of the poor. Justice (*mishpat*) is an expression of covenant wholeness, of the working out of social and economic relationships in the light of God's love for Israel. The Torah, especially such sections as the "Covenant Code" and the "Holiness Code," spells out in detail the relationship which should exist under the covenant. They emphasize a concern for the poor and oppressed, and an inherent duty to care for them. This is also the theme of the psalm.

In verse 3, "prosperity" might better be translated "shalom," i.e., peace or wholeness, the opportunity to live life in joy and fullness. A part of the covenant calling of the king is to rule so that all his subjects have this opportunity.

Verses 5-7 are a beautiful benediction for blessings on the reign of the king. What a model for a leader—in nation or church! To be one who gives life and hope as the spring rains. To be one who dispenses justice and brings shalom as long as he lives—even as long as the moon endures.

Prayer: *Help us remember the call for justice and shalom, O God. Give us perseverance to work for them for all our brothers and sisters, for as long as we live. Amen.*

Wednesday, December 30   Read Psalm 72:8-14.

The light of God shines in the powerful reign of the king in Jerusalem. Remember the Davidic covenant, which Judah understood to mean a king of David's line would always rule in Jerusalem and be Yahweh's "son." One of the national tragedies of Judah was the conviction that Yahweh would always look with favor upon the kingdom because of David. Often, that theology became the justification for complacency and self-satisfaction. But in this psalm the prayer for the world rule of the king is also a prayer for glory to Yahweh. When the king is glorified, so is his "father," Yahweh. The area over which the psalmist longs for the king to rule stretches from Tarshish (Spain) in the west to beyond "the River" (the Tigris-Euphrates Valley) in the east. It includes the kingdoms of Sheba and Seba, both located in the Yemen, where they controlled the sources of the spice trade. Sheba is often used as a symbol of wealth because of the importance to the whole Middle East of the income from the spice trade.

But the glory means nothing without justice, which is where the light really shines. Only the king's concern for the poor and needy justifies the prayer for power and glory. Without the covenant concern for the brother and sister, all the power in the world is empty. What would a king gain if he ruled the whole world at the expense of the poor, the sick, the weak, the needy, the oppressed in his own land?

Prayer: *Help us, O God of justice, to translate our concern for national power and glory into an awareness of the real glory in service to the poor and oppressed. Lead us to sensitivity to what real glory is. Amen.*

Thursday, December 31   Read Ephesians 3:1-6.

The light of God is seen in the revelation of the mystery of Christ. What is that great mystery, into which the author of Ephesians has such insight? Is it not that all humanity is one, that Jews and Gentiles share in the same hope, the same body of the church, the same promise in Christ? In the church, we see that the reunion of divided humanity is the promise of the future reunion of all creation.

The mystery was made known by revelation. The Spirit led the apostles and prophets to hear the call of God to reconciliation of ancient enemies. In their responses, they became people who were willing to be taught by God, to surrender prejudice, in order to communicate new ideals. First, the Samaritans received the gospel and became a part of the church. Ancient wounds in Israel were healed. Peter stood before the Roman centurion Cornelius and cried, "How can we deny [the Gentiles] baptism, when God has given them the Holy Spirit?" (Acts 10:47, AP). Paul and James also fought for equality for the Gentiles.

The mystery of God's grace was "given to me for you"; that is, it was intended for communication. It was a useless gift unless it was shared with those for whom the good news of a new order was intended.

The mystery was communicated so that the church might read and reflect on the new insight into the mystery. Quietness and reflection on revolutionary new ideas often lead us to "own" them, when all the exhortation and pressure in the world could not force us to adopt them.

Prayer: *All of us brothers and sisters? Even our enemies? O God, forgive us for not seeking reconciliation in home, church, nation, and world. Help us to reach out and overcome enmity and prejudice. In Jesus' name. Amen.*

New Common Lectionary, 1987
(*Disciplines* Edition)

January 1-4

Jeremiah 31:7-14
Psalm 147:12-20
Ephesians 1:3-6, 15-18
John 1:1-18

January 5-11
Epiphany

Isaiah 42:1-9
Psalm 29
Acts 10:34-43
Matthew 3:13-17

January 12-18

Isaiah 49:1-7
Psalm 40:1-11
1 Corinthians 1:1-9
John 1:29-34

January 19-25

Isaiah 9:1-4
Psalm 27:1-6
1 Corinthians 1:10-17
Matthew 4:12-23

January 26–February 1

Micah 6:1-8
Psalm 37:1-11
1 Corinthians 1:18-31
Matthew 5:1-12

February 2-8

Isaiah 58:3-9*a*
Psalm 112:4-9
1 Corinthians 2:1-11
Matthew 5:13-16

February 9-15

Deuteronomy 30:15-20
Psalm 119:1-8
1 Corinthians 3:1-9
Matthew 5:17-26

February 16-22

Isaiah 49:8-13
Psalm 62:5-12
1 Corinthians 3:10-11, 16-23
Matthew 5:27-37

February 23–March 1

Exodus 24:12-18
Psalm 2:6-11
2 Peter 1:16-21
Matthew 17:1-9

March 2-8

Genesis 2:4*b*-9, 15-17, 25; 3:1-7
Psalm 130
Romans 5:12-19
Matthew 4:1-11

March 9-15

Genesis 12:1-8
Psalm 33:18-22
Romans 4:1-17
John 3:1-17

March 16-22

Exodus 17:3-7
Psalm 95
Romans 5:1-11
John 4:5-26 (or 42)

March 23-29

1 Samuel 16:1-13
Psalm 23
Ephesians 5:8-14
John 9:1-41

March 30–April 5

Ezekiel 37:1-14
Psalm 116:1-9
Romans 8:6-11
John 11:1 (or 17)-45

April 6-12
Passion/Palm Sunday

Psalm 31:9-16
Psalm 118:19-29
Philippians 2:5-11
John 12:12-16

April 13-19
Easter

Isaiah 52:13–53:12
Acts 10:34-43
Psalm 118:14-24
Colossians 3:1-4
John 12:1-11
John 13:1-15
John 19:17-30
John 20:1-18

April 20-26

Acts 2:14a, 22-32
Psalm 16:5-11
1 Peter 1:3-9
John 20:19-31

April 27–May 3

Acts 2:14a, 36-41
Psalm 116:12-19
1 Peter 1:17-23
Luke 24:13-35

May 4-10

Acts 2:42-47
Psalm 23
1 Peter 2:19-25
John 10:1-10

May 11-17

Acts 7:55-60
Psalm 31:1-8
1 Peter 2:2-10
John 14:1-14

379

May 18-24

Acts 17:22-31
Psalm 66:8-20
1 Peter 3:13-22
John 14:15-21

May 25-31

Acts 1:6-14
Psalm 68:1-10
1 Peter 4:12-14
John 17:1-11

June 1-7
Pentecost

Acts 2:1-21 or Isaiah 44:1-8
Psalm 104:24-34
1 Corinthians 12:3b-13 or
    Acts 2:1-21
John 20:19-23 or John 7:37-39

June 8-14
Trinity

Deuteronomy 4:32-40
Psalm 33:1-12
2 Corinthians 13:5-14
Matthew 28:16-20

June 15-21

Genesis 28:10-17
Psalm 91:1-10
Romans 5:12-19
Matthew 10:24-33

June 22-28

Genesis 32:22-32
Psalm 17:1-7, 15
Romans 6:3-11
Matthew 10:34-42

June 29–July 5

Exodus 1:6-14, 22; 2:1-10
Psalm 123
Romans 7:14-25a
Matthew 11:25-30

July 6-12

Exodus 2:11-22
Psalm 69:6-15
Romans 8:9-17
Matthew 13:1-9, 18-23

July 13-19

Exodus 3:1-12
Psalm 103:1-13
Romans 8:18-25
Matthew 13:24-30, 36-43

July 20-26

Exodus 3:13-20
Psalm 105:1-11
Romans 8:26-30
Matthew 13:44-52

July 27–August 2

Exodus 12:1-14
Psalm 143:1-10
Romans 8:31-39
Matthew 14:13-21

August 3-9

Exodus 14:19-31
Psalm 106:4-12
Romans 9:1-5
Matthew 14:22-33

August 10-16

Exodus 16:2-15
Psalm 78:1-3, 10-20
Romans 11:13-16, 29-32
Matthew 15:21-28

August 17-23

Exodus 17:1-7
Psalm 95
Romans 11:33-36
Matthew 16:13-20

August 24-30

Exodus 19:1-9
Psalm 114
Romans 12:1-13
Matthew 16:21-28

August 31–September 6

Exodus 19:16-24
Psalm 115:1-11
Romans 13:1-10
Matthew 18:15-20

September 7-13

Exodus 20:1-20
Psalm 19:7-14
Romans 14:5-12
Matthew 18:21-35

September 14-20

Exodus 32:1-14
Psalm 106:7-8, 19-23
Philippians 1:21-27
Matthew 20:1-16

September 21-27

Exodus 33:12-23
Psalm 99
Philippians 2:1-13
Matthew 21:28-32

September 28–October 4

Numbers 27:12-23
Psalm 81:1-10
Philippians 3:12-21
Matthew 21:33-43

October 5-11

Deuteronomy 14:1-12
Psalm 135:1-14
Philippians 4:1-9
Matthew 22:1-14

October 12-18

Ruth 1:1-19*a*
Psalm 146
1 Thessalonians 1:1-10
Matthew 22:15-22

October 19-25

Ruth 2:1-13
Psalm 128
1 Thessalonians 2:1-8
Matthew 22:34-46

October 26–November 1
All Saints'

Revelation 7:9-17
Psalm 34:1-10
1 John 3:1-3
Matthew 5:1-12

November 2-8

Amos 5:18-24
Psalm 50:7-15
1 Thessalonians 4:13-18
Matthew 25:1-13

November 9-15

Zephaniah 1:7, 12-18
Psalm 76
1 Thessalonians 5:1-11
Matthew 25:14-30

November 16-22

Ezekiel 34:11-16, 20-24
Psalm 23
1 Corinthians 15:20-28
Matthew 25:31-46

November 23-29
Thanksgiving

Isaiah 63:16–64:8
Psalm 80:1-7
1 Corinthians 1:3-9
Mark 13:32-37

November 30–December 6

Isaiah 40:1-11
Psalm 85:8-13
2 Peter 3:8-15a
Mark 1:1-8

December 7-13

Isaiah 61:1-4, 8-11
Luke 1:46b-55
1 Thessalonians 5:16-24
John 1:6-8, 19-28

December 14-20

2 Samuel 7:8-16
Psalm 89:1-4, 19-24
Romans 16:25-27
Luke 1:26-38

December 21-27
Christmas

Isaiah 61:10–62:3
Psalm 111
Galatians 4:4-7
Luke 2:22-40

December 28–January 3, 1988

Isaiah 60:1-6
Psalm 72:1-14
Ephesians 3:1-12
Matthew 2:1-12

THE UPPER ROOM DISCIPLINES

1987